OPEN SOURCE TECHNOLOGY

Open Source Technology

By

KAILASH VADERA
HOD CSE/IT Department
Shrinathji Institute of Technology & Engg.
Nathdwara, Rajasthan

BHAVYESH GANDHI
Lecturer CSE/IT Department
Maharaja Engg. College, Udaipur
Rajasthan

UNIVERSITY SCIENCE PRESS
(An Imprint of Laxmi Publications Pvt. Ltd.)
An ISO 9001:2015 Company
BENGALURU • CHENNAI • GUWAHATI • HYDERABAD • JALANDHAR
KOCHI • KOLKATA • LUCKNOW • MUMBAI • RANCHI
NEW DELHI

OPEN SOURCE TECHNOLOGY

Printed and bound in India
Typeset at : ABRO Enterprises, Delhi.
First Edition : 2009, *Reprint* : 2013, 2016, *Second Edition* : 2017, *Edition* : 2022
ISBN : 978-81-318-0727-9

Edited by : **Sangeeta Dixit**

Branches

©	Bengaluru	080-26 75 69 30
©	Chennai	044-24 34 47 26
©	Guwahati	0361-254 36 69
©	Hyderabad	040-27 55 53 83
©	Jalandhar	0181-222 12 72
©	Kochi	0484-405 13 03
©	Kolkata	033-40 04 77 79
©	Lucknow	0522-430 36 13
©	Ranchi	0651-224 24 64

PUBLISHED IN INDIA BY

UNIVERSITY SCIENCE PRESS
(An Imprint of Laxmi Publications Pvt. Ltd.)
An ISO 9001:2015 Company
113, GOLDEN HOUSE, GURUDWARA ROAD, DARYAGANJ,
NEW DELHI - 110002, INDIA
Telephone : 91-11-4353 2500, 4353 2501
www.laxmipublications.com
info@laxmipublications.com

C—00049/022/02
Printed at : Repro Book Limited, Mumbai.

CONTENTS

PREFACE

The present textbook on "Open Source Technology" is a sincere attempt by us the make various aspects of Open Source easy and simple to understand. In this respect, we possess all the expertise and experience in the subject matter and appropriately and rightfully feels that "Open Source Technology is a Science as Art".

A textbook does not have to be boring, hard to read and nearly impossible to understand. In fact, there are two ways of saying a thing the simple way and the difficult way. The simple way is by no means simpler than the difficult way. Nevertheless, this is exactly what the author has attempted in this book to put the things in the simple way.

This book is intended for any one who is interested in Open Source Technology. It has been designed to meet the needs of beginners as well as advanced learners who wish to deal with Open Source Technology. As Open Source Technology is being used widely, this book can be used by students of computer science and IT, business administration and management.

In short, this book is for everyone who is either about Open Source Technology or interested in knowing about Open Source Technology.

This book is also the culmination of a group effort, where in other faculty and students of SITE, Nathdwara contributed their "bit" to the effort of ensuring the production of a "flawless" book. We have no doubt in our mind that this will go a long way in making this book a success. Although we have tried to make this book error free, still any suggestions regarding the improvement of this book will be welcomed.

—Authors

ACKNOWLEDGEMENT

My Sincere gratitude to Mr. Ashok Parikh (Director, SITE, Nathdwara), Prof. P.C. Sethia (Principal, SITE, Nathdwara), Dr. Satish Sharma, Mr. Nagendra Singh and Mr. Vipin Kumar Choudhary (Board of Governor of Maharaja Engg. College, Udaipur).

Thanks to my fellow collegues Mr. K.G. Vijayvargiya, Dr. S.S. Shrimali, Mr. R.C. Mehta, Ms. Shweta Kabra, Mr. Nitin Tyagi, Mr. Manish Joshi, Ms. Neha Sharma, Mr. Jatin Taldar, Mr. Rohit Srivastava, Mr. Kirti Kumar Dave, Mr. Om Prakash Dave, Ms. Garima Kothari, Mrs. Seema Vadera and Mrs. Khushboo Gandhi for their time to time suggestions and contributions.

I am thankful to my friends who have always encouraged me by appreciating and criticizing my work. I also express my deep sense of gratitude to my family members and students for their constant encouragement and full support during the preparation of the manuscript.

—Authors

Chapter 1

INTRODUCTION TO OPEN SOURCE

1.1 WHY OPEN SOURCE ?

The typical computer user owns lots of software that he bought years ago and no longer uses today. He might have upgraded his computer or changed brands, and then the program wouldn't work any longer. The software might have become old. The program may simply not do what he needs. He may have bought two or more computers, and doesn't want to pay for a second copy of the software. Whatever the reason, the software that he paid for years ago is not doing the task today. Does that really need to happen ?

What if you had the right to get a free upgrade whenever your software needed it ? What if, when you switched from a Mac to a PC, you could switch software versions for free ? What if, when the software doesn't work or isn't powerful enough, you can have it improved or even fix it yourself ? What if the software was still maintained even if the company that produced it went out of business ? What if you could use your software on your office workstation, and your home desktop computer, and your portable laptop, instead of just one computer ? You'd probably still be using the software you paid for years ago.

These are some of the rights that *Open Source* gives you.

1.2 WHAT IS OPEN SOURCE ?

Confusion about the term freedom was the very reason the term *Open source* was created. *Open source* or *Open Source Software (OSS)* is different from proprietary software. In Open Source, the source code used in the software is available to anyone to examine, evaluate, and adapt. Open source has an important impact on the way many developers view and create software. End users often use the term *open source* to cover a variety of free and *open source software*.

Open source is a development method for software that harnesses the power of distributed peer review and transparency of process. The Open Source Initiative has this for a definition of open source software :

The Open Source Definition is a bill of rights for the computer user. It defines certain rights that a software license must grant you to be certified as Open Source.

Example of open source software is :

- Linux
- Apache
- BSD
- Wikipedia
- Mozilla.

Programmers feel comfortable contributing to Open Source because they are assured of these rights :

- The right to make copies of the program, and distribute those copies.
- The right to have access to the software's source code, a necessary preliminary before you can change it.
- The right to make improvements to the program.

These rights are important to the software contributor because they keep all contributors at the same level relative to each other. Everyone who wants to be allowed to sell an Open Source program, so prices will be low and development to reach new markets will be rapid. Anyone who invests the time to build knowledge in an Open Source program can support it, and this provides users with the option of providing their own support, or the economy of a number of competing support providers. Any programmer can tailor an Open Source program to specific markets in order to reach new customers. People who do these things are not compelled to pay royalties or license fees.

The reason for the success of this somewhat communist-sounding strategy, while the failure of communism itself is visible around the world, is that the economics of information are fundamentally different from those of other products. There is very little cost associated with copying a piece of information like a computer program.

The promises of open source are :

- Better Quality
- Higher Reliability
- More Flexible
- Lower Cost
- Transparent

Open source doesn't just mean to access the source code.

The *Distribution Terms* of open source software must comply with the following criteria :

1.2.1 Free Redistribution

The license shall not restrict any party from selling or giving away the software as a component of an aggregate software distribution containing programs from several different sources. The license shall not require a royalty or other fee for such sale.

Rationale : By constraining the license to require free redistribution, we eliminate the temptation to throw away many long-term gains in order to make a few short-term sales dollars. If we didn't do this, there would be lots of pressure for cooperators to defect.

1.2.2 Source Code

The program must include source code, and must allow distribution in source code as well as compiled form. Where some form of a product is not distributed with source code, there must be a well-publicized means of obtaining the source code for no more than a reasonable reproduction cost–preferably, downloading via the Internet without charge. The source code must be the preferred form in which a programmer would modify the program. *Deliberately obfuscated* source code is not allowed. Intermediate forms such as the output of a preprocessor or translator are not allowed.

Rationale : We require access to un-obfuscated source code because you can't evolve programs without modifying them. Since our purpose is to make evolution easy, we require that modification be made easy.

1.2.3 Derived Works

The license must allow modifications and derived works, and must allow them to be distributed under the same terms as the license of the original software.

Rationale : The mere ability to read source isn't enough to support independent peer review and rapid evolutionary selection. For rapid evolution people need to be able to experiment with and redistribute modifications.

Software has little use if you can't maintain it (fix bugs, port to new systems, make improvements), and modification is necessary for maintenance. The intent here is for modification of any sort to be allowed. It must be allowed for a modified work to be distributed under the same license terms as the original work. However, it is not required that any producer of a derived work must use the same license terms, only that the option to do so be open to them. Various licenses speak differently on this subject—the BSD license allows you to take modifications private, while the GPL does not.

A concern among some software authors is that this provision could allow unscrupulous people to modify their software in ways that would embarrass the original author. They fear someone deliberately making the software perform incorrectly in a way that would make it look as if the author was a poor programmer. Others are concerned that software could be modified for criminal use, by the addition of Trojan horse functions or locally-banned technologies such as cryptography. All of these actions, however, are covered by criminal law. A common misunderstanding about software licenses is that they must specify everything, including things like "don't use this software to commit a crime." However, no license has any valid existence outside of the body of civil and criminal law. Considering a license as something apart from the body of applicable law is as silly as considering an English-language document as being apart from the dictionary, in which case none of the words would have any defined meaning.

1.2.4 Integrity of the Author's Source Code

The license may restrict source code from being distributed in modified form only if the license allows the distribution of "patch files" with the source code for the purpose of modifying the program at build time. The license must explicitly permit distribution of software built from modified source code. The license may require derived works to carry a different name or version number from the original software.

Rationale : Encouraging lots of improvement is a good thing, but users have a right to know who is responsible for the software they are using. Authors and maintainers have reciprocal right to know what they're being asked to support and protect their reputations.

Accordingly, an open source license must guarantee that source be readily available, but may require that it be distributed as pristine base sources plus patches. In this way, "unofficial" changes can be made available but readily distinguished from the base source.

Some authors were afraid that others would distribute source code with modifications that would be perceived as the work of the original author, and would reflect poorly on that author. This gives them a way to enforce a separation between modifications and their own work without prohibiting modifications. Some consider it un-aesthetic that modifications might have to be distributed in a separate "patch" file from the source code, even though Linux distributions like Debian and Red Hat use this procedure for all of the modifications they make to the programs they distribute. There are programs that automatically merge patches into the main source, and one can have these programs run automatically when extracting a source package. Thus, this provision should cause little or no hardship.

Note also that this provision says that in the case of patch files, the modification takes place at build-time. This loophole is employed in the Qt Public License to mandate a different, though less restrictive, license for the patch files, in contradiction of Section 3 of the Open Source Definition. There is a proposal to clean up this loophole in the definition while keeping Qt within Open Source.

The license must explicitly permit distribution of software built from modified source code. The license may require derived works to carry a different name or version number from the original software.

This means that Netscape, for example, can insist that only they can name a version of the program Netscape Navigator(tm) while all free versions of the program must be called Mozilla or something else.

1.2.5 No Discrimination Against Persons or Groups

The license must not discriminate against any person or group of persons.

Rationale : In order to get the maximum benefit from the process, the maximum diversity of persons and groups should be equally eligible to contribute to open sources. Therefore we forbid any open source license from locking anybody out of the process.

Some countries, including the United States, have export restrictions for certain types of software. An OSD-conformant license may warn licensees of applicable restrictions and remind them that they are obliged to obey the law; however, it may not incorporate such restrictions itself.

A license provided by the Regents of the University of California, Berkeley, prohibited an electronic design program from being used by the police of South Africa. While this was a laudable sentiment in the time of apartheid, it makes little sense today. Some people are still stuck with software that they acquired under that license, and their derived versions must carry the same restriction. Open Source licenses may not contain such provisions, no matter how laudable their intent.

1.2.6 No Discrimination Against Fields of Endeavor

The license must not restrict anyone from making use of the program in a specific field of endeavor. For example, it may not restrict the program from being used in a business, or for genetic research.

Rationale : The major intention of this clause is to prohibit license traps that prevent open source from being used commercially. We want commercial users to join our community, not feel excluded from it.

Your software must be equally usable in an abortion clinic, or by an anti-abortion organization. These political arguments belong on the floor of Congress, not in software licenses. Some people find this lack of discrimination extremely offensive!

1.2.7 Distribution of License

The rights attached to the program must apply to all to whom the program is redistributed without the need for execution of an additional license by those parties.

Rationale : This clause is intended to forbid closing up software by indirect means such as requiring a non-disclosure agreement.

The license must be automatic, no signature required. Unfortunately, there has not been a good court test in the U.S. of the power of a no-signature-required license when it is passed from a second party to the third. However, this argument considers the license in the body of contract law, while some argue that it should be considered as copyright law, where there is more precedent for no-signature licenses. A good court test will no doubt happen in the next few years, given the popularity of this sort of license and the booming nature of Open Source.

1.2.8 License Must Not be Specific to a Product

The rights attached to the program must not depend on the program's being part of a particular software distribution. If the program is extracted from that distribution and used or distributed within the terms of the program's license, all parties to whom the program is redistributed should have the same rights as those that are granted in conjunction with the original software distribution.

Rationale : This clause forecloses yet another class of license traps.

This means you can't restrict a product that is identified as Open Source to be free only if you use it with a particular brand of Linux distribution, etc. It must remain free if you separate it from the software distribution it came with.

1.2.9 License Must Not Restrict Other Software

The license must not place restrictions on other software that is distributed along with the licensed software. For example, the license must not insist that all other programs distributed on the same medium must be open source software.

Rationale : Distributors of open source software have the right to make their own choices about their own software.

Yes, the GPL is conformant with this requirement. Software linked with GPLed libraries only inherits the GPL, if it forms a single work, not any software with which they are merely distributed.

A version of Ghost Script (a Post Script-rendering program) requires that the media on which it is distributed contain only free software programs. This isn't permissible for Open Source licenses. Fortunately, the Ghost Script author distributes another (somewhat older) version of the program with a true Open Source license.

Note that there is a difference between derivation and aggregation. *Derivation* is when a program actually incorporates part of another program into itself. *Aggregation* is when you include two programs on the same CD-ROM. This section of the Open Source Definition is concerned with aggregation, not derivation. Section 4 is concerned with derivation.

1.2.10 License Must Be Technology—Neutral

No provision of the license may be predicated on any individual technology or style of interface.

Rationale : This provision is aimed specifically at licenses, which require an explicit gesture of assent in order to establish a contract between licensor and licensee. Provisions mandating so-called "click-wrap" may conflict with important methods of software distribution such as FTP download, CD-ROM anthologies, and web mirroring; such provisions may also hinder code re-use. Conformant licenses must allow for the possibility that (*a*) redistribution of the software will take place over non-Web channels that do not support click-wrapping of the download, and that (*b*) the covered code (or re-used portions of covered code) may run in a non-GUI environment that cannot support popup dialogues.

Free software is open source software, but not all open source software's are free.

This would get us in trouble if any of these licenses are ever changed to be non-open source—we'd have to issue a revision of the Open Source Definition immediately. It really belongs in explanatory text, not in the Open Source Definition itself.

1.3 OPEN SOURCE PRINCIPLES

As you know Open Source is a term most commonly applied to software and it refers to set of principles and practices where by the design and production information is shared openly, with out the normal restriction encountered when developing software with in a commercial environment where intellectual property is closely guarded.

The brief explanation of each principle is as follows :

1.3.1 Licensees are Free to Use Open Source Software for Any Purpose Whatsoever

An open source license may not interfere in any way with the use of the software by licensees. Restrictions on use, such as "for research and noncommercial purposes only," are not allowed in open source licenses. The phrase *free to use* is also intended to mean, "without any conditions that would impede use," such as a requirement for the licensee to report uses to the licensor, or to disclose the means or manner of internal uses of the software. Note also that the first word, *licensees,* means that *open source software is only available under the terms of a license to which each licensee must agree.*

1.3.2 Licensees are Free to Make Copies of Open Source Software and to Distribute them without Payment of Royalties to a Licensor

This principle does not mean that a licensor cannot sell open source software. It merely says that a licensee need not pay the licensor for additional copies he makes himself, even if those copies are distributed to others. As a practical matter, this open source principle drives the price of mere copies of open source software toward its marginal cost of production and distribution.

1.3.3 Licensees are Free to Create Derivative Works of Open Source Software and to Distribute them without Payment of Royalties to a Licensor

Quality software is built upon the foundations of earlier software. Many advocates of free and open source software contend that the requirement for open source licenses to permit the unhindered creation and distribution of *derivative works* is essential to meet the goal of the intellectual property laws as stated in the U.S. Constitution, "to promote the progress of science and the useful arts." Under this open source principle, a licensor cannot charge a royalty for the privilege to create and distribute derivative works, or require a licensee to pay a royalty for copies of a derivative work that are distributed, or impose any restrictions on the type or character of those derivative works.

1.3.4 Licensees are Free to Access and use the Source Code of Open Source Software

Source code is written in a human language to instruct a computer how to perform certain functions. Since the source code must be changed in order to instruct the computer to perform different functions, access to the source code is essential to make the third open source principle—the freedom to create derivative works of open source software—a practical reality. Source code is a means to an end, not the end itself. The phrase *free to access* merely requires the licensor to make source code available to licensees upon request at zero prices, not necessarily to distribute the source code to everyone.

1.3.5 Licensees are Free to Combine Open Source and Other Software

Open source licenses may not impose conditions or restrictions on other software with which the licensed software is merely combined or distributed. This prevents restrictions regarding what other software can be placed on computer storage media or in computer memory. Open source is one of many possible business and licensing models for software distribution, and customers must be free to select and use those software alternatives. This open source principle does not mean that licensors cannot impose reciprocal conditions upon licensees who create and distribute derivative works, for the activity of creating derivative works is not the same as merely combining software on media or on computers.

1.4 OPEN STANDARDS REQUIREMENTS FOR SOFTWARE

The Requirement. An "Open Standard" must not prohibit conforming implementation in open source software.

1.4.1 The Criteria

To comply with the Open Standards Requirement, an "Open Standard" must satisfy the following criteria. If an "Open Standard" does not meet these criteria, it will be discriminating against open source developers.

1.4.1.1 No Intentional Secrets

The standards MUST NOT withhold any detail necessary for interoperable implementation. As flows are inevitable, the standard MUST define a process for fixing flaws identified during implementation and interoperability testing and to incorporate said changes into a revised version or super sending version of the standards to release under terms that do not violate the OSR.

1.4.1.2 Availability

The standard MUST be freely and publicity available (ex. From a stable web site) under royalty-free terms at reasonable and non-discriminatory cost.

1.4.1.3 Patents

All patents essential to implementation of the standards Must :

1. Be licensed under royalty-free terms for unrestricted use, or
2. Be covered by a promise of non-assertion when practiced by open source software.

1.4.1.4 No Agreements

There MUST NOT any requirement for execution of a license agreement, NDA, grant, click-through or any other form of paperwork to deploy conforming implementation of the standard.

1.4.1.5 No OSR-Incomplete Dependencies

Implementation of the standard MUST NOT require any other technology that fails to meet the criteria of this requirement.

1.5 WHERE OSS HAS SUCCEEDED

- There are many open source projects.
  - SourceForge.net, a leading site for open source development, lists nearly 80,000.
  - A small number of open source projects are highly successful.

  - Provide widely used alternative to traditional commercial or "closed source" software.
  - Many more projects are used by small communities of experts.
- The most successful projects tend to be infrastructure software, not applications.

1.6 OPEN SOURCE SUCCESSES

- More on server than client side
  - More expert users of servers
  - Server operating systems
    - Linux
  - Certain server software
    - Web
    - Mail
    - DNS
  - So far less so with other server software
    - Database (MySQL rising, less easy to measure)
- Software for technical users.

1.7 FREE SOFTWARE

Free software is a software that can be used, studied, and modified without restriction, and which can be copied and redistributed in modified or unmodified form either without restriction, or with restrictions only to ensure that further recipients can also do these things. To make these acts possible, the human readable form of the program (called the source code) must be made available. The source code may be either accompanied by a software license saying that the copyright holder permits these acts (a free software license), or be released into public domain, so that these rights can be automatically hold.

Alternative terms for free software have been coined in an attempt to make the use of "free" less ambiguous. The most common is "open source software", which has since evolved to refer to a subtly different sense of freedom. Free software is also known as "**software libre**", "free, libre and open source software" ("FLOSS"), and "free and open source software" ("FOSS").

Free software is distinct from freeware; freeware is proprietary software made available free of charge. One can use, but not study, modify or redistribute freeware.

Since free software may be freely redistributed and generally available at very little cost. Free software business models are usually based on adding value such as support, training, customization, integration, or certification. At the same time, some business models which work with non-free software are not compatible with free software, such as those that depend on a user having no choice but to pay for a license in order to lawfully use a software product.

The free software movement was launched in 1983 to make these freedoms available to every computer user. Software that does not provide these freedoms is referred to as proprietary software or non-free software.

Free software is software that may be modified and redistributed freely by anyone, with no significant restrictions on how the code may be changed, the uses to which it may be put, or the parties with whom it may be shared.

Today, free software is a large body of high-quality code on which much of the Internet depends for critical functions, and it constitutes the core operating system for an increasing number of desktop machines as well. But free software is much more than just a collection of programs. It is also a political movement, a programming methodology, and a business model—although not necessarily to the same people at the same time. Indeed, even the term free software is controversial; as we'll see later, some people prefer to call it open source software. The story of how free software became so technologically successful, even as it became ideologically fractious, starts in the early days of the computer industry.

1.8 WHAT IS FREE SOFTWARE ?

We maintain this free software definition to show clearly what must be true about a particular software program for it to be considered free software.

Free software is a matter of liberty, not price. To understand the concept, you should think of free as in free speech, not as in free beer.

Free software is a matter of the users' freedom to run, copy, distribute, study, change and improve the software.

Free in Free Software is referring to freedom, not price. Having been used in this meaning since the 80s, the first documented complete definition appears to be the GNU's Bulletin, vol. 1 no. 1 [1], published February 1986. In particular, four freedoms define Free Software as :

1.8.1 The Freedom to Run the Program, for any Purpose

Placing restrictions on the use of Free Software, such as time ("30 days trial period", "license expires January 1st, 2004") purpose ("permission granted for research and non-commercial use", "may not be used for benchmarking") or geographic area ("must not be used in country X") makes a program non-free.

1.8.2 The Freedom to Study How the Program Works, and Adapt it to Your Needs

Placing legal or practical restrictions on the comprehension or modification of a program, such as mandatory purchase of special licenses, signing of a Non-Disclosure Agreement (NDA) or for programming languages that have multiple forms or representation making the preferred human way of comprehending and editing a program ("source code") inaccessible also makes it proprietary (non-free). Without the freedom to modify a program, people will remain at the mercy of a single vendor.

1.8.3 The Freedom to Redistribute Copies So You can Help Your Neighbor

Software can be copied/distributed at virtually no cost. If you are not allowed to give a program to a person in need, that makes a program non-free. This can be done for a charge, if you so choose.

1.8.4 The Freedom to Improve the Program, and Release Your Improvements to the Public, so that the Whole Community Gets Benefits

Not everyone is an equally good programmer in all fields. Some people don't know how to program at all. This freedom allows those who do not have the time or skills to solve a problem to indirectly access the freedom to modify. This can be done for a charge.

These freedoms are rights, not obligations, although respecting these freedoms for society may at times oblige the individual. Any person can choose to not make use of them, but may also choose to make use of all of them. In particular, it should be understood that Free Software does not exclude commercial use. If a program fails to allow commercial use and commercial distribution, it is not Free Software. Indeed a growing number of companies base their business model completely or at least partially on Free Software, including some of the largest proprietary software vendors. Free Software makes it legal to provide help and assistance, it does not make it mandatory.

Free Software shares much of its philosophy with Open Source software, but many people within the open source community feel that there are important distinctions between the terms, as described in the section Free Software vs. Open source software.

Often Free Software is referred as "free as in speech, not as in beer", stressing the idea that the Free-software movement is concerned with freedom, not with price. Throughout this book the reader should assume that the word "free" is referring to freedom.

1.9 WHAT ARE SOME EXAMPLES OF FREE SOFTWARE ?

Some free software are :

1. *Operating Systems* : Linux, BSD, Darwin and Open Solaris
2. GCC Compiler, GDB debugger and C/C++ libraries.
3. *Servers* : BIND name server, Send mail transport, Apache web server and Samba file server.
4. *Relational Database systems* : MySql and PostgresSQL.
5. *Programming language* : Java, Perl, PHP, Python, Lua, Ruby and Tcl.
6. *GUI Related* : X Windows System, GNOME, KDE, and Xfce desktop environments.
7. *GRASS* : Open Source Geography Information System (GIS).
8. OpenOffice.org office suite, Mozilla and Firefox web browser and GIMP graphics editor.
9. Typesetting and document preparation system Tex and Latex.
10. *OGG* : Free Software multimedia file type that can function like an mp3 or mp4.

If you're a desktop user, you're probably using Free Software quite a bit. Every software package released by the **Mozilla Foundation**, including the Firefox Browser, and the Thunderbird E-Mail client, among dozens of other programs, is Free Software. You've probably heard of Open Office, the Gamin IM application, the GIMP image manipulation software, the Azures Bit Torrent Client, the VLC Media Player, and the Audacity audio editing software. All of these are Free Software, and you can download them for free right now, use them for as long as you like, and share them with whomever you like. While you're at it, I'd recommend reading Tools of the Trade for more Free Software suggestions. But those were the Desktop Applications. The software that's running the Internet, as we know it today is made up primarily of Free Software. First, the Operating Systems : Linux, FreeBSD, and Open Solaris are all Free Software Operating Systems. Each has several "flavors", often referred as 'distributions', or 'distros' for short. These are the Operating Systems that are being used by the large majority of small, medium, and large businesses all over the world to run their servers. By servers I mean all types of servers—from Web Server computers to Databases. Make no mistake, however : Both Linux and FreeBSD have Desktop-dedicated versions which you can download and try for free, and use in conjunction with whichever Operating System you're using now. I'd recommend trying out Ubuntu since it's the easiest and most user-friendly, all the while not sacrificing Linux's powerful features.

But by "running the internet" I wasn't just referring to the Operating Systems. The most popular Web Server software, by a large margin, is the **Apache Web Server**. One of the most powerful and versatile Databases is **MySQL**. They both are not only Free Software, but also special hardware to try them out on your local machine. You can just go and download the 'desktop versions' (these are really the normal versions with a GUI, mostly for development purposes) from their respective websites, and setup a server environment on your own desktop, no matter what Operating system you're running.

What about the scripting languages ? Are they standards or languages ? That depends. In the case of JavaScript, for example, it's a standard. It's called ECMA Script or ECMA-262. In that case, it's a matter of how you run that standard, and since the specification for that standard is open, there are plenty of Free JavaScript Interpreters are there. Now as for other scripting languages : The three most used scripting/interpreted languages are the "P" languages — **Perl, PHP**, and **Python**. All of them are Free. You can go to their respective websites and download their interpreters, source codes, specifications, versions, documentation, mods, apps, etc., to your hearts content.

Even proprietary software has Free Software within it. These are commonly libraries that are included within the program that provide some specific function for the program.

1.10 FREE SOFTWARE LICENSE PROVIDER

Most Free Software is released fewer than one of the following license agreements :

1.10.1 GNU General Public License

The strict GPL license is the most common, and the most demanding of users of software released under it. The Linux Kernel is released under (version 2 of) this license, as well as the GNU Compiler Collection (The GCC).

1.10.2 GNU Lesser General Public License

This license was originally released as a compromise between the strict GPL license and the more permissive licenses such as the BSD license and the MIT license. It does not carry the "inheritance" element that the GPL license does, which means that commercial software may use software released under this license without having to be released under the GPL, or the LGPL license itself.

1.10.3 BSD Licenses

Sometimes referred to as "BSD-Style" licenses, these licenses are more permissive that the GNU licenses. The original was used for the Berkley Software Distribution (BSD), a Unix-like operating system for which the license was named.

1.10.4 Mozilla License

The Mozilla Public License was developed for software released by the Mozilla Foundation (it was actually developed prior to that, but today that is its primary use). It is a "weak copy-left" license, that has since been adopted, in modified versions, by several other companies and organizations. Mozilla Firefox, Mozilla Thunderbird, and the Mozilla Application Suite are some of the software programs released under this license.

1.10.5 MIT License

This license, which originated at the Massachusetts Institute of Technology, is a public domain license. It is one of the most permissive types of licenses, and is the license under which the X Windows System is released.

1.10.6 Apache License

Technically, this license is incompatible with the GPL, since it explicitly allows modifications to the software itself to remain secret and said modifications to be sold. This does not mean that software released under this license is not Free Software, since it does require the party releasing the software to adhere to the 4 Freedoms. The Apache Web Server is released under this license.

1.10.7 The "as-is" Release Model

This usually means that the released code is simply placed in the public domain, with no restrictions whatsoever apart from not "claiming rights" to that code, and not claiming that the user wrote it. There are actually quite a few dedicated-purpose libraries released under this license, which do something very specific, very efficiently.

1.11 FREE SOFTWARE VS. OPEN SOURCE SOFTWARE

The primary distinction of open source software is that it's not about freedom; it's about what software do things better.

As a whole the movement is often called "Free and Open source Software" (FOSS). While many people point to the differences between the two, this book will focus on what unites the two. For the purposes of clarity the abbreviation FOSS will be used when describing issues that apply to all open source software projects, whereas OSS will be used when describing issues that apply only to software with open source licenses that allow future developers to close the source code, and FSS will be used when talking about issues that apply only to software with free licenses requiring future developers maintain the previous style of licensing (if not the license itself).

Critics have said that the term "open source" fosters an ambiguity of a different kind such that it confuses the mere availability of the source with the freedom to use, modify, and redistribute it. Developers have used the alternative terms Free/Open Source Software (FOSS), or Free/Libre/Open Source Software (FLOSS), consequently, to describe open source software, which is also free software.

The term "Open Source" was originally intended to be trademarkable, however, the term was deemed too descriptive, so no trademark exists. The OSI would prefer that people treat Open Source as if it were a trademark, and use it only to describe software licensed under an OSI approved license.

There have been instances where software vendors have labeled proprietary software as "open source" because it interfaces with popular OSS (such as Linux). Open source advocates consider this to be both confusing and incorrect. *OSI Certified* is a trademark licensed only to people who are distributing software licensed under a license listed on the Open Source Initiative's list.

Open source software and free software are different terms for software, which comes with certain rights, or freedoms, for the user. They describe two approaches and philosophies towards free software. Open source and free software (or software libre) both describe software, which is free from onerous licensing restrictions. It may be used, copied, studied, modified and redistributed without restriction. Free software is not the same as freeware, software available at zero prices.

The definition of open source software was written to be almost identical to the free software definition. There are very few cases of software that is free software but is not open source software, and vice versa. The difference in the terms is where they place the emphasis. "Free software" is defined in terms of giving the user freedom. This reflects the goal of the free software movement. "Open source" highlights that the source code is viewable to all and proponents of the term usually emphasize the quality of the software and how this is caused by the development models which are possible and popular among free and open source software projects.

Free software licenses are not written exclusively by the FSF. The FSF and the OSI both list licenses, which meet their respective definitions of free software. Open source software and free software share an almost identical set of licenses. One exception is an early version of the Apple Public Source License, which was accepted by the OSI but rejected by the FSF because it did not allow private modified versions; this restriction was removed in later version of the license. There are now new versions that are approved by both the OSI and the FSF.

The Open Source Initiative believes that more people will be convinced by the experience of freedom. The FSF believes that more people will be convinced by the concept of freedom.

The FSF believes that knowledge of the concept is an essential requirement, insists on the use of the term free, and separates itself from the open source movement. The Open Source Initiative believes that free have three meanings : free as in beer, free as in freedom, and free as in untellable. The problem with the term "open source" is it says nothing about the freedom to modify and redistribute, so people who think that source access without freedom is a sufficient definition use it. This possibility for misuse is the case for most of the licenses that make up Microsoft's "shared source" initiative.

1.12 PUBLIC DOMAIN

Public domain comprises the body of knowledge and innovation (especially creative works such as writing, art, music, and inventions) in relation to which no person or other legal entity can establish or maintain proprietary interests within a particular legal jurisdiction. This body of information and creativity is considered to be part of a common cultural and intellectual heritage, which, in general, anyone may use or exploit, whether for commercial or non-commercial purposes. About 15 percent of all books are in the Public domain, including 10 percent of all books that are still in print.

Fig. 1.1. Logo of Public Domain.

If an item ("work") is not in the public domain, it may be the result of a proprietary interest such as a copyright, patent, or other Sui generics right. The extent to which members of the public may use or exploit the work is limited to the extent of the proprietary interests in the relevant legal jurisdiction. However, when the copyright, patent or other proprietary restrictions expire, the work enters the public domain and may be used by anyone for any purpose.

1.12.1 Public Domain Software

Another common form of open source software is software that has entered into the public domain. This is software that is unrestricted by copyright or licenses, and therefore free to use for any purpose. Before the rise of the open source software movement a great deal of software written in academic circles was released into the public domain for peer-review. This practice has changed with the rise of a more intentional open source movement, resulting in much software that was once public domain, now being released as FOSS. The public domain is where many resources used in open source projects come from, but there are few (if any) major projects that operate totally within the public domain.

Programs that are uncopyrighted because their authors intended to share them with everyone else are in the public domain. The UNIX community has developed a number of such programs over the years. Programs in the public domain can be used without restriction as components of other programs. When reusing such code, it is good to understand its history so that you can be sure it really is in the public domain.

DEFINITION : Programs that are uncopyrighted because their authors intended to share them with everyone else are in the public domain. The UNIX community has developed a number of such programs over the years. Programs in the public domain can be used without restriction as components of other programs. When reusing ... Definition continues below.

1.13 FOSS DOES NOT MEAN ANY COST

This is a common misunderstanding about FOSS; in no small part because nearly all FOSS programs are available free of charge. For example when the text editor Emacs was first released Richard Stallman charged from time to time to get copies. Developers have the choice to charge under most FOSS licenses, although they rarely choose to. The only requirement to be a truly FOSS project is that the publisher provides the source code with the program, and to allow the user to edit that code.

On top of the initial cost of purchasing software, there are other ongoing costs associated with all software. This can come in the form of support agreements, the cost of customization, training costs support personnel and other sources. This is true of both traditional commercial software and FOSS programs. There is a large and active debate about which type of software is more expensive over the long run for large corporations, for individual users there is little to no question that FOSS is cheaper by far.

1.14 HISTORY

The history given here is not intended to be a complete and perfect rendering of the history of the open source movement. Indeed it would be quite impossible to do so, as we are currently in the middle of the movement, and proper histories cannot be written about current events. Instead this chapter is intended to give the reader a general understanding of how the open source movement got started, so they can better understand the current debates.

In the beginning (1960's and 1970's) nearly all code was provided as a form of open source. Since you had to get programs to run on many different machines, companies that wanted customers to be able to run their software they had to provide the source code to compile themselves. Frequently licensing agreements did not encumber this code, or those licenses were never enforced. Often the users would notice flaws in the programs, fix them, and provide the improvements back to the publisher at no charge. Unix user groups often shared code with each other as well, creating an even larger body of code to work from. At the time most companies believed that hardware would always generate far more profit than software.

At the same time when academics wrote programs as part of their research, they would often release the code into the public domain to others to learn from their work. The first email server, ftp server, and web server were all public domain projects that were created by academics and shared as public domain software.

Over time the hardware became more standardized. This allowed software publishers to tighten up on what segments of code they would allow their users to see and edit. This tightening started to frustrate users, especially academics; since they could no longer fix the problem they found, and from time to time found that they couldn't use the hardware or software they wanted to. This trend mostly continued in mainstream software, strengthen by the rise of Microsoft.

During the late 1970's, many small businesses attempted to survive writing software for the new microcomputers. None were able to rely on hardware sales or after sale support contracts to subsidize software development. Few of these people, whether from an academic tradition of freely distributed software or not, were willing to make their products available without fee. Perhaps most famously, Bill Gates (a co-founder of Microsoft) realized that software, not hardware, held the prospect of being the greatest profit source in the new world of computing. When IBM needed an operating system for their personal computers instead of writing their own, Microsoft licensed an early version of DOS, but retained the licensing rights for other hardware manufacturers. This choice changed the face of computing by creating a standard operating system that most personal computers would run on, it lead directly to Microsoft's dominance of personal computing, and later allowed them major access to the server side market as well. Microsoft has grown into the largest software producer in the world, competing in almost every segment of the market. There are many people that feel that the only way to compete with Microsoft is through open source projects, which leverage a far larger support base than most companies can provide.

In this sea of activity, the FOSS movement primarily grew out of two places : the Berkeley Software Distribution licenses from the University of California and Richard Stallman's Free Software Foundation Gnu Public License.

1.14.1 BSD

During the 1970s, after Ken Thompson of Bell Labs spent a year teaching at the University of California at Berkeley, several research groups there began to develop software for the UNIX operating system. And, as Bell Labs had no plans to port the system to the then new DEC VAX computer system, the Computer Science Research Group at Berkeley undertook the port. That port became very popular at other universities, and the CSRG began distribution of it, with their modifications and additions, under the name Berkeley Software Distribution. The researchers at Berkeley frequently found ways to improve or add to the existing versions of UNIX. Bell Labs accepted some of the BSD changes, and passed on others. Over time the CSRG found ways to improve the basic aspects of UNIX (*e.g.*, the file system). Concurrently, AT&T made improvements of their own, causing the two versions to move in different (although similar) directions. As development progressed on the Berkeley version of UNIX, it grew further and further away from the work that AT&T was doing on their version (the last version of which was System V). In the early 1990s there was a major legal skirmish over the Berkeley Software Distribution (BSD) between AT&T, the University of California at Berkeley, and the Unix System Laboratories (USL), to which AT&T had turned over the marketing and development of UNIX. The suit resulted in most of BSD being found to be unencumbered by copyright restrictions by those who controlled the original Bell Labs code. By the mid-1990s, the CSRG released 4.4BSD-Lite, Release 2 as their final product as they were closed down by the Regents of the University of California. The BSD releases were the root of the various versions of BSD that are common today, most notably FreeBSD, Net BSD and Open BSD. Throughout its development, BSD was distributed in an open manner, resulting in contributions from many different contributors.

1.14.2 The Free Software Foundation and the GNU Project

In 1983, Richard Stallman (then of MIT) became frustrated with the growing commercialization of the computer development work that had been done at MIT, and with the increasing limitations imposed on software users. After a time, he began to create software that gave control to users. His vision was to create an entire operating system totally free of the restrictions being imposed by proprietary licensing. His first major software development effort (even before he became disenchanted with trends in the software industry) was the text editor, GNU Emacs. His next was a LISP system, a wick compiler, and finally the GNU project.

In 1985 Stallman founded the Free Software Foundation (FSF) to help generate support for the GNU Project. FSF has grown into one of the most important organizations in the FOSS movement. While the primary FSF mission continues to be the completion of the GNU operating system, FSF has also taken on the role of "free-software evangelist" by protecting and supporting free software. FSF also holds the copyrights too much of the source code written for the GNU project, ensuring that it always remains freely available to users.

Over the next 10 years Stallman gathered a group of people together who essentially developed the entire core utilities found in UNIX and the Unix-like operating systems. In the UNIX spirit, these consist of hundreds (perhaps thousands) of small utility programs and tools. This project is still operating and is known as the GNU Project. Many of these programs have become standard on the BSD variants as well (see above). In 1994, Linux Torvalds released the first version of the Linux kernel, and when combined with the GNU utilities already available from the GNU Project, the Linux operating system came to be. The Debian distribution of Linux is called GNU/Linux, in recognition of Stallman's position that it is a joint production, to recognize that the GNU Project provides most of the essential utilities. The GNU Project continues its slow progress on its own operating system kernel, which will be known as Hurd. Hurd is intended to be offered as the official GNU replacement for the UNIX kernel, though it is currently at a beta development stage.

While the FSF has become somewhat controversial, it has certainly had a major impact on computing. Millions of copies of the GNU software are used every day throughout the world.

1.14.3 Free Software Foundation

The *Free Software Foundation (FSF)* is a non-profit corporation founded by Richard Stallman on 4 October 1985 to support the free software movement, a copy left-based movement which aims to promote the universal freedom to distribute and modify computer software without restriction . The FSF is incorporated in the Commonwealth of Massachusetts, United States of America.

From its founding until the mid-1990s, FSF's funds were mostly used to employ software developers to write free software for the GNU Project. Since the mid-1990s, the FSF's employees and volunteers have mostly worked on legal and structural issues for the free software movement and the free software community.

Being consistent with its goals, only free software is used on all of the FSF's computers.

1.14.4 GNU Project

The *GNU Project* is free software, mass collaboration project, announced in 1983 by Richard Stallman. It initiated the GNU operating system, software development for which began in January 1984. GNU is a recursive acronym that stands for "GNU's Not Unix".

The founding goal of the project was, in the words of its initial announcement, to develop "a sufficient body of free software to get along without any software that is not free." To make this happen, the GNU Project began working on an operating system called *GNU*. This goal of making a free software operating system was achieved in 1992 when the last gap in the GNU system, a kernel, was filled by a third-party Unix-style kernel called *"Linux"* being released as free software.

Current work of the GNU Project includes software development, awareness building, and political campaigning.

1.14.5 Berkeley Software Distribution

Berkeley Software Distribution (BSD), sometimes called *Berkeley Unix*, is the UNIX derivative distributed by the University of California, Berkeley, starting in the 1970s.

Historically, BSD has been considered as a branch of UNIX—'BSD UNIX', because it had shared the initial code base and design with the original UNIX by AT&T and collaborated on the development in the pioneer days of UNIX. It was widely identified with the versions of UNIX available for workstation-class systems, which can be attributed to the ease with which it could be licensed and the familiarity it found among the founders of many technology companies during the 1980s. The familiarity often came from using similar systems—notably DEC's ULTRIX and Sun Microsystems SunOS—during their education. Though BSD itself was largely superseded by the System V Release 4 and OSF/1 systems in the 1990s (both of which incorporated BSD code), the modified code base as open source—mostly derived from 4.4BSD-Lite have seen increasing use and development recently.

Today, the term of "BSD" is often non-specifically used to refer to any of the BSD descendants, *e.g.*, FreeBSD, NetBSD or OpenBSD, which forms a branch of Unix-like operating systems.

1.15 WHY "FREE SOFTWARE" IS BETTER THAN "OPEN SOURCE"

"Open Source" misses the point of Free Software is an updated version of this article. While free software by any other name would give you the same freedom, it makes a big difference which name we use : different words convey different ideas. In 1998, some of the people in the free software community began using the term "open source software" instead of "free software" to describe what they do. The term "open source" quickly became associated with a different approach, a different philosophy, different values, and even a different criterion for which licenses are acceptable. The Free Software movement and the Open Source movement are today separate movements with different views and goals, although we can and do work together on some practical projects.

The fundamental difference between the two movements is in their values, their ways of looking at the world. For the Open Source movement, the issue of whether software should be open source is a practical question, not an ethical one. As one person put it, "Open source is a development methodology; free software is a social movement." For the Open Source movement, non-free software is a suboptimal solution. For the Free Software movement, non-free software is a social problem and free software is the solution.

1.16 PROPRIETARY VS. OPEN SOURCE LICENSING MODEL

Proprietary/Close Source S/W	*Open Source S/W*
Licensor distributes object code only; source code is kept a trade secret.	Licensor distributed source code.
Modifications are prohibited.	Modification are permitted.
All upgrades, support and development are done by licensor.	Licensee may do its own development and support or hire any third party to do it.
Fees are for the software license, Maintenance, and upgrades.	Fees, if any, are for integration, packing, support, and consulting.
Sublicensing is prohibited, or is a very limited right.	Sublicensing id permitted; licensee may have to distribute the source code to program and modification.
Microsoft Windows is an example of Close Source S/W.	Wikipedia is an example of Open Source S/W.

1.17 WHY SOME COMPANIES USE OPEN SOURCE SOFTWARE ?

Some companies use open source software because :

- Cost savings
- Stability
- Access and broad rights to source code
- Access to skilled community of developers
- Ability to define and expedite new development.

1.18 WHY SOME COMPANIES DON'T USE OPEN SOURCE SOFTWARE ?

Some companies don't use open source software because :

- "Free like a puppy"
- Migration costs
- Uncertainty about open development model

- Lack of IP warranties and indemnities
- Copy left provisions of GPL, LGPL and similar licenses.

SUMMARY

Open Source or *Open Source Software (OSS)* is different from proprietary software. In Open Source, the source code used in the software is available to anyone to examine, evaluate, and adapt. *Open source* is a development method for software that harnesses the power of distributed peer review and transparency of process. The Open Source Definition is a bill of rights for the computer user. It defines certain rights that a software license must grant you to be certified as Open Source.

Example of open source software is : Linux, Apache, BSD, Wikipedia, Mozilla.

Free software is software that can be used, studied, and modified without restriction, and which can be copied and redistributed in modified or unmodified form either without restriction, or with restrictions only to ensure that further recipients can also do these things. Free software is also known as "*software libre*", "Free, Libre and Open Source Software" ("FLOSS"), and "Free and Open Source Software" ("FOSS").

Free in Free Software is referring to freedom, not price. Having been used in this meaning since the 80s, the first documented complete definition appears to be the GNU's Bulletin, vol. 1 no. 1 [1], published February 1986. In particular, four freedoms define Free Software

Example : Linux, BSD, Darwin and Open Solaris

Public domain comprises the body of knowledge and innovation (especially creative works such as writing, art, music, and inventions) in relation to which no person or other legal entity can establish or maintain proprietary interests within a particular legal jurisdiction. Programs that are uncopyrighted because their authors intended to share them with everyone else are in the public domain. The UNIX community has developed a number of such programs over the years.

REVIEW QUESTIONS

1. What is the reason for using Open Source Technology ? Explain it.
2. What is Open Source and give the proper definition of open source ?
3. What are the distribution criteria of open source technology ?
4. Explain the principles of open source and give the requirements of open source.
5. Where the open source has successor ?
6. What is Free Software ? Explain it and write the difference between open source and free software.
7. What is Public Domain ? Explain it.
8. Explain the difference between Open Source and Close Source Software.
9. Explain how the FOSS does not mean any cost.
10. Explain the History of BSD.
11. Explain the History of FSF.
12. Explain the History of GNU project.

❑❑❑

Chapter 2

PRINCIPLES AND OPEN SOURCE METHODOLOGY

2.1 HISTORY

In late 1970s and early 1980s, two different groups were establishing the roots of the current open source software movement :

- On the US East coast, Richard Stallman, formerly a programmer at the MIT AI Lab, resigned, and launched the GNU Project and the Free Software Foundation. The ultimate goal of the GNU Project was to build a free operating system, and Richard started by coding some programming tools (a compiler, an editor, etc.). As a legal tool, the GNU General Public License (GPL) was designed not only to ensure that the software produced by GNU will remain free, but to promote the production of more and more free software. On the philosophical side, Richard Stallman also wrote the GNU Manifesto, stating that availability of source code and freedom to redistribute and modify software are fundamental rights.
- On the US West coast, the Computer Science Research Group (CSRG) of the University of California at Berkeley was improving the Unix system, and building lots of applications, which quickly become "BSD Unix". Mainly DARPA contracts, and a dense network of Unix hackers around the world helped to debug, maintain and improve the system funded these efforts. During many time that software was not redistributed outside the community of holders of a Unix AT&T license. But in the late 1980s, it was finally distributed under the "BSD license", one of the first open source licenses. Unfortunately, at that time every user of BSD UNIX also needed an AT&T Unix license, since some parts of the kernel and several important utilities, which were needed for a usable system, were still proprietary.

During the 1980s and early 1990s, open source software continued its envelopment, initially in several relatively isolated groups. USENET and the Internet helped to coordinate transnational efforts, and to build up strong user communities. Slowly, much of the software already developed was integrated, merging the work of many of these groups. As a result of this integration, complete environments could be built on top of Unix using open source software. In many cases, system admen's even replaced the standard tools with GNU programs. At that time, many applications were already the best ones in their field (Unix utilities, compilers, etc.). Especially interesting is the case of the X Window System, which was one of the first cases of open source software funded by a consortium of companies.

During 1991–1992, the whole landscape of open source software, and of software development in general, was ready to change. Two very exciting events were taking place, although in different communities :

- In California, Bill Jolitz was implementing the missing portions to complete the Net/2 distribution, until it was ready to run on I386-class machines. Net/2 was the result of the effort of the CSRG to make an unencumbered version of BSD Unix (free of AT&T copyrighted code). Bill called his work 386BSD, and it quickly became appreciated within the BSD and Unix communities. It included not only a kernel, but also many utilities, making a complete operating system.

  The work was covered by the BSD license, which also made it a completely free software platform. It also included free software under other licenses (like for instance the GNU compiler).

- In Finland, Linus Torvalds, a student of computer science, unhappy with Tanenbaum's Minix, was implementing the first versions of the Linux kernel. Soon, many people were collaborating to make that kernel more and more usable, and adding many utilities to complete GNU/Linux, a real operating system. The Linux kernel, and the GNU applications used on top of it are covered by GPL.

In 1993, both GNU/Linux and 386BSD were reasonably stable platforms. Since then, 386BSD has evolved into a family of BSD based operating systems (NetBSD, FreeBSD, and OpenBSD), while the Linux kernel is healthy evolving and being used in many GNU/Linux distributions (Slack ware, Debian, Red Hat, Suse, Mandrake, and many more).

During the 1990s, many open source projects have produced a good quantity of useful (and usually high-quality) software. Some of them (chosen with no special reason in mind) are Apache (widely used as a WWW server), Perl (an interpreted language with lots of libraries), XFree86 (the most widely used X11 implementation for PC-based machines), GNOME and KDE (both providing a consistent set of libraries and applications to present the casual user with an easy to use and friendly desktop environment), Mozilla (the free software project funded by Netscape to build a WWW browser), etc. Of all these projects, GNOME and KDE are especially important, because they address usability by non-technical people. Their results are already visible and of good quality, finally allowing everybody to benefit from open source software. The software being produced by these projects dispels the common myth that open source software is mainly focused on server and developer-oriented systems. In fact, both projects are currently producing lots of desktop personal productivity applications.

The late 1990s are very exciting times with respect to open source software. Open source systems based on GNU/Linux or *BSD are gaining public acceptance, and have become a real alternative to proprietary systems, competing head to head with the market leaders (like Windows NT in servers). In many niches, the best choice is already open source (an outstanding case is Apache as Web server, with a market share consistently over 50%).

The announce of the liberation of Netscape Communicator, in 1998, was the starting point of a rush of many big companies to understand open source software. Apple, Corel and IBM, for instance, are trying different approaches to use, promotion or development of open source software. Many companies of all sizes (from the small startup composed of a couple of programmers to the recently public Red Hat) are exploring new economic models to succeed in the competitive software market. The media has also started to give attention to the formerly marginal open source software movement, which is now composed not only of individuals and non-profit organizations, but also of small and medium companies.

Looking at all these events, the following question easily arises : *Are we at the beginning of a new model of the software industry* ? This is a question, which is difficult to answer, since there is no known and reliable method for looking into the future. However, through this document, we hope to provide readers with some information, which can be useful, can use to reach their own answer.

The free software movement was launched in 1983. In 1998, a group of individuals advocated that the term free software is replaced by Open Source Software (OSS) as an expression, which is less ambiguous and more comfortable for the corporate world. Software developers may want to publish their software with an open source license, so that any body may also develop the same software or understand how it works. Open source software generally allows any body to make a new version of the software, port it to new operating systems and processor architectures, share it with others or market it. The aim of open source is to let the product be more understandable, modifiable, duplicatable, reliable or simply accessible, while it is still marketable.

The Open Source Definition, notably, presents an open source philosophy, and further defines a boundary on the usage, modification and redistribution of open source software. Software licenses grant rights to users, which would otherwise be prohibited by copyright. These include rights on usage, modification and redistribution. Several open source software licenses have qualified within the boundary of the Open Source Definition. The most prominent example is the popular GNU General Public License (GPL). While open source presents a way to broadly make the sources of a product publicly accessible, the open source licenses allow the authors to fine tune such access.

The "open source" label came out of a strategy session held in Palo Alto in reaction to Netscape's January 1998 announcement of a source code release for Navigator (as Mozilla). A group of individuals at the session included Todd Anderson, Larry Augustin, John Hall, Sam Ockman, Christine Peterson and Eric S. Raymond. They used the opportunity before the release of Navigator's source code to clarify a potential confusion caused by the ambiguity of the word "free" in English. The 'open source' movement is generally thought to have begun with this strategy session. Many people, nevertheless, claimed that the birth of the Internet, since 1969, started the open source movement, while others do not distinguish between open source and free software movements.

2.2 OPEN SOURCE INITIATIVES

Open Source Initiative (OSI) is a non-profit corporation dedicated to managing and promoting the Open Source Definition for the good of the community, specifically through the OSI Certified Open Source Software certification mark and program. You can read about successful software products that have these properties, and about our certification mark and program, which allow you to be confident that software really, is "Open Source." We also make copies of approved open source licenses here.

The basic idea behind open source is very simple. When programmers can read, redistribute, and modify the source code for a piece of software, the software evolves. People improve it, people adapt it, and people fix bugs. And this can happen at a speed that, if one is used to the slow pace of conventional software development, seems astonishing.

We in the open source community have learned that this rapid evolutionary process produces better software than the traditional closed model, in which only a very few programmers can see the source and everybody else must blindly use an opaque block of bits.

Open Source Initiative exists to make this case to the commercial world.

Open source software is an idea whose time has finally come. For twenty years it has been building momentum in the technical cultures that built the Internet and the World Wide Web. Now it's breaking out into the commercial world, and that's changing all the rules. This site is still evolving as we think through the implications of open source in the commercial world.

2.2.1 History of Initiatives

The movement was formally launched in 1998 by Jon "maddog" Hall, Larry Augustin, Eric S. Raymond, Bruce Perens, and others. Raymond is probably the single person most identified with the movement; he was and remains its self-described principal theorist, but does not claim to lead it in any exclusive sense. The open source movement is steered by a loose collegium of elders that includes Raymond, its other co-founders, and such notables as Linus Torvalds, Larry Wall, and Guido van Rossum.

The founders were dissatisfied with what they saw as the confrontational attitude of the free software movement, and favored advocating free software exclusively on the grounds of technical superiority (a claim previously made by Raymond in his essay *The Cathedral and the Bazaar*). It was hoped that open source and the associated propaganda would become a more persuasive argument to businesses. Raymond's comment was *"If you want to change the world, you have to co-opt the people who write the big checks."* (Cygnus Support had been pursuing exactly this approach for a number of years already, but not advertising it widely.)

The group adopted the Open Source Definition for open source software, based on the Debian Free Software Guidelines, which in turn was based on The Free Software Definition. They also established the *Open Source Initiative* (OSI) as a steward organization for the movement. However, they were unsuccessful in their attempt to secure a trademark for 'open source', to act as an imprimatur and to prevent misuse of the term. Despite this, the OSI developed considerable influençe in the corporate sphere and has been able to hold abuse of the term to a tolerable minimum through vigorous jawboning. With the Free Software Foundation (FSF), it has become one of the hacker community's two principal advocacy organizations.

The early period of the open source movement coincided with and partly drove the dot-com boom of 1998-2000, and saw a large growth in the popularity of Linux and the formation of many open source-friendly companies. The movement also caught the attention of the mainstream software industry, leading to open source software offerings by established software companies such as Corel (Corel Linux), Sun Microsystems (OpenOffice.org), and IBM (OpenAFS). By the time the dot-com boom busted in 2001, many of the early hopes of open source advocates had already borne fruit, and the movement continued from strength to strength in the cost-cutting climate of the 2001-2003 recession.

2.2.2 Actions

The actions are:

1. Writing and spreading free software
2. Building awareness
3. Legislation
4. Internal conflict

2.3 OPEN STANDARDS PRINCIPLES

An Open Standard is more than just a specification. The principles behind the standard, and the practice of offering and operating the standard, are what make the standard Open. Bruce Perens, who also created the Open Source Definition and the Debian Social Contract, created Open Standards Principles and Practice.

Open Source Principles are :

2.3.1 Availability

Open Standards are available for all to read and implement. Thus :

1. The best practice is for the standards text and reference implementation to be available for free downloads via the Internet.
2. Any software project should be able to afford a copy without undue hardship. The cost should not far exceed the cost of a college textbook.
3. Licenses attached to the standards documentation must not restrict any party from implementing the standard using any form of software license.
4. The best practice is for software reference platforms to be licensed in a way that is compatible with all forms of software licensing, both Free Software (Open Source) and proprietary. However, see *Predatory Practices* regarding license restrictions that may be appropriate for a software reference platform.

2.3.2 Maximize End-User Choice

Open Standards create a fair, competitive market for implementations of the standard. They do not lock the customer in to a particular vendor or group. Thus :

1. They must allow a wide range of implementations, by businesses, academia, and public projects.
2. They must support a range of pricing from very expensive to zero-price.

2.3.3 No Royalty

Open Standards are free for all to *implement*, with no royalty or fee. *Certification* of compliance by the standards organization may have a fee. Thus :

1. Patents embedded in standards must be licensed royalty-free, with non-discriminatory terms.
2. Certification programs should include a low or zero cost self-certification, but may include higher-cost programs with enhanced branding.

2.3.4 No Discrimination

Open Standards and the organizations that administer them do not favor one implementer over another for any reason other than the technical standards compliance of a vendor's implementation. Certification organizations must provide a path for low and zero-cost implementations to be validated, but may also provide enhanced certification services. Thus :

1. A standards organization that wishes to support itself through certification branding should establish a premium track and a low-cost or zero-cost track. Generally, the premium track will provide a certification lab outside of the vendor's facility to verify a vendor's implementation and enhanced branding : a certification mark that indicates a greater certainty of verification and financial support of the standard. The low or zero-cost track would provide self-certification by the vendor and baseline branding.

2.3.5 Extension or Subset

Implementations of Open Standards may be extended, or offered in subset form. However, certification organizations may decline to certify subset implementations, and may place requirements upon extensions.

2.3.6 Predatory Practices

Open Standards may employ license terms that protect against subversion of the standard by *embrace-and-extend* tactics. The license may require the publication of reference information and a license to create and redistribute software compatible with the extensions. It may not prohibit the implementation of extensions.

1. The standards organization may wish to apply an agreement similar to the *Sun Industry Standards Source License* to the standard documentation and its accompanying reference implementation. The Sun agreement requires publication of a reference implementation (not the actual commercial implementation) for any extensions to the standard. This makes it possible for a standards organization to actively preserve interoperability without stifling innovation.

2.3.7 Modularity

Modularity is the principle of maintaining well-defined boundaries between components. Adhering to open standards where possible is a noticeable trait in open source software because it helps define these boundaries.

2.3.8 Early and Often

Early and often entails making things available as early as possible. This includes not only the software but also plans and design. Applying this principle means putting an imperfect version out earlier rather than keeping something back until it is more polished.

Many open source projects achieve the early and often using a couple of common methods :

- **Source code availability :** The source code of the software is often made available either on a daily as a zip file or lives in a source code repository such as CVS or Subversions. Community members using these systems have to compile or build the software from its source code. This is typically used by a small percentage of the community that is actively working on, or interested in, the source code.
- **Milestones builds :** On a periodic basis the administrators or core developers of the project compile the software and make the resulting executables for downloading. These downloads are typically used by the members of the community that are interested in the functionality of the software. Many open source projects release milestones builds and these practices can be considered to be a form of methodology.
- **Nightly builds :** On a nightly basis the source code is compiled to generate the executable binaries. These builds are made available for community members that want to test the latest source code.

2.4 METHODOLOGIES

2.4.1 Software Engineering Methodology

"Given unlimited resources, the majority of software problems can probably be solved but the challenge for software engineers is to produce high-quality software with a finite amount of resources and to a predicted schedule."

2.4.1.1 Engineering Software

Developing a software system is usually not done in a single night of hard work, but is a complex and time-consuming process. In order to control this process, reducing the complexity and uncertainties surrounding the to-be software system, we try to adhere to some kind of framework that introduces certain degrees of structure to the overall development process. Software engineering methodologies are the framework that tells us how we should go about developing our software systems. These frameworks define different phases of the development process, such as planning, requirements analysis, design, testing and maintenance. The choice of which methodology to use in a development project is closely related to the size of the software system and the environment it is supposed to function in. The environment in itself constitutes a larger system—though most often not a computer software system, but rather some kind of organization. The different paradigms presented in this chapter all spring from this view of the world as a system of systems.

2.4.1.2 The Life-Cycle Paradigm

The life-cycle paradigm of software engineering is sometimes called the "waterfall model", as it demands a sequential approach to the development process. The work is started at the system level and passes through phases of analysis, design, coding, testing and maintenance. Six activities constitute the overall development process.

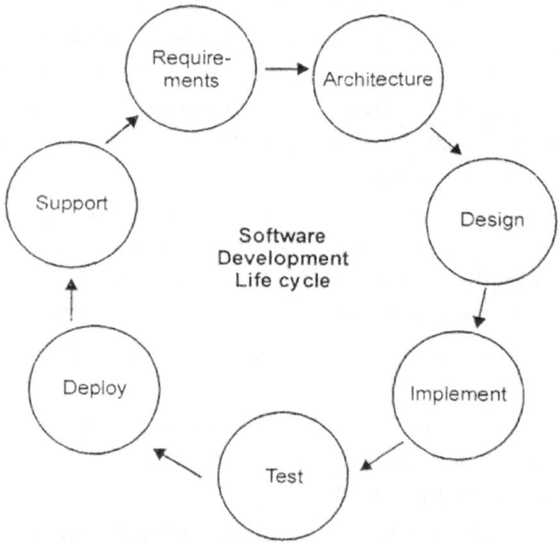

Fig. 2.1. Life Cycle Paradigm.

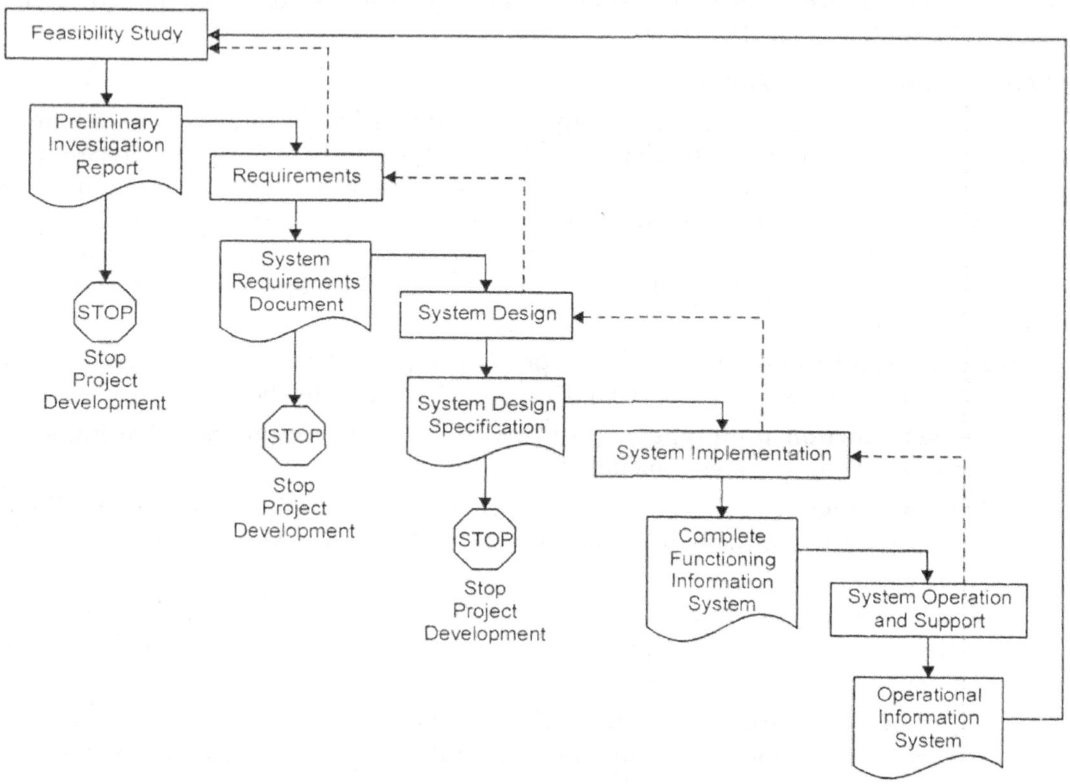

Fig. 2.2. Waterfall Model.

- **System engineering and analysis :** This activity is characterized by system-level requirements gathering for all system elements, which then is reduced to a subset of requirements that are relevant to the software system being developed. Overall design and analysis tasks are also executed in order to understand the full system of which the software system being developed is only a part.
- **Software requirements analysis :** This activity is usually executed together with the customer, as the goal is to document all function, performance and interfacing requirements for the software.
- **Design :** When creating the design of the software system the requirements are transformed into a representation of software that can be assessed for quality before the actual coding begins. Data structures, architecture, procedural detail and interface characterization are outlined and documented in a design specification.
- **Coding :** This activity is the transition of the design specification into a software program.
- **Testing :** This activity is to be executed using documented test methods in order to ensure that as many errors as possible is unveiled, and that the software is in accordance with the requirements.
- **Maintenance :** Rather than being an atomic activity, maintenance reapplies all other activities, as new requirements are defined in order to adapt the software to the changes occurring in its environment and to correct errors encountered after the software has been deployed.

2.4.1.3 The Prototyping Paradigm

Contrary to the static, procedural approach offered by the life-cycle paradigm, the prototyping paradigm can be used. Similarly to the life-cycle paradigm, this process begins by gathering requirements of the system. The developers meet with customers, determine the overall objectives of the software and identify any known requirements. A quick design then occurs, focusing on areas visible to the users, such as user interface and basic functionality. The design model is then used to implement a first prototype, which may take one of three forms :

- **Interaction prototype :** This is a paper or computer software prototype that makes it possible for users to understand how to interact with the software system.
- **Subset function prototype :** This is a working software program that implements a subset of the required functionality.
- **Existing program :** This is an existing program that implements most or all of the required functionality, but has features that should be improved in a later development effort.
- **A throwaway prototype :** This is may be usable software program, but is not suitable as the final software product, for various reasons such as poor performance, maintainability or overall quality.
- **A prototype to refine and deliver :** This kind of prototype is enhanced and possibly reworked in various areas so that it is suitable to deliver as the final software product.

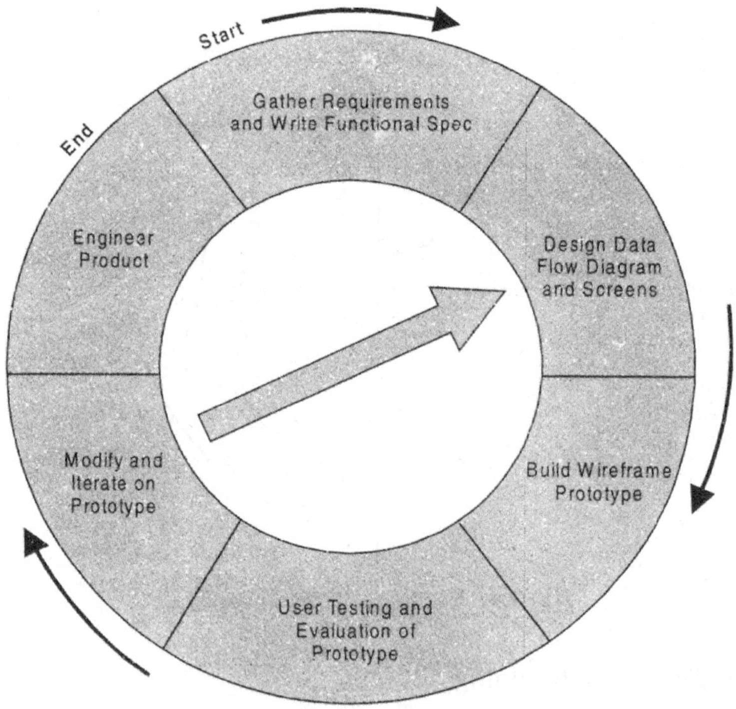

Fig. 2.3. The Prototyping Paradigm.

When the prototype is created, the customer reviews it. Typically this review gives feedback to the developers that help remove uncertainties in the requirements of the software system, and starts an iteration of refinement in order to further clarify requirements by improving the prototype, or by building new prototypes.

2.4.1.4 The Spiral Model Paradigm

In addition to some of the aspects of the life-cycle and prototyping paradigms, the spiral model adds an element of risk analysis to the development process. The model is presented as a spiral, in which a circuit around four major activities represents each iteration :

- **Planning :** Determine objectives and constraints of the project, and define the alternatives.
- **Risk analysis :** Analysis of alternatives, and identification/resolution of risks.
- **Engineering :** Development of the "next-level" product.
- **Customer evolution :** Evaluation of the product engineered.

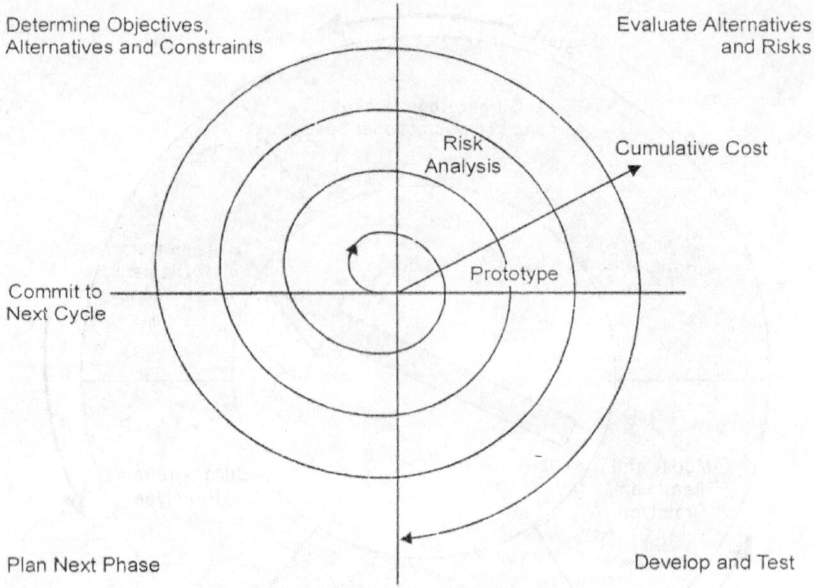

Fig. 2.4. The Spiral Model Paradigm.

2.4.2 An Open Source Methodology

One of the buzzwords of the movement in the field of computer programming is the concept of "open source" software and computing. The term refers to software created by a community of programmers rather than a single vendor. The best example is the popular Web Browser known as Mozilla. The "Source code" of the software was created by programmers from different organizations and is made freely available to others to modify and copy as they wish. Open source software and operating system have proven so popular that many for profit corporations are adapting open source products into their business models some general conclusion about open source software development methodology.

2.4.2.1 What is Open Source Methodology for Development ?

Our interest steams from personal experience of using open source software as well as from our academic background within systems science. At times we have got a feeling of trespassing on unexplored fields and these are the times we feel have been most rewarding. As we have seen many positive aspects of this development process, we have to come believe that traditional development methods a really may have something to learn from the open source community. What is then our experience of our approach ?

This material is very extensive, and has demanded a large portion of critical interpretation. We hope to have put forward the characteristics of open source software development, in a way that has been natural and easy to read. When discussing open source, we are not only discussing a methodology, principle or phenomenon open source is in itself way of viewing software and the governing principles of the development process. Commercialism and idealism found in the open source community is in itself a subject well worthy. There are many other aspects of open source software development that are interesting and deserve to be explored.

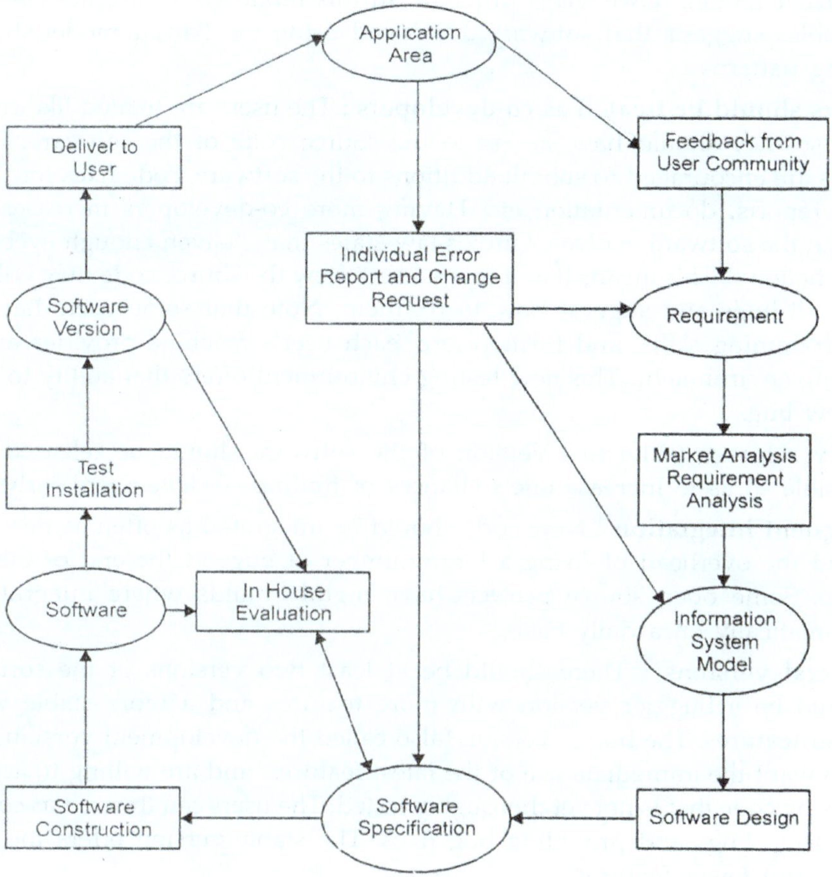

Fig. 2.5. OST Methodology.

2.5 PHILOSOPHY

In his 1997 essay the Cathedral and the Bazaar, open source evangelist Eric S. Raymond suggests a model for developing OSS known as the Bazaar model. Raymond likens the development of software by traditional methodologies to building a cathedral, *"carefully crafted by individual wizards or small bands of mages working in splendid isolation"*. He suggests that all software should be developed using the bazaar style, which he described as *"a great babbling bazaar of differing agendas and approaches."*

In the Cathedral model, development takes place in a centralized way. Roles are clearly defined. Roles include people dedicated to designing (the architects), people responsible for managing the project, and people responsible for implementation. Traditional software engineering follows the Cathedral model. Fred P. Brooks in his book *The Mythical Man-Month* advocates this sort of model. He goes further to say that in order to preserve the architectural integrity of a system; as few architects should do the system design as possible.

The Bazaar model, however, is different. In this model, roles are not clearly defined. Gregorio Robles suggests that software developed using the Bazaar model should exhibit the following patterns :

- **Users should be treated as co-developers :** The users are treated like co-developers and so they should have access to the source code of the software. Furthermore users are encouraged to submit additions to the software, code fixes for the software, bug reports, documentation etc. Having more co-developers increases the rate at which the software evolves. Linux's law states that, "Given enough eyeballs all bugs are shallow." This means that if many users view the source code they will eventually find all bugs and suggest how to fix them. Note that some users have advanced programming skills, and furthermore, each user's machine provides an additional testing environment. This new testing environment offers that ability to find and fix a new bug.
- **Early releases :** The first version of the software should be released as early as possible so as to increase one's chances of finding co-developers early.
- **Frequent integration :** New code should be integrated as often as possible so as to avoid the overhead of fixing a large number of bugs at the end of the project life cycle. Some open source projects have nightly builds where integration is done automatically on a daily basis.
- **Several versions :** There should be at least two versions of the software. There should be a buggier version with more features and a more stable version with fewer features. The buggy version (also called the development version) is for users who want the immediate use of the latest features, and are willing to accept the risk of using code that is not yet thoroughly tested. The users can then act as co-developers, reporting bugs and providing bug fixes. The stable version offers the users fewer bugs and fewer features.
- **High modularization :** The general structure of the software should be modular allowing for parallel development.
- **Dynamic decision-making structure :** There is a need for a decision making structure, whether formal or informal, that makes strategic decisions depending on changing user requirements and other factors. Cf. Extreme programming.

Most well known OSS products follow the Bazaar model as suggested by Eric Raymond. These include projects such as Linux, Netscape, Apache, the GNU Compiler Collection, and Perl to mention a few.

There is no one philosophy that brings people to open source software. There is however two main branches of thought in which many people share some similar views and have helped create a strong movement. To understand the open source movement as a whole you need to understand both of these main philosophies.

2.6 SOFTWARE FREEDOM

An earlier software movement similar to Open Source is the Free Software Movement (embodied in the Free Software Foundation). The free software movement is a new social movement, which aims to protect the rights of user to access and modify software. There are generally three primary components of software freedom as following :

1. **Freedom to Use** : Many believe that software should not have limitations on their private use, aside from restrictions on the creator's liability. In contrast, some commercial packages (like Microsoft Windows) disallow certain usages while a more expensive product allows such a use. According to US copyright law, this right is implicit unless limited by private contracts.
2. **Freedom to Modify** : Possibly more important than the freedom to use is the freedom to modify existing programs. Although certainly related to the overall open source ideal, this freedom also implies that your modifications remain yours. Some open source licenses require the modifier to assign the rights to their work to the originator of the license (Microsoft's Shared Source program is generally considered one example). Obviously, very few completely commercial software packages give users this freedom. In US copyright law, this is an implicit exclusive right of the creator of a work. To give others this right, the creator must agree to do so.
3. **Freedom to Distribute** : A final key freedom is the ability to distribute software, modified or unmodified. Software packages that limit their distribution limit others freedom to do with it what they will. It can also prevent them from providing their improvement to the community. Similar to the freedom to modify, some open source licenses also limit the freedom to distribute, often requiring changes to be submitted back to some central repository. As with the right to modify, this is an exclusive right of the creator.

Notably absent from these freedoms is the requirement that free software be economically free. Several licenses do not prevent merchants from selling the software whether modified or unmodified. In fact, several groups have historically charged for various pieces of software, which are generally considered free software. Depending on the license, the merchant may still be under other restrictions.

An example of a license that provides software freedom with some restrictions on the distributor of the software is the GNU General Public License, or GPL. Richard Stallman et al., for the GNU Project, wrote the GPL. The GPL has all of the above freedoms listed within. The most important difference from the above baseline is what the Creative Commons calls a "Share and Share Alike" clause. If you distribute a modification to a particular software package under the GPL, then you must agree that your portion of the work is also licensed by the GPL.

2.7 OPEN SOURCE SOFTWARE DEVELOPMENT

Software development process Activities and steps
Requirements | Architecture | Design | Implementation | Testing | Deployment
Models
Agile | Clean room | Iterative | RAD | RUP | Spiral | Waterfall | XP | Scrum
Supporting disciplines
Configuration management | Documentation | Software Quality Assurance (SQA) | Project management | User experience design

Open source software development is the process by which open source software (or similar software whose source is publicly available) is developed. These are software products "available with its source code and under an open source license to study, change, and improve its design". Examples of popular Open source software product are Mozilla Firefox and the OpenOffice.org Suite. The Open source software development method is very unstructured, because no clear development tools, phases, etc., have been defined like with development methods such as DSDM. Instead, every project has its own phases. There are, however, generalities between Open source development projects.

The second main branch of open source philosophy revolves around the opportunity for a new software development model. Open source is also about sharing ideas, and spreading the effort of creating software over a large number of interested developers. This sharing can lead to better software in shorter development times. It also allows for better feedback directly to the developers than is often present in traditional development models. Major companies like Apple and IBM have recognized that there can be a significant advantage to writing software in this way. Apple by way of the Darwin project and IBM through several significant donations of software and patents to open source groups have paved the way for other companies to seriously consider using this development model.

Open source software development can be divided into several phases. A diagram displaying the process-data structure of Open source software development is placed on the right side. In this picture, the phases of Open source software development are displayed, along with the corresponding data elements. This diagram is made using the Meta-Modeling and Meta-Process Modeling techniques.

The process starts with a choice between the adopting of an existing project, or the starting of a new project. The difference between these two is explained in the section 'New projects vs. existing projects'. If a new project is started, the process goes to the Initiation phase. If an existing project is adopted, the process goes directly to the Execution phase.

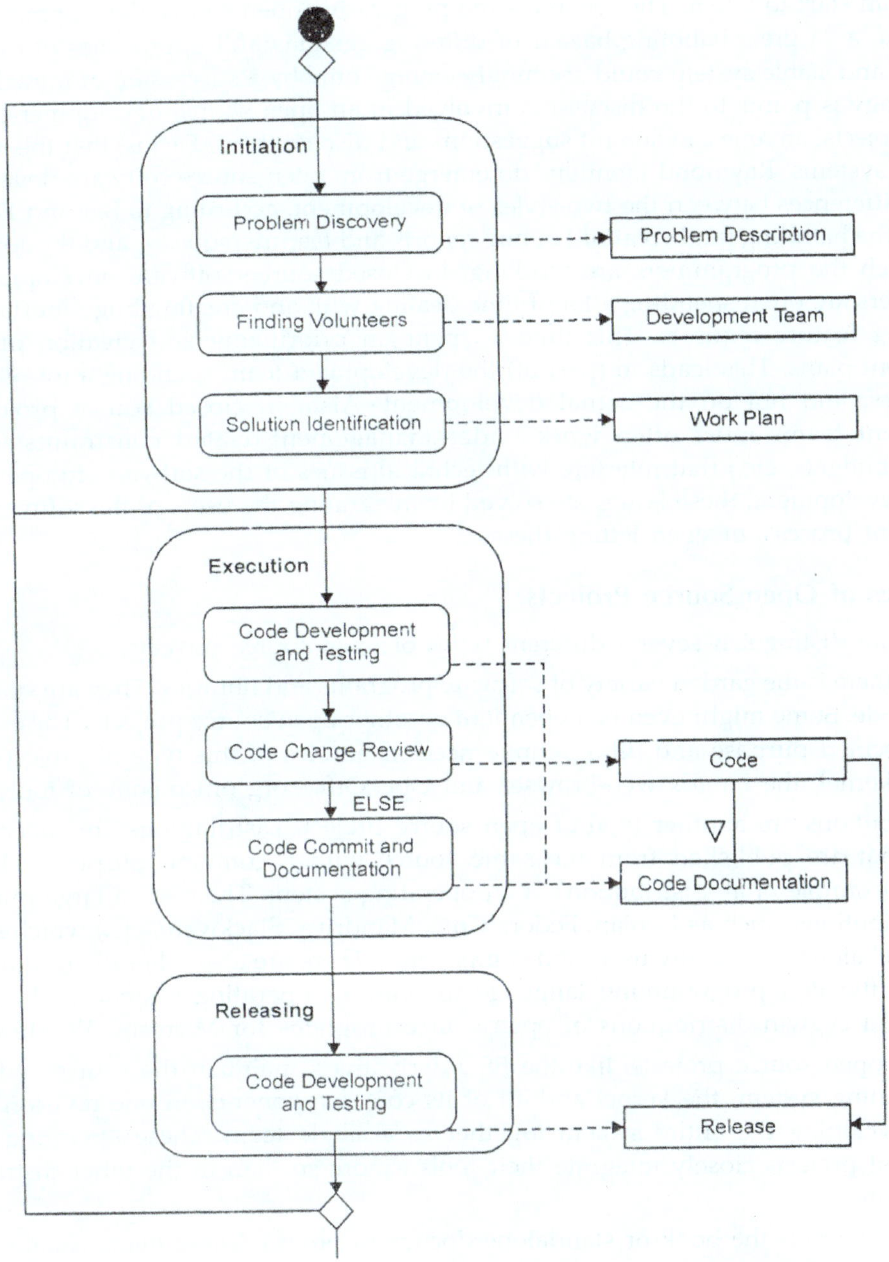

Fig. 2.6. Process data model for Open Source Software development.

2.7.1 History

In 1997, Eric S. Raymond wrote *the Cathedral and the Bazaar*. In this book, Raymond makes the distinction between two kinds of software development. The first is the conventional closed source development. These kind of development methods are, according to Raymond, like the building of a cathedral; central planning, tight organization and one process from start to finish. The second is the progressive open source development, which is more like a "a great babbling bazaar of differing agendas and approaches out of which a coherent and stable system could seemingly emerge only by a succession of miracles." The latter analogy is points to the discussion involved in an open source development process. In some projects, anyone can submit suggestions and discuss them. Fact is, that the 'coherent and stable systems' Raymond mentions do emerge from open source software development projects. Differences between the two styles of development, according to Bar and Fogel, are in general the handling (and creation) of bug reports and feature requests, and the constraints under which the programmers are working. In closed source software development, the programmers are often spending a lot of time dealing with and creating bug reports, as well as handling feature requests. This time is spent on prioritizing and creation of further development plans. This leads to (part of) the development team spending a lot of time on these issues, and not on the actual development. Also, in closed source projects, the development teams must often work under management-related constraints (such as deadlines, budgets, etc.) that interfere with technical issues of the software. In open source software development, these issues are solved by integrating the users of the software in the development process, or even letting these.

2.7.2 Types of Open Source Projects

One can distinguish several different types of open source projects.

First, there is the garden variety of software programs and libraries. They are standalone pieces of code. Some might even be dependent on other open source projects. These projects serve a specified purpose and fill a definite need. Examples of this type of project include the Linux kernel, the Firefox web-browser and OpenOffice.org office suite of tools.

Distributions are another type of open source project. Distributions are collections of software that are published from the same source with a common purpose. The most prominent example of a "distribution" is an operating system. There are a large number of Linux distributions (such as Debian, Fedora Core, Mandriva, Slackware, etc.) which ship the Linux kernel along with many user-land components. There are also other distributions, like ActivePerl, the Perl programming language for various operating system, and even the OpenCD and cygwin distributions of open source programs for Microsoft Windows.

Other open source projects, like the BSD derivatives, maintain the source code of an entire operating system, the kernel and all of its core components, in one revision control system; developing the entire system together as a single team. These operating system development projects closely integrate their tools : more so than in the other distribution-based systems.

Finally, there is the book or standalone document project. These items usually do not shipped as part of an open source software package. The Linux Documentation Project hosts many such projects that document various aspects of the GNU/Linux operating system. There are many other examples of this type of open source project.

2.7.3 Starting an Open Source Project

There are several ways in which work on an open source project can start :

1. An individual who senses the need for a project announces the intent to develop the project in public. The individual may receive offers of help from others. The group may then proceed to work on the code.
2. A developer working on a limited but working codebase, releases it to the public as the first version of an open source program. The developer continues to work on improving it, and possibly is joined by other developers.
3. The source code of a mature project is released to the public, after being developed as proprietary software or inhouse software.
4. A well-established open source project can be forked by an interested outside party. Several developers can then start a new project, whose source code then diverges from the original.

Eric Raymond observed in his famous essay "The Cathedral and the Bazaar" that announcing the intent for a project is usually inferior to releasing a working project to the public.

It's a common mistake to start an own project when contributing to an existing similar project would be more effective (NIH syndrome). To start a successful project it is very important to investigate what's already there.

2.7.4 Participants in OSS Development Projects

Participants in OSS development projects fall into two broad categories : The Core and the Peripheral. The Core or Inner Circle are developers who modify the primary code that constitutes the project. The Peripheral usually consists of users of the software. They report bugs, submit fixes, and suggest changes.

The participants can be divided into the following :

1. Project leaders who have the overall responsibility (Core). Most of them might have been involved in coding the first release of the software. They control the overall direction of individual projects.
2. Volunteer developers (Core/Periphery) who do actual coding for the project. These include :
   - o Senior members with broader overall authority.
   - o Peripheral developers producing and submitting code fixes.
   - o Occasional contributors.
   - o Maintainers who work on different aspects of the project.
3. Everyday users (Periphery) who perform testing, identify bugs, deliver bug reports, etc.
4. Posters (Periphery) who participate frequently in newsgroups and discussions, but do not do any coding.

Projects often exhibit an early geographical trend, even if there is international interest. For example, most of the core founders of the KDE Desktop Environment were German.

2.7.5 Tools used for Open Source Development

1. Communication Channels

Developers and users of an open source project are not all necessarily working on the project in proximity. They require some electronic means of communications. E-mail is one of the most common forms of communication among open source developers and users. Often, electronic mailing lists are used to make sure e-mail messages are delivered to all interested parties at once. This ensures that at least one of the members can reply to it (in private or to the whole mailing list). In order to communicate in real time, many projects use an instant messaging method such as IRC (although there are many others available). Web forums have recently become a common way for users to get help with problems they encounter when using an open source product. Wikis have become common as a communication medium for developers and users.

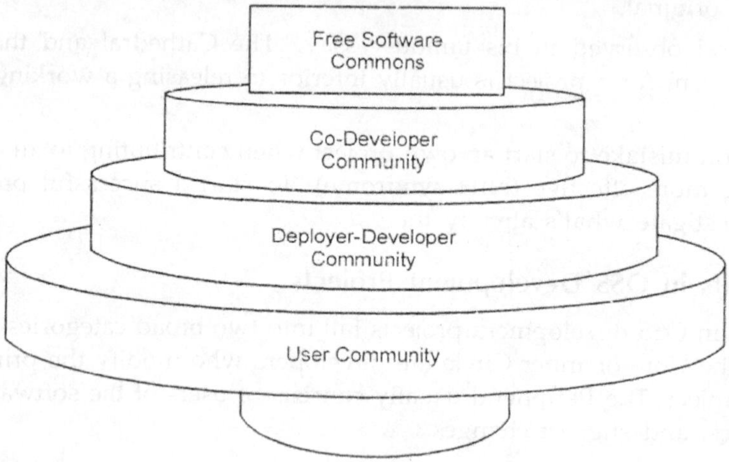

Fig. 2.7. Open Source Community.

2. Software Engineering Tools

I. Version control systems

In OSS development the participants, who are mostly volunteers, are distributed amongst different geographic regions so there is need for tools to aid participants to collaborate in the development of source code.

Concurrent Versions System (CVS) is a prominent example of a source code collaboration tool being used in OSS projects. CVS helps manage the files and codes of a project when several people are working on the project at the same time. CVS allows several people to work on the same file at the same time. This is done by moving the file into the users' directories and then merging the files when the users are done. CVS also enables one to easily retrieve a previous version of a file.

The Subversion Revision Control System (SVN) was created to replace CVS. It is quickly gaining ground as an OSS project version control system.

There are many other version control systems.

Bug trackers and task lists

Most large-scale projects require a bug tracker (usually web or otherwise Internet based) to keep track of the status of various issues in the development of the project. A simple text file is not sufficient, because they have many such bugs, and because they wish to facilitate reporting and maintenance of bugs by users and secondary developers. Some popular bug trackers include :

- Bugzilla—a sophisticated bug tracker from the Mozilla house. Web-based.
- Mantis—a web-based PHP/MySQL bug tracker.
- Trac—integrating a bug tracker with a wiki, and an interface to the Subversion version control system.
- Request tracker—written in Perl. Given as a default to CPAN modules - see rt.cpan.org.
- GNATS—The GNU Bugtracking system.
- SourceForge and its forks provide a bug tracker as part of its services. As a result many projects hosted at SourceForge.net and similar services default to using it.
- LibreSource.

3. Testing Tools

Since OSS projects undergo frequent integration, tools that help automate testing during system integration are used. An example of such tool is Tinderbox. Tinderbox enables participants in an OSS project to detect errors during system integration. Tinderbox runs a continuous build process and informs users about the parts of source code that have issues and on which platform(s) these issues arise. Furthermore, this tool identifies the author of the offending code. The author is then held responsible for ensuring that error is resolved. Mainly because normal testing tools are quite expensive, open source testing tools are gaining popularity.

A debugger is a computer program that is used to debug (and sometimes test or optimize) other programs. GNU Debugger (GDB) is an example of a debugger used in Open source software development. This debugger offers remote debugging, what makes it especially applicable to Open source software development. Also, some memory leak detectors have been designed to work with GDB.

A memory leak tool or memory debugger is a programming tool for finding memory leaks and buffer overflows. A memory leak is a particular kind of unnecessary memory consumption by a computer program, where the program fails to release memory that is no longer needed. Examples of memory leak detection tools used by Mozilla are the XPCOM Memory Leak tools. Validation tools are used to check if pieces of code conform to the specified syntax. They are most often used in the context of HTML/XML, but can also be used with programming languages. An example of a validation tool is LCLint, now called Splint.

4. Package Management

A package management system is a collection of tools to automate the process of installing, upgrading, configuring, and removing software packages from a computer. The Red Hat Package Manager (RPM) for .rpm and Advanced Packaging Tool (APT) for .deb file format, are package management systems used by a number of Linux distributions.

5. Automated Tests

Software testing is an integral part of open source development. While many open source packages were known to be released with some glaring bugs even in some stable releases, most open source software eventually becomes very stable.

Traditionally, in most of the open source there was a general lack of awareness for automated tests, in which one writes automated test scripts and programs that run the software and try to find out if it behaves correctly. Recently, however, this awareness has been growing, possibly because of influence from Extreme Programming, and because of some high-profile software packages that incorporated such test suites.

Most open source software is either command line or alternatively APIs and as such is very easy to test automatically.

2.8 LICENSES

2.8.1 What is License ?

A *license* is the permission or right granted to engage in some act without which the act might be otherwise unlawful. A person, institution, must grant a license or government that has the legal authority to do so. The term "license" also refers to the document that specifically describes these permissions and rights.

The license must be automatic, no signature required, however, this argument considers the license in the body of contract law, while some argue that it should be considered as copyright law, where there is one precedent for no-signature license. A good court test will no doubt happen in the next few years, given the popularity of this sort of license and the booming nature of Open Source.

Open source licenses define the privileges and restrictions a licensor must follow in order to use, modify or redistribute the open source software. Open source software includes software with source code in the public domain and software distributed under an open source license.

Examples of open source licenses include Apache License, BSD license, GNU General Public License, GNU Lesser General Public License, MIT License, Eclipse Public License and Mozilla Public License.

The proliferation of open source licenses is one of the few negative aspects of the open source movement because it is often difficult to understand the legal implications of the differences between licenses.

To understand the Open Source Definition, we need to look at some common licensing practices as they relate to Open Source.

- **Public Domain**

  A common misconception is that much free software is *public domain*. This happens simply because the idea of free software or Open Source is confusing to many people, and they mistakenly describe these programs as public-domain because that's the closest concept that they understand. The programs, however, are clearly copyrighted and covered by a license, just a license that gives people more rights than they are used to.

A public-domain program is one upon which the author has deliberately surrendered his copyright rights. It can't really be said to come with a license; it's your personal property to use as you see fit. Because you can treat it as your personal property, you can do what you want with a public-domain program. You can even re-license a public-domain program, removing that version from the public domain, or you can remove the author's name and treat it as your own work.

If we are doing a lot of work on a public-domain program, consider applying your own copyright to the program and re-licensing it. For example, if you don't want a third party to make their own modifications that they then keep private, apply the GPL or a similar license to your version of the program. The version that you started with will still be in the public domain, but your version will be under a license that others must need if they use it or derive from it.

You can easily take a public-domain program private, by declaring a copyright and applying your own license to it or simply declaring "All Rights Reserved."

- **Free Software Licenses in General**

If you have a free software collection like a *Linux* disk, you may believe the programs on that disk are your property. ınat's not entirely true. Copyrighted programs are the property of the copyright holder, even when they have an Open Source license like the GPL. The program's license grants you some rights, and you have other rights under the definition of *fair use* in copyright law.

It's important to note that an author does not have to issue a program with just one license. You can GPL a program, and also sell a version of the same program with a commercial, non-Open source license. Many people who want to make a program Open Source and still make some money from it use this exact strategy. Those who do not want an Open Source license may pay for the privilege, providing a revenue stream for the author.

All of the licenses we will examine have a common feature : they each disclaim all warranties. The intent is to protect the software owner from any liability connected with the program. Since the program is often being given away at no cost, this is a reasonable requirement—the author doesn't have a sufficient revenue stream from the program to fund liability insurance and legal fees.

If free-software authors lose the right to disclaim all warranties and find themselves getting sued over the performance of the programs that they've written, they'll stop contributing free software to the world. It's to our advantage as users to help the author protect this right.

- **The GNU General Public License**

Please see Appendix B for the full text of the GPL. The GPL is a political manifesto as well as a software license, and much of its text is concerned with explaining the rationale behind the license. This political dialogue has put some people off, and thus provided some of the reason that people have written other free software licenses. However, the GPL was assembled with the assistance of law professors, and is much better written than most of its ilk. I'd strongly urge that you use the GPL, or its library variant the LGPL, if you can. If you choose another license, or write your own, be sure about your reasons. People who write their own licenses should consider that this is not a step to be taken lightly. The unexpected complications of an ill-considered license can create a decades-long burden for software users.

The text of the GPL is not itself under the GPL. Its license is simple : *Everyone is permitted to copy and distribute verbatim copies of this license document, but changing it is not allowed.* An important point here is that the text of the licenses of Open Source software are generally *not* themselves Open Source. Obviously, a license would offer no protection if anyone could change it.

The provisions of the GPL satisfy the Open Source Definition. The GPL does not require any of the provisions permitted by paragraph 4 of the Open Source Definition, *Integrity of the Author's Source Code.*

The GPL does not allow you to *take modifications private.* Your modifications must be distributed under the GPL. Thus, the author of a GPL-ed program is likely to receive improvements from others, including commercial companies who modify his software for their own purposes.

The GPL doesn't allow the incorporation of a GPL-ed program into a proprietary program. The GPL's definition of a proprietary program is any program with a license that doesn't give you as many rights as the GPL.

There are a few loopholes in the GPL that allow it to be used in programs that are not entirely Open Source. Software libraries that are normally distributed with the compiler or operating system you are using may be linked with GPL-ed software; the result is a partially-free program. The copyright holder (generally the author of the program) is the person who places the GPL on the program and has the right to violate his own license. This was used by the KDE authors to distribute their programs with *Qt* before Troll Tech placed an Open Source license on *Qt*. However, this right does not extend to any third parties who redistribute the program—they must follow all of the terms of the license, even the ones that the copyright holder violates, and thus it's problematical to redistribute a GPL-ed program containing *Qt*. The KDE developers appear to be addressing this problem by applying the LGPL, rather than the GPL, to their software.

The political rhetoric in the GPL puts some people off. Some of them have chosen a less appropriate license for their software simply because they eschew Richard Stallman's ideas and don't want to see them repeated in their own software packages.

The GNU Library General Public License

The LGPL is a derivative of the GPL that was designed for software libraries. Unlike the GPL, an LGPL-ed program can be incorporated into a proprietary program. The C-language library provided with Linux systems is an example of LGPL-ed software—it can be used to build proprietary programs, otherwise Linux would only be useful for free software authors.

An instance of an LGPL-ed program can be converted into a GPL-ed one at any time. Once that happens, you can't convert that instance, or anything derived from it, back into an LGPL-ed program.

The rest of the provisions of the LGPL are similar to those in the GPL—in fact, it includes the GPL by reference.

- **The X, BSD, and Apache Licenses**

  The X license and its relatives the BSD and Apache licenses are very different from the GPL and LGPL. These licenses let you do nearly anything with the software licensed under them. This is because the software that the X and BSD licenses originally covered was funded by monetary grants of the U.S. Government. Since the U.S. citizens had already paid for the software with their taxes, they were granted permission to make use of that software as they pleased.

  The most important permission, and one missing from the GPL, is that you can take X-licensed modifications private. In other words, you can get the source code for a X-licensed program, modify it, and then sell binary versions of the program without distributing the source code of your modifications, and without applying the X-license to those modifications. This is still Open Source, however, as the Open Source Definition does not require that modifications always carry the original license.

  Many other developers have adopted the X-license and its variants, including the *BSD (Berkeley System Distribution)* and the *Apache* web server project. An annoying feature of the BSD license is a provision that requires you to mention (generally in a footnote) that the software was developed at the University of California any time you mention a feature of a BSD-licensed program in advertising. Keeping track of which software is BSD-licensed in something huge like a Linux distribution, and then remembering to mention the University whenever any of those programs are mentioned in advertising, is somewhat of a headache for business people. At this writing, the *Debian GNU/Linux* distribution contains over 2,500 software packages, and if even a fraction of them were BSD-licensed, advertising for a Linux system like Debian might contain many pages of footnotes! However, the *X Consortium* license does not have that advertising provision. If you are considering using a BSD-style license, use the X-license instead.

- **The Artistic License**

  Although this license was originally developed for Perl, it's since been used for other software. It is, in my opinion, a sloppily-worded license, in that it makes requirements and then gives you loopholes that make it easy to bypass the requirements. Perhaps that's why almost all Artistic-license software is now dual-licensed, offering the choice of the Artistic License or the GPL.

  Section 5 of the Artistic License prohibits sale of the software, yet allows an aggregate software distribution of more than one program to be sold. So, if you bundle an Artistic-licensed program with a five-line *hello-world's*, you can sell the bundle. This feature of the Artistic License was the sole cause of the "aggregate" loophole in paragraph 1 of the Open Source Definition. As use of the Artistic License wanes, we are considering removing the loophole. That would make the *Artistic* a non-Open source license. This isn't a step we would take lightly, and there will probably be more than a year of consideration and debate before it happens.

  The Artistic License requires you to make modifications free, but then gives you a loophole (in Section 7) that allows you to take modifications private or even place parts of the Artistic-licensed program in the public domain!

- **The Netscape Public License and the Mozilla Public License**

  Netscape developed NPL when they made their product *Netscape Navigator* Open Source. Actually, the Open source version is called *Mozilla;* Netscape reserves the trademark *Navigator* for their own product. Eric Raymond and I acted as unpaid consultants during the development of this license. I tried, unsuccessfully, to persuade Netscape to use the GPL, and when they declined, I helped them compose a license that would comply with the Open Source Definition.

  An important feature of the NPL is that it contains special privileges that apply to Netscape and nobody else. It gives Netscape the privilege of relicensing modifications that you've made to their software. They can take those modifications private, improve them, and refuse to give you the result. This provision was necessary because when Netscape decided to go Open Source, it had contracts with other companies that committed it to provide *Navigator* to them under a non-Open source license.

  Netscape created the *MPL,* or *Mozilla Public License,* to address this concern. The MPL is much like the NPL, but does not contain the clause that allows Netscape to re-license your modifications.

  The NPL and MPL allow you to take modifications private.

  Many companies have adopted a variation of the MPL for their own programs. This is unfortunate, because the NPL was designed for the specific business situation that Netscape was in at the time it was written, and is not necessarily appropriate for others to use. It should remain the license of Netscape and Mozilla, and others should use the GPL or the X licenses.

2.8.2 Choosing a License

The propagation of many different and incompatible licenses works to the detriment of Open Source software because fragments of one program cannot be used in another program with an incompatible license.

Steer clear of the Artistic License unless you are willing to study it carefully and edit out its loopholes. Then, make a few decisions :

1. Do you want people to be able to *take modifications private* or not ? If you want to get the source code for modifications back from the people who make them, apply a license that mandates this. The GPL and LGPL would be good choices. If you don't mind people taking modifications private, use the X or Apache license.
2. Do you want to allow someone to merge your program with his or her own proprietary software ? If so, use the LGPL, which explicitly allows this without allowing people to make modifications to your own code private, or use the X or Apache licenses, which do allow modifications to be kept private.
3. Do you want some people to be able to buy commercial-licensed versions of your program that are not Open Source ? If so, dual-license your software. I recommend the GPL as the Open Source license; you can find a commercial license appropriate for you to use in books like *Copyright Your Software* from Nolo Press.
4. Do you want *everyone* who uses your program to pay for the privilege ? If so, perhaps Open Source isn't for you. If you're satisfied with having only some people

pay you, you can work that and keep your program Open Source. Most of the Open Source authors consider their programs to be contributions to the public good, and don't care if they are paid at all.

The table below gives a comparison of licensing practices :

License	*Can be mixed with non-free software*	*Modifications can be taken private and not returned to you*	*Can be relicensed by anyone*	*Contains special privileges for the original copyright holder over your modifications*
GPL				
LGPL	X			
BSD	X	X		
NPL	X	X		X
MPL	X	X		
Public Domain	X	X	X	

Note : X Means Yes

2.8.3 Some Important Licenses

While there are many open source licenses in use today, a few have emerged as more popular (and therefore more important) than most as following :

2.8.3.1 Apache License

The *Apache License* (Apache Software License previous to version 2.0) is a free software license authored by the Apache Software Foundation (ASF). The Apache License (versions 1.0, 1.1, and 2.0) requires preservation of the copyright notice and disclaimer, but it is not a Copyleft license — it allows use of the source code for the development of free and open source software as well as proprietary and closed source software.

All software produced by the ASF or any of its projects or subjects is licensed according to the terms of the Apache License. Some non-ASF software is licensed using the Apache License as well : as of September 2007, over 2000 non-ASF projects located at SourceForge.net are available under the terms of the Apache License.

The Apache Software Foundation (ASF) is a non-profit corporation to support Apache software projects. Apache's projects are characterized by a collaborative, consensus based development process, an open and pragmatic software license. Among the ASF's objectives are to provide legal protection to volunteers working on Apache projects, and to protect the Apache brand name from being used by other organizations.

There are currently two forms of the Apache in wide use today : versions 1.1 and 2.0. While 2.0 is considered by ASF to be the current version and most users have happily switched, a few large groups objected to new clauses inserted into 2.0 regarding patents, and have refused to use any software with the new license (most notable the Open BSD project).

Apache License	
Author	Apache Software Foundation
Version	2.0
Copyright	Apache Software Foundation
Published	January 2004
DFSG compatible	Yes
Free software	Yes
OSI approved	Yes
GPL compatible	Yes - GPLv3
Copyleft	No
Linking from code with a different license	Yes

2.8.3.2 BSD Licenses

BSD licenses represent a family of permissive free software licenses. The original was used for the Berkeley Software Distribution, an Unix-like operating system for which the license is named. The original owners of BSD were the Regents of the University of California because BSD was first written at the University of California, Berkeley. The first version of the license was revised, and the resulting licenses are more properly called modified BSD licenses. Permissive licenses, sometimes with important differences pertaining to license compatibility, are referred to as "BSD-style licenses". Several BSD-like licenses, including the New BSD license, have been vetted by the Open Source Initiative as meeting their definition of open source.

The licenses have few restrictions compared to other free software licenses such as the GNU General Public License or even the default restrictions provided by copyright, putting it relatively closer to the public domain. The BSD licenses have been referred to as *copy center*, as a comparison to standard copyright and Copyleft free software : "Take it down to the copy center and make as many copies as you want."

BSD is both a license, and a class of licenses (generally referred to as BSD-like). The modified BSD license (in wide use today) is very similar to the license originally used for the BSD version of Unix (see BSD history above). The BSD license is a simple license that merely requires that all code licensed under the BSD license be licensed under the BSD license IF redistributed in source code format. BSD (unlike some other licenses) does not require that source code be distributed at all.

BSD is actually very close, though still distinct, from a public domain license. Like works in the public domain, BSD-like licenses permit nearly free modification and distribution of a work. There are only two significant ways in which BSD-like licenses differ from public domain. First, the BSD license carries the requirement that the license, along with its statement of copyright, is carried along with the work, or modified copies. This does not however limit code under different licenses from being combined with it. Second, the BSD-like licenses have a standard disclaimer of guarantees, such as fitness for a particular use and merchantability. This latter portion should not come as any surprise, since practically all software packages carry a clause nearly identical to this one.

In summary, the major difference between BSD-like licenses and the public domain is that BSD licensed works must remain attributed to the original creator(s). Some BSD licenses take this further, and require similar copyright statements in advertising materials for a distributed software product. Most however are simply limited this basic requirement.

For those who are opposed to the GPL for its limitations on modification and distribution, the BSD license is often quite acceptable. Due to the inherent lack of limitations, BSD code can be incorporated into any other project, commercial or otherwise, removing a lot of the worries of licensing issues from code. Similarly, for those who endorse the licenses such as the GPL for their ability to protect software freedoms, the BSD is looked upon as a step in the right direction, but not enough to guarantee said freedoms. They often encourage the use of more GPL like licenses for this reason.

"New" BSD License	
Author	Regents of the University of California
Version	N/A
Copyright	Public Domain
Published	1990[1]
DFSG compatible	Yes
Free software	Yes
OSI approved	Yes
GPL compatible	Yes
Copyleft	No
Linking from code with a different license	Yes

2.8.3.3 (GPL or (GNU)

The GNU General Public License is a free software license, created by the Free Software Foundation (FSF); version 2 was released in 1991. It is usually abbreviated to GNU GPL, or, simply, GPL. FSF recently announced that they have started work on version 3 of this license, and should be releasing the new version in the spring of 2007. The motivations for these changes have not been articulated yet, but based on a lecture by Richard Stallman held at New York's Cooper Union on November 29, 2005, the changes are related to the World Intellectual Property Organization's (WIPO) work on world copyright standardization.

The GPL protects the 3 main articles of software freedom as defined in the section on Software Freedom. The GPL also contains a clause requiring publishers of GPL licensed programs that make modifications to the software, to distribute that modification under the GPL. This clause, which causes others to give the GPL the label "viral", since it apparently "infects" any code, which it touches. In practice, this clause is not that invasive. If such a violation is found, detaching the GPL code from the modified code by placing it in a different file is generally sufficient to return to compliance with the license.

It is important to note that the GPL is not a contract, in the same way that End User License Agreements are. It provides no restrictions on use aside from those already set by copyright law. However, to utilize any rights, which are not explicitly given to you, you have to accept the conditions of the GPL. For example, you cannot distribute a work without the creator's consent. If the work is under the GPL, then the GPL lists the conditions under which the creator has agreed to give you consent.

2.8.3.4 LGPL

An important corner-case of the GPL requires that only GPL code can link with GPL libraries, even if the library is contained in a separate file, and the code, which uses it, contains no GPL code unto itself. Some as too strict sees this, since such an action could be considered a "use" of the library, not as a modification. In order to allow for such a distinction, the LGPL was created. The LGPL fixes precisely this problem : If someone uses an LGPL work as a library which is symbolically linked with a project, the rest of the project does not have to be put under the LGPL. On the other hand, if any modifications are made to the LGPL'ed work, which are distributed along with the software package as a whole, the changes must be made public, similar to the rules of the GPL. The "L" in the LGPL stands for different things for different people. Initially it was considered as a "Library" license, since the clause specifically dealt with issues of linking. However, the GNU Foundation describes this as the "Lesser" GPL, since it gives fewer protections to the work than the GPL does. While the GNU Foundation does not frown upon the use of the LGPL, it encourages the use of the GPL when possible.

2.9 COPYRIGHT

2.9.1 Why Do We Have Copyright ?

Compared to other legal concepts, copyright is a relatively new invention in human history. The development of copyright regulation reflects the social and technological transformation around human creative activity and distribution of the resultant profits. While granting exclusive private rights to authors or copyright holders has been considered as a way of encouraging human creative activity, copyright law also claims to recognize

Fig. 2.8. Logo of Copyright.

the larger public interest, particularly with respect to education, research and access to information.

Copyright law uses various means to balance public and private interests. In the Statute of Anne (1710), the earliest modern copyright law, authorities are allowed to limit and control the price of printed books according to their best judgment. In the United States Constitution, authors are granted exclusive rights to their writings within a limited time. In copyright law, fair use exceptions are specified to avoid the drawbacks of excessive assertion of exclusive rights and to attain a balance between conflicting interests.

2.9.2 What can be Copyrighted ?

Copyright applies to the expression of ideas in different forms, including literary, dramatic, musical, artistic, and other intellectual works. The ideas expressed in such works are themselves not copyrightable. Since the 1980s, the copyright ability of software became internationally accepted.

2.9.3 How do We Copyright Our Work ?

Now-a-days, copyright law does not require formalities. The author does not need to publish, register, pay a registration fee of any kind, nor attach a copyright notice to her work, for her copyright to take effect. Copyright is automatically applied to a work once it is created13 and the creator of the work automatically becomes the copyright holder.

Copyright is a legal concept enacted by most national governments, that gives the creator of an original work exclusive rights to it, usually for a limited period of time. At its most general, it is literally "the right to copy", but also gives the copyright holder the right to be credited for the work, to determine who (if anyone) can perform it or adapt it to other forms, to benefit financially from the work, and other related rights. It is one form of intellectual property (distinct from patents, trademarks, and trade secrets), and applies to any particular expression of an idea or information, which is substantial and self-contained in a fixed form. The symbol for copyright is "©". (The letter C inside parentheses – "(c)" – although a common practice, has never been legally recognized as a symbol for copyright.)

2.9.4 Scope

Copyright may apply to a wide range of creative, intellectual, or artistic forms or "works". These include poems, theses, plays, and other literary works, movies, choreographic works (dances, ballets, etc.), musical compositions, audio recordings, paintings, drawings, sculptures, photographs, software, radio and television broadcasts of live and other performances, and, in some jurisdictions, industrial designs. Graphic designs or industrial designs may have separate or overlapping laws applied to them in some jurisdictions. Copyright is one of the concepts covered by the umbrella term *intellectual property*.

Copyright does not cover ideas or information themselves, only the form or manner in which they are expressed. For example, the copyright to a Mickey Mouse cartoon restricts others from making copies of the cartoon or creating derivative works based on Disney's particular anthropomorphic mouse, but doesn't prohibit the creation of other works about anthropomorphic mice in general, so long as they're different enough to not be judged copies of Disney's. In many jurisdictions, copyright law makes exceptions to these restrictions for the purpose of commentary and other related uses (See Fair Use, Fair Dealing). Other laws may impose legal restrictions which copyright does not—such as trademarks and patents.

Copyright laws are standardized somewhat through international conventions such as the Berne Convention which have been ratified by most countries, and are required by international organizations such as European Union or World Trade Organization from their member states.

2.9.5 Exclusive Rights

Several exclusive rights typically attach to the holder of a copyright :

- to produce copies or reproductions of the work and to sell those copies (including, typically, electronic copies).
- to import or export the work.
- to create derivative works (works that adapt the original work).
- to perform or display the work publicly.
- to sell or assign these rights to others.
- to transmit or display by radio or video.

2.10 COPYLEFT

The "reversed *c* in a full circle" is the copyleft symbol. It is the copyright symbol mirrored. Unlike the copyright symbol, it has no legal meaning.

Copyleft is a play on the word copyright and is the practice of using copyright law to remove restrictions on distributing copies and modified versions of a work for others and requiring that the same freedoms be preserved in modified versions.

Fig. 2.9. Copyleft Logo.

Copyleft is a form of licensing and may be used to modify copyrights for works such as computer software, documents, music, and art. In general, copyright law allows an author to prohibit others from reproducing, adapting, or distributing copies of the author's work. In contrast, an author may, through a Copyleft licensing scheme, give every person who receives a copy of a work permission to reproduce, adapt or distribute the work as long as the same Copyleft licensing scheme also binds any resulting copies or adaptations. A widely used and originating Copyleft license is the GNU General Public License. Similar licenses are available through Creative Commons—called Share-alike.

Copyleft may also be characterized as a copyright licensing scheme in which an author surrenders some but not all rights under copyright law. Instead of allowing a work to fall completely into the public domain (where no copyright restrictions are imposed), Copyleft allows an author to impose some but not all copyright restrictions on those who want to engage in activities that would otherwise be considered copyright infringement. Under Copyleft, copyright infringement may be avoided if the would-be infringe perpetuates the same Copyleft scheme. For this reason Copyleft licenses are also known as **viral** or **reciprocal licenses.**

2.10.1 What is Copyleft ?

Copyleft is a general method for making a program or other work free, and requiring all modified and extended versions of the program to be free as well. The simplest way to make program free software is to put it in the public domain, uncopyrighted. This allows people to share the program and their improvements, if they are so minded. But it also allows uncooperative people to convert the program into proprietary software. They can make changes, many or few, and distribute the result as a proprietary product. People who receive the program in that modified form do not have the freedom that the original author gave them; the middleman has stripped it away.

In the GNU project, our aim is to give all users the freedom to redistribute and change GNU software. If middlemen could strip off the freedom, we might have many users, but those users would not have freedom. So instead of putting GNU software in the public domain, we "Copyleft" it. Copyleft says that anyone who redistributes the software, with or without changes, must pass along the freedom to further copy and change it. Copyleft guarantees that every user has freedom.

Copyleft also provides an incentive for other programmers to add to free software. Important free programs such as the GNU C++ compiler exist only because of this.

Copyleft also helps programmers who want to contribute improvements to free software get permission to do that. These programmers often work for companies or universities that would do almost anything to get more money. A programmer may want to contribute her changes to the community, but her employer may want to turn the changes into a proprietary software product.

When we explain to the employer that it is illegal to distribute the improved version except as free software, the employer usually decides to release it as free software rather than throw it away.

To Copyleft a program, we first state that it is copyrighted; then we add distribution terms, which are a legal instrument that gives everyone the rights to use, modify, and redistribute the program's code *or any program derived from it* but only if the distribution terms are unchanged. Thus, the code and the freedoms become legally inseparable.

Proprietary software developers use copyright to take away the users' freedom; we use copyright to guarantee their freedom. That's why we reverse the name, changing "copyright" into "Copyleft."

Copyleft is a general concept; there are many ways to fill in the details. In the GNU Project, the specific distribution terms that we use are contained in the GNU General Public License (available in HTML, text, and Texinfo format). The GNU General Public License is often called the GNU GPL for short. There is also a Frequently Asked Questions page about the GNU GPL. You can also read about why the FSF gets copyright assignments from contributors.

An alternate form of Copyleft, the GNU Lesser General Public License (LGPL) (available in HTML, text, and Texinfo format), applies to a few (but not all) GNU libraries. To learn more about properly using the LGPL, please read the article *why you shouldn't use the Lesser GPL for your next library*.

The GNU Free Documentation License (FDL) (available in HTML, text and Texinfo) is a form of Copyleft intended for use on a manual, textbook or other document to assure everyone the effective freedom to copy and redistribute it, with or without modifications, either commercially or noncommercial.

The appropriate license is included in many manuals and in each GNU source code distribution.

All these licenses are designed so that you can easily apply them to your own works, assuming you are the copyright holder. You don't have to modify the license to do this, just include a copy of the license in the work, and add notices in the source files that refer properly to the license.

Using the same distribution terms for many different programs makes it easy to copy code between various different programs. Since they all have the same distribution terms, there is no need to think about whether the terms are compatible. The Lesser GPL includes a provision that lets you alter the distribution terms to the ordinary GPL, so that you can copy code into another program covered by the GPL.

If you would like to Copyleft your program with the GNU GPL or the GNU LGPL, please see the license instructions page for advice. Please note that you must use the entire text of our licenses, if you use one. Each is an integral whole, and partial copies are not permitted.

If you would like to Copyleft your manual with the GNU FDL, please see the instructions at the end of the FDL text, and the GFDL instructions page. Again, partial copies are not permitted.

2.10.2 History

An early example of copyleft was the Tiny BASIC project started in the newsletter of the People's Computer Company in 1975. Dennis Allison wrote a specification for a simple version of the BASIC programming language. This design did not support text strings and only used integer arithmetic. The goal was for the program to fit in 2 to 3 kilobytes of memory.

The Tiny BASIC contents of the newsletter soon became *Dr. Dobb's Journal of Tiny BASIC* with a subtitle of "Calisthenics & Orthodontia, Running Light Without Overbyte." Hobbyists began writing BASIC language interpreters for their microprocessor based home computers and sending the source code to Dr. Dobb's Journal and other magazines to be published. By the middle of 1976, Tiny BASIC interpreters were available for the Intel 8080, the Motorola 6800 and MOS Technology 6502 processors. This was a very successful open source project.

The May 1976 issue of *Dr. Dobb's Journal* had Li-Chen Wang's Palo Alto Tiny BASIC for the Intel 8080 microprocessor. The listing began with the usual title, author's name and date but it also had "@COPYLEFT ALL WRONGS RESERVED". A fellow Homebrew Computer Club member, Roger Rauskolb, modified and improved Li-Chen Wang's program and this was published in the December 1976 issue of *Interface Age* magazine. Roger added his name and preserved the COPYLEFT Notice.

A later instance of copyleft arose when Richard Stallman was working on a Lisp interpreter. Symbolics asked to use the Lisp interpreter, and Stallman agreed to supply them with a public domain version of his work. Symbolics extended and improved the Lisp interpreter, but when Stallman wanted access to the improvements that Symbolics had made to his interpreter, Symbolics refused. Stallman then, in 1984, proceeded to work towards eradicating this emerging behavior and culture of proprietary software, which he named software hoarding.

As Stallman deemed it impractical in the short term to eliminate current copyright law and the wrongs he perceived it perpetuating, he decided to work within the framework of existing law; he created his own copyright license, the Emacs General Public License, the first copyleft license. This later evolved into the GNU General Public License, which is now one of the most popular Free Software licenses. For the first time a copyright holder had taken steps to ensure that the maximum number of rights be perpetually transferred to a program's users, no matter what subsequent revisions anyone made to the original program. This original GPL did not grant rights to the public at large, only those who had already received the program; but it was the best that could be done under existing law. The new license was not at this time given the copyleft label.

Richard Stallman stated that it comes from Don Hopkins, whom he calls a very imaginative fellow, who mailed him a letter in 1984 or 1985 on which was written : "Copyleft—all rights reserved." The term "kopyleft" with the notation "All Rights Reserved" was also in use in the early 1970s within the Principia Discordia, which may have inspired Hopkins or influenced other usage. And in the arts Ray Johnson had earlier coined the term independently as it pertained to his making of and distribution of his mixed media image in his mail art and ephemeral gifts, for which he encouraged the making of derivative works (While the phrase itself appears briefly as (or on) one of his pieces in the 2002 documentary *How to Draw a Bunny*, Johnson himself is not referenced in the 2001 documentary *Revolution OS*.)

There are definitional problems with the term "copyleft" which contribute to controversy over it. The term originated as an amusing back-formation from the term "copyright", and was originally a noun, meaning the copyright license terms of the GNU General Public License originated by Richard Stallman as part of the Free Software Foundation's work. Thus, "your program is covered by the copyleft" is almost considered to mean the same as the program being GPL'd. When used as a verb, as in "he copylefted his most recent version", it is less precise and can refer to any of several similar licenses, or indeed a notional imaginary license for discussion purposes.

2.10.3 Applying Copyleft

Common practice for using copyleft is to codify the copying terms for a work with a license. Any such license typically gives each person possessing a copy of the work the same freedoms as the author, including (from the Free Software Definition) :

1. the freedom to use and study the work,
2. the freedom to copy and share the work with others,
3. the freedom to modify the work,
4. and the freedom to distribute modified and therefore derivative works.

These freedoms do not ensure that a derivative work will be distributed under the same liberal terms. In order for the work to be truly copyleft, the license has to ensure that the author of a derived work can only distribute such works under the same or equivalent license.

In addition to restrictions on copying, copyleft licenses address other possible impediments. These include ensuring the rights cannot be later revoked and requiring the work and its derivatives are provided in a form that facilitates modification. In software, this requires that the source code of the derived work is made available together with the software itself.

Copyleft licenses necessarily make creative use of relevant rules and laws. For example, when using copyright law, those who contribute to a work under copyleft usually must gain, defer or assign copyright holder status. By submitting the copyright of their contributions under a copyleft license, they deliberately give up some of the rights that normally follow from copyright, including the right to be the unique distributor of copies of the work.

Some laws used for copyleft licenses vary from one country to another, and may also be granted in terms that vary from country to country. For example, in some countries it is acceptable to sell a software product without warranty, in standard GNU GPL style in most European countries it is not permitted for a software distributor to waive all warranties regarding a sold product. For this reason the extent of such warranties are specified in most European copyleft licenses. Regarding that, see the CeCILL license, a license that allows one to use GNU GPL in combination with a limited warranty.

2.10.4 Types of Copyleft and Relation to Other Licenses

Copyleft is a distinguishing feature of some free software licenses. Copyleft even became a "Divisive" issue in the ideological "Strief" between the Open Source Initiative and the free software movement. Many free software licenses are not copyleft licenses because they do not require the licensee to distribute derivative works under the same license. There is an ongoing debate as to which class of license provides the greater degree of freedom. This debate hinges on complex issues such as the definition of freedom and whose freedoms are more important, or whether to maximize the freedom of all potential future recipients of a work (*freedom from* the creation of proprietary software). Non-copyleft free software licenses maximize the freedom of the initial recipient (*freedom to* create proprietary software).

In common with the Creative Commons share-alike licensing system, GNU's Free Documentation License allows authors to apply limitations to certain sections of their work, exempting some parts of their creation from the full copyleft mechanism. In the case of the GFDL, these limitations include the use of invariant sections, which may not be altered by future editors. The initial intention of the GFDL was as a device for supporting the documentation of copylefted software. However, the result is that it can be used for any kind of document.

1. Strong and Weak Copyleft

The Copyleft governing a work is considered to be "stronger", to the extent that the copyleft provisions can be efficiently imposed on all kinds of derived works. "Weak copyleft" refers to licenses where not all derived works inherit the copyleft license; whether a derived work inherits or not often depends on the manner in which it was derived.

"Weak copyleft" licenses are generally used for the creation of software libraries, to allow other software to link to the library, and then be redistributed without the legal requirement for the work to be distributed under the library's copyleft license. Only changes to the weak copylefted software itself become subject to the copyleft provisions of such a license, not changes to the software that links to it. This allows programs of any license to be compiled and linked against copylefted libraries such as G Lib C (the GNU project's implementation of the C standard library), and then redistributed without any re-licensing required.

The most well known free software license that uses strong copyleft is the GNU General Public License. Free software licenses that use "weak" copyleft include the GNU Lesser General Public License and the Mozilla Public License. Examples of non-copyleft free software licenses include the X11 license, Apache license and the BSD licenses.

The Design Science License is a strong copyleft license that can apply to any work that is not software, documentation, or art, such as music, sports photography, and video. It is hosted on the Free Software Foundation website's license list, but it is not considered compatible with the GPL by the Free Software Foundation.

2. Full and Partial Copyleft

"Full" and "partial" copyleft relate to another issue : Full copyleft is when all parts of a work (except the license itself) can be modified by consecutive authors. Partial copyleft exempts some parts of the work from the copyleft provisions, thus permitting unrestricted modification, or in some other way does not impose all the principles of copylefting on the work. For example, in artistic creation full copylefting is sometimes not possible or desirable.

I. Share-alike

Many share-alike licenses are partial (or non-full) copyleft licenses. Share-alike, however, imposes the requirement that any freedom that is granted regarding the original work (or its copies), must be granted on exactly the same terms in any derived work : this further implies that any *full* copyleft license is automatically a share-alike license (but not the other way around!). Instead of using *copyright's* "all rights reserved" motto, or *full copyleft's* "no rights reserved", *share-alike* licenses rather use the "some rights reserved" statement. Some permutations of the Creative Commons licenses are examples of share-alike.

2.10.5 A Brief Note about Copyrights and Copyleft

Software licensing should not be confused with copyright protections. Open source licensing explicitly relies on copyright law protections and no code licensed under most of those licenses is a release to the public domain. The author of software can limit the use of he created, since the code is a written work and subject to copyright law provisions. A creator can limit use of the software as desired, since copyright is a privilege of exclusive use. Copyright protections allow a copyright holder (not necessarily an author) to control use and distribution of software via licensing. That license may allow changes (as does the GPL) or prohibit them (as do most commercial EULA agreements).

The concept of Copyleft also grew out of the work by GNU and others in the open source movement. While copyright is intended to most protect written works from unauthorized use, and most commercial copyright licenses do so by prohibiting changes or distribution, Copyleft licenses encourage free and widespread use.

2.11 PATENT

In the past few years the issue of software patents has become one of the most pressing to those in the open source movement. In the United States and some other countries software is subject to patent protections. While only some other countries have placed similar restrictions on the production of software the patent system in the US has become problematic worldwide.

2.11.1 What is Patent ?

A **patent** is a set of exclusive rights granted by a state to an inventor or his assignee for a fixed period of time in exchange for a disclosure of an invention.

The procedure for granting patents, the requirements placed on the patentee and the extent of the exclusive rights vary widely between countries according to national laws and international agreements. Typically, however, a patent application must include one or more claims defining the invention which must be new, inventive, and useful or industrially applicable. The exclusive right granted to a patentee in most countries is the right to prevent or exclude others from making, using, selling, offering to sell or importing the invention.

2.11.2 Definition

The term "patent" usually refers to a right granted to anyone who invents or discovers any new and useful process, machine, article of manufacture, or composition of matter, or any new and useful improvement thereof. The additional qualification "utility patents" is used in countries such as the United States to distinguish them from other types of patents but should not be confused with utility models granted by other countries. Examples of particular species of patents for inventions include biological patents, business method patents, chemical patents and software patents.

Some other types of intellectual property rights are referred to as "patents" in some jurisdictions : industrial design rights are called "design patents" in some jurisdictions (they protect the visual design of objects that are not purely utilitarian), plant breeders' rights are sometimes called *"plant patents"*, and utility models or *Gebrauchsmuster* are sometimes called *"petty patents"* or *"innovation patents"*. This article relates primarily to the patent for an invention, although so-called petty patents and utility models may also be granted for inventions. Certain grants made by the monarch in pursuance of the royal prerogative were sometimes called *"letters patent"*, which was a government notice to the public of a grant of an exclusive right to ownership and possession. These were often grants of a patent-like monopoly and predate the modern British origins of the patent system.

For other uses of the term "patent" see Land patent which were land grants by early state governments in the USA. This reflects the original meaning of "letters patent" that had a broader scope than current usage.

2.11.3 Law

1. Effects

A patent is not a right to practice or use the invention. Rather, a patent provides the right to *exclude others* from making, using, selling, offering for sale, or importing the patented invention for the term of the patent, which is usually 20 years from the filing date. A patent is, in effect, a limited property right that the government offers to inventors in exchange for their agreement to share the details of their inventions with the public. Like any other property right, it may be sold, licensed, mortgaged, assigned or transferred, given away, or simply abandoned.

The rights conveyed by a patent vary country-by-country. For example, in the United States, a patent covers research, except "purely philosophical" inquiry. A U.S. patent is infringed by any "making" of the invention, even a making that goes toward development of a new invention — which may itself become subject of a patent. In contrast, Australian law permits others to build on top of a patented invention, by carving out exceptions from infringement for those who conduct research (*e.g.*, for academic purposes) on the invention.

A patent being an exclusionary right does not, however, necessarily give the owner of the patent the right to exploit the patent. For example, many inventions are improvements of prior inventions which may still be covered by someone else's patent. If an inventor takes an existing, patented mouse trap design, adds a new feature to make an improved mouse trap, and obtains a patent on the improvement, he or she can only legally build his or her improved mouse trap with permission from the patent holder of the original mouse trap, assuming the original patent is still in force. On the other hand, the owner of the improved mouse trap can exclude the original patent owner from using the improvement.

Some countries have "working provisions" which require that the invention be exploited in the jurisdiction it covers. Consequences of not working an invention vary from one country to another, ranging from revocation of the patent rights to the awarding of a compulsory license awarded by the courts to a party wishing to exploit a patented invention. The patentee has the opportunity to challenge the revocation or license, but is usually required to provide evidence that the reasonable requirements of the public have been met by the working of invention.

2. Enforcement

Patents can generally only be enforced through civil lawsuits (for example, for a US patent, by an action for patent infringement in a United States federal court), although some territories (such as France and Austria) have criminal penalties for wanton infringement. Typically, the patent owner will seek monetary compensation for past infringement, and will seek an injunction prohibiting the defendant from engaging in future acts of infringement. In order to prove infringement, the patent owner must establish that the accused infringer practices all of the requirements of at least one of the claims of the patent (noting that in many jurisdictions the scope of the patent may not be limited to what is literally stated in the claims, for example due to the "doctrine of equivalents").

An important limitation on the ability of a patent owner to successfully assert the patent in civil litigation is the accused infringer's right to challenge the validity of that patent. Civil courts hearing patent cases can and often do declare patents invalid. The grounds on which a patent can be found invalid are set out in the relevant patent legislation and vary between countries. Often, the grounds are a sub-set of the requirements for patentability in the relevant country. Whilst an infringer is generally free to rely on any available ground of invalidity (such as a prior publication, for example), some countries have sanctions to prevent the same validity questions being relitigated. An example is the UK Certificate of contested validity.

The vast majority of patent rights, however, are not determined through litigation, but are resolved privately through patent licensing. Patent licensing agreements are effectively contracts in which the patent owner (the licensor) agrees not to sue the licensee for infringement of the licensor's patent rights, usually in return for a royalty or other payment. It is common for companies engaged in complex technical fields to enter into dozens of license agreements associated with the production of a single product. Moreover, it is equally common for competitors in such fields to license patents to each other under cross-licensing agreements in order to gain access to each other's patents. A cross license agreement could be highly desirable to the mouse trap developers discussed above, for example, because it would permit both parties to profit off each other's inventions.

The United Nations Statistics Division reports that USA was the top market for patents in force in 2000 closely followed by the EU and Japan.

3. *Ownership*

In most countries, both natural persons and corporate entities may apply for a patent. The entity or entities then become the owners of the patent when and if it issues. However, it is nearly always required that the inventor or inventors be named and an indication be given on the public record as to how the owner or owners acquired their rights to the invention from the inventor or inventors.

In the United States, however, only the natural person(s) (*i.e.*, the inventor/s) may apply for a patent. If a patent issues, then each person listed as an inventor owns the patent separately from the other. For example, if two inventors are listed on a patent, then each one may grant licenses to the patent independently of the other, absent an agreement to the contrary.

It is common in the United States for inventors to assign their ownership rights to a corporate entity. Inventors that work for a corporation, for example, often are required to assign their ownership rights to their corporation as a condition of their employment. Independent inventors often assign their ownership rights to a single entity so that only one entity has the right to grant a license.

The ability to assign ownership rights increases the liquidity of a patent as property. Inventors can obtain patents and then sell them to third parties. The third parties then own the patents as if they had originally made the inventions themselves.

4. *Governing Laws*

The grant and enforcement of patents are governed by national laws, and also by international treaties, where those treaties have been given effect in national laws. Patents are, therefore, territorial in nature.

Commonly, a nation forms a patent office with responsibility for operating that nation's patent system, within the relevant patent laws. The patent office generally has responsibility for the grant of patents, with infringement being the remit of national courts.

There is a trend towards global harmonization of patent laws, with the World Trade Organization (WTO) being particularly active in this area. The TRIPs Agreement has been largely successful in providing a forum for nations to agree on an aligned set of patent laws. Conformity with the TRIPs agreement is a requirement of admission to the WTO and so compliance is seen by many nations as important. This has also led to many developing nations, which may historically have developed different laws to aid their development, enforcing patents laws in line with global practice.

A key international convention relating to patents is the Paris Convention for the Protection of Industrial Property, initially signed in 1883. The Paris Convention sets out a range of basic rules relating to patents, and although the convention does not have direct legal effect in all national jurisdictions, the principles of the convention are incorporated into all notable current patent systems. The most significant aspect of the convention is the provision of the right to claim priority : filing an application in any one member state of the Paris Convention preserves the right for one year to file in any other member state, and receive the benefit of the original filing date. Because the right to a patent is intensely date-driven, this right is fundamental to modern patent usage.

The authority for patent statutes in different countries varies. In the United States, the Constitution empowers Congress to make laws to "promote the Progress of Science and useful Arts..." The laws Congress passed are codified in title 35 of the United States Code and created the United States Patent and Trademark Office. In the UK, substantive patent law is contained in the Patents Act 1977 as amended.

In addition, there are international treaty procedures, such as the procedures under the European Patent Convention (EPC) [administered by the European Patent Organisation (EPOrg)], and the Patent Cooperation Treaty (PCT) (administered by WIPO and covering 137 countries), that centralise some portion of the filing and examination procedure. Similar arrangements exist among the member states of ARIPO, OAPI, the analogous treaties among African countries.

5. Application

A patent is requested by filing a written application at the relevant patent office. The application contains a description of how to make and use the invention and, under some legislations, if not self evident, the usefulness of the invention. The patent application may or must also comprise "claims". Claims define the invention and embodiments for which the applicant wants patent rights.

To obtain a patent, an applicant must provide a written description of the invention in sufficient detail for a person skilled in the art (*i.e.,* the relevant area of technology) to make and use the invention. This written description is provided in what is known as the patent specification, which is often accompanied by illustrating drawings. Some countries, such as the United States, further require that the specification disclose the "best mode" of the invention (*i.e.,* the most effective way, to the best of the inventor's knowledge, to make or practice the invention). In addition, at the end of the specification, the applicant must provide one or more claims that define what the applicant regards as their invention. A claim, unlike the body of the specification, is a description designed to provide the public with notice of precisely what the patent owner has a right to exclude others from making, using, or selling. Claims are often analogized to a deed or other instrument that, in the context of real property, sets the metes and bounds of an owner's right to exclude. The claims define what a patent covers. A single patent may contain numerous claims, each of which is regarded as a distinct invention.

For a patent to be granted, that is to take legal effect, the patent application must meet the legal requirements related to patentability.

Once a patent application has been filed, most patent offices examine the application for compliance with the requirements of the relevant patent law. If the application does not comply, the objections are usually communicated to the applicant or their patent agent or attorney, who can respond to the objections to attempt to overcome them and obtain the grant of the patent.

In most countries, there is no requirement that the inventor build a prototype or otherwise reduce his or her invention to actual practice in order to obtain a patent. The description of the invention, however, must be sufficiently complete so that another person with ordinary skill in the art of the invention can make and use the invention without undue experimentation.

Once granted the patent is subject in most countries to renewal fees, generally due each year, to keep the patent in force.

In *Egbert v. Lippmann*, 104 U. S. 333 (1881) (the "corset case"), the United States Supreme Court affirmed a decision that an inventor who had "slept on his rights for eleven years" without applying for a patent could not obtain one at that time. This decision has been codified as 35. U.S.C. §102, which bars an inventor from obtaining a patent if the invention has been in public use for more than one year prior to filing.

6. Economics

I. Rationale

There are four primary incentives embodied in the patent system : to invent in the first place; to disclose the invention once made; to invest the sums necessary to experiment, produce and market the invention; and to design around and improve upon earlier patents.

1. Patents provide incentives for economically efficient research and development (R&D). Many large modern corporations have annual R&D budgets of hundreds of millions or even billions of dollars. Without patents, R&D spending would be significantly less or eliminated altogether, limiting the possibility of technological advances or breakthroughs. Corporations would be much more conservative about the R&D investments they made, as third parties would be free to exploit any developments. This second justification is closely related to the basic ideas underlying traditional property rights.
2. In accordance with the original definition of the term "patent," patents facilitate and encourage disclosure of innovations into the public domain for the common good. If inventors did not have the legal protection of patents, in many cases, they would prefer or tend to keep their inventions secret. Awarding patents generally makes the details of new technology publicly available, for exploitation by anyone after the patent expires, or for further improvement by other inventors. Furthermore, when a patent's term has expired, the public record ensures that the patentee's idea is not lost to humanity.

3. In many industries (especially those with high fixed costs and either low marginal costs or low reverse engineering costs — computer processors, software, and pharmaceuticals for example), once an invention exists, the cost of commercialization (testing, tooling up a factory, developing a market, etc.) is far more than the initial conception cost. (For example, the internal "rule of thumb" at several computer companies in the 1980s was that post-R&D costs were 7-to-1). Unless there is someway to prevent copies from competing at the marginal cost of production, companies will not make that productization investment.
4. Patent rights create an incentive for companies to develop workarounds to patented inventions, thereby creating improved or alternative technologies that might not otherwise be developed.

   One interesting side effect of modern patent usage is that the smalltime inventor can use the exclusive right status to become a licensor. This allows the inventor to accumulate capital quickly from licensing the invention and may allow rapid innovation to occur because he or she may choose to not manage a manufacturing buildup for the invention. Thus the inventor's time and energy can be spent on pure innovation, allowing others to concentrate on manufacturability.

II. Criticism

While each of the four incentives is achieved by the patent system in some contexts, the patent system has countervailing costs, and those costs fall more heavily in some contexts than others. There are many critics and criticisms of patents and this has resulted in the formation of a large number of groups who oppose patents in general, or specific types of patents, and who lobby for their abolishment.

Patents have always been criticized for being granted on already known inventions. In 1938, for example, R. Buckminster Fuller, inventor of the geodesic dome wrote :

"At present (1938), the (US patent) files, are so extraordinarily complex and the items so multitudinous that a veritable army of governmental servants is required to attend them and sort them into some order of distinguishable categories to which reference may be made when corresponding with patent applicants for the purposes of examiner citation of "prior art" disclosure. This complexity makes it inevitable that the human-equation involved in government servants relative to carelessness or mechanical limitations should occasion the granting of multitudes of "probably" invalid patent claims."

Patents have also been criticized for conferring a "negative right" upon a patent owner, permitting them to exclude competitors from using or exploiting the invention, even if the competitor subsequently develops the same invention independently. This may be subsequent to the date of invention, or to the priority date, depending upon the relevant patent law (see First to file and first to invent).

Patents may hinder innovation as well. A holding company, pejoratively known as a "patent troll", owns a portfolio of patents, and sues others for infringement of these patents while doing little to develop the technology itself.

Another theoretical problem with patent rights was proposed by law professors Michael Heller and Rebecca Sue Eisenberg in a 1998 *Science* article. Building from Heller's theory of the tragedy of the anticommons, the professors postulated that intellectual property rights may become so fragmented that, effectively, no one can take advantage of them as to do so would require an agreement between the owners of all of the fragments.

Since at least the early 1980s, patent offices have accepted that computer programs can lie within the realm of patentable subject matter, although the regulations for when a computer program is a patentable invention differ markedly between countries.

In response to perceived problems with the grant of patents, and the evolving nature of technology and industry, there is debate about, and reform of, patent systems around the world. The TRIPs agreement, developed by the WTO has led to the alignment of many patent systems with regard to certain controversial issues, such as what can be protected by patents and the issue of compulsory licences in cases of national need.

7. History

There is evidence suggesting that something like patents was used among some ancient Greek cities. The creator of a new recipe was granted an exclusive right to make the food for one year, and a similar practice existed in some Roman cities. Patents in the modern sense originated in Italy in 1474. At that time the Republic of Venice issued a decree by which new and inventive devices, once they had been put into practice, had to be communicated to the Republic in order to obtain the right to prevent others from using them.

England followed with the Statute of Monopolies in 1623 under King James I, which declared that patents could only be granted for "projects of new invention." During the reign of Queen Anne (1702–1714), the lawyers of the English Court developed the requirement that a written description of the invention must be submitted. These developments, which were in place during the Colonial period, formed the basis for modern English and United States patent law.

In the United States, during the colonial period and Articles of Confederation years (1778–1789), several states adopted patent systems of their own. The first Congress adopted a Patent Act, in 1790, and the first patent was issued under this Act, on July 31, 1790 (and the subject matter of that patent was for the making of potash).

Economics of FOSS *Open Source Initiative (OSI)* is a non-profit corporation dedicated to managing and promoting the Open Source Definition for the good of the community, specifically through the OSI Certified Open Source Software certification mark and program. You can read about successful software products that have these properties, and about our certification mark and program, which allow you to be confident that software really, is "Open Source." We also make copies of approved open source licenses here.

- An Open Standard is more than just a specification. The principles behind the standard, and the practice of offering and operating the standard, are what make the standard Open.

Software Engineering Methodology

"Given unlimited resources, the majority of software problems can probably be solved but the challenge for software engineers is to produce high-quality software with a finite amount of resources and to a predicted schedule."

I. The Life-Cycle Paradigm

The life-cycle paradigm of software engineering is sometimes called the "waterfall model", as it demands a sequential approach to the development process. The work is started at the system level and passes through phases of analysis, design, coding, testing and maintenance. Six activities constitute the overall development process.

II. The Prototyping Paradigm

Contrary to the static, procedural approach offered by the life-cycle paradigm, the prototyping paradigm can be used. Similarly to the life-cycle paradigm, this process begins by gathering requirements of the system. The developers meet with customers, determine the overall objectives of the software and identify any known requirements. A quick design then occurs, focusing on areas visible to the users, such as user interface and basic functionality.

III. The Spiral Model Paradigm

In addition to some of the aspects of the life-cycle and prototyping paradigms, the spiral model adds an element of risk analysis to the development process. *Open Source Methodology* : One of the buzzwords of the movement in the field of computer programming is the concept of "open source" software and computing. *Open source software development* is the process by which open source software (or similar software whose source is publicly available) is developed. These are software products 'available with its source code and under an open source license to study, change, and improve its design". Examples of popular Open source software product are Mozilla Firefox and the OpenOffice.org Suite. The Open source software development method is very unstructured, because no clear development tools, phases, etc., have been defined like with development methods such as DSDM. A *license* is the permission or right granted to engage in some act without which the act might be otherwise unlawful. A person, institution, must grant a license or government that has the legal authority to do so. The term "license" also refers to the document that specifically describes these permissions and rights. *Copyleft* is a play on the word copyright and is the practice of using copyright law to remove restrictions on distributing copies and modified versions of a work for others and requiring that the same freedoms be preserved in modified versions.

2.12 ZERO MARGINAL COST

At the heart of the economics of FOSS is the zero marginal cost of goods in a digital environment. In this respect, the emergence of FOSS represents a confirmation of classical microeconomic price theory - that an equilibrium price in a perfect market approximates the marginal cost. From this perspective, FOSS can be understood as a pioneer in reaching what can be understood as an evolutionarily stable dynamic Nash equilibrium in truly free market.

Most products have some fixed cost and some marginal cost of production. The fixed cost would be the factory; the marginal cost would be the labor, materials, transportation, packages, marketing etc. The price of the usually starts high, and competition brings it down overtime to be close to the marginal cost.

Creative products like music, novels and movies typically have high fixed cost and low marginal cost. As technology has improved the marginal cost of music, novels and movies has down close to zero, and we now have a great deal of piracy. Software is similar to music, novel and movies, except software industry has had to deal with the problem of piracy for longer. Economic theory suggests with good competition, the price of these product should eventually go down to the marginal cost. For all of these products the sellers have tied the product you really want to something physical and a physical object has a non-zero marginal cost. However, with electronic distribution, people want the music without paying for the CD, the movie without a DVD, a novel without a book, and software without the installation of CD, and manuals. The marginal cost of distribution is close to zero, so in theory, the price should eventually get to zero.

2.13 INCOME-GENERATION OPPORTUNITIES

While contributing time and effort in developing, enhancing and documenting FOSS does not provide any direct income, the development of expertise in FOSS provides a broad range of income-generating opportunities—from generating in-house savings from enhancements to FOSS to consulting opportunities in installing, training, customizing and the provision of technical support for FOSS installations. In Part I : The Networked Information Economy of *The Wealth of Networks : How Social Production Transforms Markets and Freedom* (Yale University Press, 2006) Yochai Benkler provides an excellent analysis—with IBM's strategy as a key example—of ways that income and wealth are being generated through open source and open content strategies.

2.13.1 Problems with Traditional Commercial Software

First it should be noted that the commercial software industry is one of the largest and most important industries in the world. The rise of the Open Source movement does not necessarily spell the end of the commercial software industry. On the contrary, many people argue that commercial software can be strengthening by the use of open source techniques. Commercial software is designed to provide a product worth paying for and most of it is (that's why the industry is so big). Despite it's price tag, commercial software, is often far from perfect.

Commercial products will be updated frequently in order to reflect the fluctuating demands of the market and customer needs. These needs can lead to software practices that rearrange and rewrite the software too frequently, or release beta versions as commercial endeavors resulting in high rates of bugs in early versions. Some commercial programs are over designed and written in sloppy code leading to bloat, slow, running programs. Open Source by contrast is driven by the needs of the end users. The skills of the coders is in taking personal pride in what they do, not rushing to meet artificially imposed deadlines (except their own). Thereby their code is often of a superior caliber than that of programmers in the commercial environment. There is also usually a very extensive degree of feedback as the programmers test their products within a wide network of people.

Another problem with traditional commercial software is its closed nature. There is usually no or limited freedom to tamper with the copyrighted product. Also, companies often force users to follow upgrade paths that they may not wish to follow. Open source software enables the individual to customize the software to his end needs in all freedom. Another heavily criticized aspect of commercial software is that customers are frequently locked-in to a product because to keep using data files you are often forced to continue to use the same program. If you wish to share files with users that have upgraded, you often have to upgrade yourself or be written off as irrelevant. Since open source software allows competing programs to share different data file types, there is no reason to be trapped into anyone program. If a newer version has a new file format, then there often are converters that allow users of older versions to keep up their data files up to date.

2.14 INTERNATIONALIZATION

The open nature of Open Source Software allows for extensive internationalization of software. OS's can be modified for any language, for example recently a version of Linux was translated into Welsh (spoken in Wales). While many major commercial projects are provided in multiple languages, it is often too expensive to translate them into more than 3 or 4 languages. Many FOSS projects are available in 10 or more languages, as a programmer who wants the package to be available in their native tongue can in computing, *Internationalization* means of adapting computer software for non-native environments, especially other nations and cultures. Internationalization is the process of designing a software application so that it can be adapted to various languages and regions without engineering changes. Localization is the process of adapting software for a specific region or language by adding locale-specific components and translating text.

2.14.1 Scope

Focal points of internationalization and localization efforts include :

- Language
  - Computer-encoded text
- Alphabets/scripts; different systems of numerals; left-to-right script vs. right-to-left scripts. Most recent systems use the Unicode standard to solve many of these character encoding problems.
- Spelling variants for different countries where the same language is spoken, *e.g., localization* (en-US, en-CA, en-GB-oed) vs. *localization* (en-GB, en-AU).
  - Graphical representations of text (printed materials, online images containing text).
  - Spoken (Audio).
  - Subtitling of film and video.
- Date/time format, including use of different calendars.
- Formatting of numbers (decimal points, positioning of separators, character used as separator).
- Time zones (UTC in internationalized environments).
- Currency.

- Images and colors : issues of comprehensibility and cultural appropriateness.
- Names and titles.
- Government assigned numbers (such as the Social Security number in the US, National Insurance number in the UK) and passports.
- Telephone numbers, addresses and international postal codes.
- Weights and measures.
- Paper sizes.
- Any other aspect of the product or service that is subject to regulatory compliance the distinction between internationalization and localization is subtle but important. Internationalization is the adaptation of products for *potential* use virtually everywhere, while localization is the addition of special features for use in a *specific* locale. The processes are complementary, and must be combined to lead to the objective of a system that works globally. Subjects unique to localization include :
- Language translation.
- National varieties of languages (see language localization).
- Special support for certain languages such as East Asian languages.
- Local customs.
- Local content.
- Symbols.
- Order of sorting.
- Aesthetics.
- Cultural values and social context.

2.14.2 Methods

The current prevailing practice is for applications to place text in resource strings, which are loaded during program execution as needed. These strings, stored in resource files, are relatively easy to translate. Programs are often built to reference resource libraries depending on the selected locale data.

Thus to get an application to support multiple languages one would design the application to select the relevant language resource file at runtime. Resource files are translated to the required languages. This method tends to be application-specific and at best, vendor-specific. The code required to manage date entry verification and many other locale-sensitive data types also must support differing locale requirements. Modern development systems and operating systems include sophisticated libraries for international support of these types. However many development environments still lack full Unicode support, which drastically hampers the translation effort, especially to East Asian languages.

Software localization is a process of translating software user interfaces from one language to another and adapting it to suit a foreign culture. This process is labor-intensive and often requires significant efforts from development teams. There are tools that can simplify the localization process. A lot of these projects get outsourced to specialized companies to cut costs.

Software localization can also refer to adapting software from one culture to another. During localization, some references to history or culture are replaced with an equivalent native reference, which ideally does not change the meaning of the statement.

In console gaming, localization also describes the controversial process of designing consoles and cartridges so as to make cartridges unplayable outside of the geographic regions for which they were intended. For example, a European cartridge might not function in a North American machine. Additionally, it entails the change of dialogue and plot elements to better suit the country's audience. One reason for doing this is local censorship variations; the rules of censorship for Nintendo of America may be different than those in Japan.

Relation to Localization

In software development, after a product has been internationalized, "localization" refers to the process of making it ready for a specific market.

So you can refer to a product as being "internationalized" if it has been developed to meet most of the needs of an international community, but not yet customized to a specific region. The customization to a specific region is called "localization".

SUMMARY

Open Source Initiative (OSI) is a non-profit corporation dedicated to managing and promoting the Open Source Definition for the good of the community, specifically through the OSI Certified Open Source Software certification mark and program. You can read about successful software products that have these properties, and about our certification mark and program, which allow you to be confident that software really, is "Open Source." We also make copies of approved open source licenses here.

An Open Standard is more than just a specification. The principles behind the standard, and the practice of offering and operating the standard, are what make the standard Open. Bruce Perens, who also created the Open Source Definition and the Debian Social Contract, created open Standards Principles and Practice.

Software Freedom

An earlier software movement similar to Open Source is the Free Software Movement (embodied in the Free Software Foundation). The free software movement is a new social movement, which aims to protect the rights of user to access and modify software. There are generally three primary components of software freedom as following :

Open source software development is the process by which open source software (or similar software whose source is publicly available) is developed. These are software products "available with its source code and under an open source license to study, change, and improve its design". A *license* is the permission or right granted to engage in some act without which the act might be otherwise unlawful. A person, institution, must grant a license or government that has the legal authority to do so. The term "license" also refers to the document that specifically describes these permissions and rights.

Copyright is a legal concept enacted by most national governments, that gives the creator of an original work exclusive rights to it, usually for a limited period of time. At its most general, it is literally "the right to copy", but also gives the copyright holder the right to be credited for the work, to determine who (if anyone) can perform it or adapt it to other forms, to benefit financially from the work, and other related rights. *Copyleft* is a play on the word copyright and is the practice of using copyright law to remove restrictions on distributing copies and modified versions of a work for others and requiring that the same freedoms be preserved in modified versions.

REVIEW QUESTIONS

1. What is open source ? What is the scope of open source ?
2. Explain the term open source media, government.
3. Explain the open source culture.
4. What is OSI ? Why it is used ?
5. Give the importance of open source initiatives.
6. What is the meaning of software freedom ?
7. What do you mean by "open source" ?
8. What source code will you be realising, and how it will be licensed ?
9. What is "zero marginal cost" ? Why it is used ?
10. Draw and explain process data model for open source software development.
11. What is patent ? Why it is used ?
12. Give the defination of patent also explain the law of patent.
13. What is enforcement in the term of patent ?
14. Explain the ownership of patent.
15. Give the difference between "law" and "government law".
16. Explain the open source principles.
17. Explain open source methodologies.
18. Describe all the steps of open source development model.
19. Give the difference between "copy left" and "copy right".
20. Discuss concept of software internationalization and it's related problems.
21. What is the meaning of zero marginal cost ? How it is related to free software ?

□□□

Chapter 3 CASE STUDIES

3.1 APACHE

The *Apache License* (Apache Software License previous to version 2.0) is a free software license authored by the Apache Software Foundation (ASF). The Apache License (versions 1.0, 1.1, and 2.0) requires preservation of the copyright notice and disclaimer, but it is not a Copyleft license — it allows use of the source code for the development of free and open source software as well as proprietary and closed source software.

All software produced by the ASF or any of its projects or subjects is licensed according to the terms of the Apache License. Some non-ASF software is licensed using the Apache License as well as of September 2007, over 2000 non-ASF projects located at SourceForge.net are available under the terms of the Apache License.

The Apache Software Foundation (ASF) is a non-profit corporation to support Apache software projects. Apache's projects are characterized by a collaborative, consensus based development process, an open and pragmatic software license. Among the ASF's objectives are to provide legal protection to volunteers working on Apache projects, and to protect the Apache brand name from being used by other organizations.

There are currently two forms of the Apache in wide use today : versions 1.1 and 2.0. While 2.0 is considered by ASF to be the current version and most users have happily switched, a few large groups objected to new clauses inserted into 2.0 regarding patents, and have refused to use any software with the new license (most notable the Open BSD project).

The Apache web server is currently the most popular web server in the world. Nearly 70% of all websites are served by Apache.

The Apache project grew out of an attempt to improve upon the original web server https. Https was a public domain software project that was largely abandoned in the early 1990's. At that time it was the most popular web server in use, and several developers recognized that development needed to continue. Since https was in the public domain they were able to continue work on the program and include a great number of improvements. They quickly organized themselves into the Apache Foundation, to have a stable organization to oversee the on-going work on their new web server. Apache's version of https quickly overtook the original https as the most popular web server in use.

Overtime the Apache Foundation grew to house many related open source projects. Including Tom Cat, a popular Java server let server, and many others.

After many years of developing Apache 1.x, the Apache Foundation found that some of the original architecture of Apache was starting to show it's age, and further extensions were becoming impossible. Therefore a team of mostly volunteer developers started to develop Apache 2. Apache 2 is a complete re-write of Apache, and has allowed the Apache Foundation to add new flexibility of their flagship product.

The stature of the Apache Foundation has also allowed them to become a repository for significant donations of software to the open source community. Most notably 2 large donations from IBM to the Apache Foundation in 2004.

3.1.1 History

The first version of the Apache web server was created by Robert McCool, who was heavily involved with the National Center for Supercomputing Applications web server, known simply as NCSA Https. When Rob left NCSA in mid-1994, the development of https stalled, leaving a variety of patches for improvements circulating through e-mails.

Rob McCool was not alone in his efforts. Several other developers helped form the original "Apache Group" : Brian Behlendorf, Roy T. Fielding, Rob Hartill, David Robinson, Cliff Skolnick, Randy Terbush, Robert S. Thau, Andrew Wilson, Eric Hagberg, Frank Peters, and Nicolas Pioch.

Version 2 of the Apache server was a substantial re-write of much of the Apache 1.x code, with a strong focus on further modularization and the development of a portability layer, the Apache Portable Runtime. The Apache 2.x core has several major enhancements over Apache 1.x. These include UNIX threading, better support for non-Unix platforms (such as Microsoft Windows), a new Apache API, and IPv6 support. The first alpha release of Apache 2 was in March 2000, with the first general availability release on 6 April 2002.

Version 2.2 introduced a new authorization API that allows for more flexibility. It also features improved cache modules and proxy modules.

3.1.2 Features

Apache supports a variety of features, many implemented as compiled modules which extend the core functionality. These can range from server-side programming language support to authentication schemes. Some common language interfaces support mod_perl, mod_python, Tcl, and PHP. Popular authentication modules include mod_access, mod_auth, and mod_digest. A sample of other features include SSL and TLS support (mod_ssl), a proxy module, a useful URL re-writer (also known as a re-write engine, implemented under mod_re-write), custom log files (mod_log_config), and filtering support (mod_include and mod_ext_filter).

Popular compression methods on Apache include the external extension module, mod_gzip, implemented to help with reduction of the size (weight) of web pages served over HTTP. Apache logs can be analyzed through a web browser using free scripts such as AW Stats/W3Perl or Visitors.

Virtual hosting allows one Apache installation to serve many different actual websites. For example, one machine, with one Apache installation could simultaneously serve www.example.com, www.test.com, test47.test-server.test.com, etc.

Apache features configurable error messages, DBMS-based authentication databases, and content negotiation. It is also supported by several Graphical User Interfaces (GUIs) which permit easier, more intuitive configuration of the server.

3.1.3 Usage

Apache is primarily used to serve both static content and dynamic Web pages on the World Wide Web. Many web applications are designed expecting the environment and features that Apache provides.

Apache is the web server component of the popular LAMP web server application stack, alongside MySQL, and the PHP/Perl/Python programming languages.

Apache is redistributed as part of various proprietary software packages including the Oracle Database or the IBM Web Sphere application server. Mac OS X integrates Apache as its built-in web server and as support for its WebObjects application server. It is also supported in someway by Borland in the Kylix and Delphi development tools. Apache is included with Novell NetWare 6.5, where it is the default web server.

Apache is used for many other tasks where content needs to be made available in a secure and reliable way. One example is sharing files from a personal computer over the Internet. A user who has Apache installed on their desktop can put arbitrary files in the Apache's document root which can then be shared.

Programmers developing web applications often use a locally installed version of Apache in order to preview and test code as it is being developed.

Microsoft Internet Information Services (IIS) is the main competitor to Apache, trailed by Sun Microsystems' Sun Java System Web Server and a host of other applications such as Zeus Web Server. Some of the biggest web sites in the world are run using Apache. Google's search engine front end is based on a modified version of Apache, named Google Web Server (GWS). Wikimedia projects, including Wikipedia are also run on Apache servers.

3.1.4 Licenses

The Apache Software Foundation uses various licenses to distribute software and documentation, to accept regular contributions from individuals and corporations, and to accept larger grants of existing software products.

These licenses help us achieve our goal of providing reliable and long-lived software products through collaborative open source software development. In all cases, contributors retain full rights to use their original contributions for any other purpose outside of Apache while providing the ASF and its projects the right to distribute and build upon their work within Apache.

3.1.5 Licensing of Distributions

All software produced by The Apache Software Foundation or any of its projects or subjects is licensed according to the terms of the documents listed below.

1. **Apache License, Version 2.0 (current)**

   The 2.0 version of the Apache License was approved by the ASF in 2004. The goals of this license revision have been to reduce the number of frequently asked questions, to allow the license to be reusable without modification by any project (including non-ASF projects), to allow the license to be included by reference instead of listed in every file, to clarify the license on submission of contributions, to require a patent license on contributions that necessarily infringe the contributor's own patents, and to move comments regarding Apache and other inherited attribution notices to a location outside the license terms (the NOTICE file).

   The result is a license that is supposed to be compatible with other open source licenses, while remaining true to the original goals of the Apache Group and supportive of collaborative development across both nonprofit and commercial organizations. The Apache Software Foundation is still trying to determine if this version of the Apache License is compatible with the GPL.

   All packages produced by the ASF are implicitly licensed under the Apache License, Version 2.0, unless otherwise explicitly stated. More developer documentation on how to apply the Apache License to your work can be found in *Applying the Apache License, Version 2.0.* See the License FAQ.

2. **Apache License, Version 1.1 (historic)**

   The 1.1 version of the Apache License was approved by the ASF in 2000. The primary change from the 1.0 license is in the 'advertising clause; derived products are no longer required to include attribution in their advertising materials, only in their documentation.

   Individual packages licensed under the 1.1 version may have used different wording due to varying requirements for attribution or mark identification, but the binding terms were all the same.

3. **Apache License, Version 1.0 (historic)**

   This is the original Apache License which applies only to older versions of Apache packages (such as version 1.2 of the Web server).

4. **Contributor License Agreements**

   The ASF desires that all contributors of ideas, code, or documentation to the Apache projects complete, sign, and submit (via postal mail, fax or e-mail) an Individual Contributor License Agreement (CLA) [PDF form]. The purpose of this agreement is to clearly define the terms under which intellectual property has been contributed to the ASF and thereby allow us to defend the project should there be a legal dispute regarding the software at some future time. A signed CLA is required to be on file before an individual is given commit rights to an ASF project.

For a corporation that has assigned employees to work on an Apache project, a Corporate CLA (CCLA) is available for contributing intellectual property via the corporation that may have been assigned as part of an employment agreement. Note that a Corporate CLA does not remove the need for every developer to sign their own CLA as an individual, to cover any of their contributions which are not owned by the corporation signing the CCLA.

CLAs may be submitted by traditional postal mail, fax, or by emailing a scan of the signed copy to secretary@.

5. **Software Grants**

   When an individual or corporation decides to donate a body of existing software or documentation to one of the Apache projects, they need to execute a formal Software Grant agreement with the ASF. Typically, this is done after negotiating approval with the ASF Incubator or one of the PMCs, since the ASF will not accept software unless there is a viable community available to support a collaborative project.

3.1.6 The Apache Software License, Version 1.1

Redistribution and use in source and binary forms, with or without Modification, are permitted provided that the following conditions are met :

1. Redistributions of source code must retain the above copyright notice, this list of conditions and the following disclaimer.
2. Redistributions in binary form must reproduce the above copyright notice, this list of conditions and the following disclaimer in the documentation and/or other materials provided with the Distribution.
3. The end-user documentation included with the redistribution, if any, must include the following acknowledgment :"This product includes software developed by the Apache Software Foundation (http ://www.apache.org/)."Alternately, this acknowledgment may appear in the software itself, if and wherever such third-party acknowledgments normally appear.
4. The names "Apache" and "Apache Software Foundation" must not be used to endorse or promote products derived from this Software without prior written permission. For written permission, please contact apache@apache.org.
5. Products derived from this software may not be called "Apache", nor may "Apache" appear in their name, without prior written permission of the Apache Software Foundation.

3.2 BERKELEY SOFTWARE DISTRIBUTION

Berkeley Software Distribution (BSD), sometimes called **Berkeley Unix,** is the UNIX derivative distributed by the University of California, Berkeley, starting in the 1970s.

Historically, BSD has been considered as a branch of UNIX — 'BSD UNIX', because it had shared the initial codebase and design with the original UNIX by AT&T and collaborated on the development in the pioneer days of UNIX. It was widely identified with the versions of UNIX available for workstation-class SYSTEMS, which can be attributed to the ease with which it could be licensed and the familiarity it found among the founders of many technology companies during the 1980s. The familiarity often came from using similar systems — notably DEC's ULTRIX and Sun Microsystems SunOS — during their education. Though BSD itself was largely superseded by the System V Release 4 and OSF/1 systems in the 1990s (both of which incorporated BSD code), the modified codebase as open source — mostly derived from 4.4BSD-Lite have seen increasing use and development recently.

BSD Unix	
Website	N/A
Company/developer	CSRG, UC Berkeley
OS family	Unix
Source model	Open source
Latest stable release	4.4-Lite2 / 1995
Kernel type	Monolithic
License	BSD licenses
Working state	Superseded by derivatives (see below)

Today, the term of "BSD" is often non-specifically used to refer to any of the BSD descendants, *e.g.*, FreeBSD, NetBSD or OpenBSD, which forms a branch of Unix-like operating systems.

3.2.1 History

1. PDP-11 Beginnings

The earliest distributions of UNIX from Bell Labs in the 1970s included the source code to the operating system, allowing researchers at universities to modify and extend UNIX. The first UNIX system at Berkeley was a PDP-11 installed in 1974, and the computer science department used it for extensive research thereafter.

Other universities became interested in the software at Berkeley, and so in 1977 Bill Joy, then a graduate student at Berkeley, assembled and sent out tapes of the *first Berkeley Software Distribution (1BSD)*. 1BSD was an add-on to Sixth Edition Unix rather than a complete operating system in its own right; its main components were a Pascal compiler and Joy's ex line editor.

The *Second Berkeley Software Distribution (2BSD)*, released in 1978, included updated versions of the 1BSD software as well as two new programs by Joy that persist on Unix systems to this day : the vi text editor (a visual version of ex) and the C shell.

Later releases of 2BSD contained ports of changes to the VAX-based releases of BSD back to the PDP-11 architecture. 2.9BSD from 1983 included code from 4.1cBSD, and was the first release that was a full OS (a modified Version 7 Unix) rather than a set of applications and patches. The most recent release, **2.11BSD**, was first released in 1992, with maintenance updates from volunteers continuing until 2006 (patch 445 was released on December 26, 2006).

2. VAX Versions

A VAX computer was installed at Berkeley in 1978, but the port of Unix to the VAX architecture, UNIX/32V, did not take advantage of the VAX's virtual memory capabilities. The kernel of 32V was largely rewritten by Berkeley students to include a virtual memory implementation, and a complete operating system including the new kernel, ports of the 2BSD utilities to the VAX, and the utilities from 32V was released as **3BSD** at the end of

1979. 3BSD was also alternatively called Virtual VAX/UNIX or VMUNIX (for Virtual Memory Unix), and BSD kernel images were normally called /vmunix until 4.4BSD.

The success of 3BSD was a major factor in the Defense Advanced Research Projects Agency's (DARPA) decision to fund Berkeley's Computer Systems Research Group (CSRG), which would develop a standard Unix platform for future DARPA research in the VLSI Project. CSRG released **4BSD**, containing numerous improvements to the 3BSD system, in October 1980.

4BSD (November 1980) offered a number of enhancements over 3BSD, notably job control in the previously-released cash, deliver mail (the antecedent of send mail), "reliable" signals, and the Curses programming library.

4.1BSD (June 1981) was a response to criticisms of BSD's performance relative to the dominant VAX operating system, VMS. The 4.1BSD kernel was systematically tuned up by Bill Joy until it could perform as well as VMS on several benchmarks. (The release would have been called *5BSD*, but the name was changed to avoid confusion with AT&T's UNIX System V release. One early, never-released test version was in fact called 4.5BSD.)

4.2BSD would take over two years to implement and contained several major overhauls. Before its official release came three intermediate versions : *4.1a* incorporated a modified version of BBN's preliminary TCP/IP implementation; *4.1b* included the new Berkeley Fast File System, implemented by Marshall Kirk McKusick; and *4.1c* was an interim release during the last few months of 4.2BSD's development.

The official 4.2BSD release came in August 1983. It was notable as the first version released after the 1982 departure of Bill Joy to co-found Sun Microsystems; Mike Karels and Marshall Kirk McKusick took on leadership roles within the project from that point forward. On a lighter note, it also marked the debut of BSD's daemon mascot in a drawing by McKusick that appeared on the cover of the printed manuals distributed by USENIX.

4.3BSD was released in June 1986. Its main changes were to improve the performance of many of the new contributions of 4.2BSD that had not been as heavily tuned as the 4.1BSD code. Prior to the release, BSD's implementation of TCP/IP had diverged considerably from BBN's official implementation. After several months of testing, DARPA determined that the 4.2BSD version was superior and would remain in 4.3BSD. (See also History of the Internet.)

After 4.3BSD, it was determined that BSD would move away from the aging VAX platform. The Power 6/32 **platform** (codenamed "Tahoe") developed by Computer Consoles Inc. seemed promising at the time, but was abandoned by its developers shortly thereafter. Nonetheless, the **4.3BSD-Tahoe** port (June 1988) proved valuable as it led to a separation of machine-dependent and machine-independent code in BSD which would improve the system's future portability.

Until this point, all versions of BSD had incorporated proprietary AT&T UNIX code and therefore required licenses from AT&T for their use. Source code licenses had become very expensive by this point, and several outside parties had expressed interest in a separate release of the networking code, which had been developed entirely outside AT&T and would not be subject to the licensing requirement. This led to **Networking Release 1 (Net/1)**, which was made available to non-licensees of AT&T code and was freely redistributable under the terms of the BSD license. It was released in June 1989.

4.3BSD-Reno came in early 1990. It was an interim release during the early development of 4.4BSD, and its use was considered a "gamble", hence the naming after the gambling center of Reno, Nevada. This release was clearly moving towards POSIX compliance, and, according to some, away from the BSD philosophy (as POSIX is very much based on System V, and Reno was quite bloated compared to previous releases).

In August 2006, *Information Week* magazine rated 4.3BSD as the "Greatest Software Ever Written", commenting that "BSD 4.3 represents the single biggest theoretical undergirded of the Internet."

Net/2 and legal troubles

After Net/1, BSD developer Keith Bostic proposed that more non-AT&T sections of the BSD system be released under the same license as Net/1. To this end, he started a project to re-employment most of the standard UNIX utilities without using the AT&T code. For example, vi, which had been based on the original Unix version of end, was rewritten as nvi (new vi). Within eighteen months, all the AT&T utilities had been replaced, and it was determined that only a few AT&T files remained in the kernel. These files were removed, and the result was the June 1991 release of **Networking Release 2 (Net/2)**, a nearly complete operating system that was freely distributable.

Net/2 was the basis for two separate ports of BSD to the Intel 80386 architecture : the free 386BSD by William Jolitz and the proprietary BSD/386 (later renamed BSD/OS) by Berkeley Software Design (BSDi). 386BSD itself was short-lived, but became the initial code base of the NetBSD and FreeBSD projects that were started shortly thereafter.

BSDi soon found itself in legal trouble with AT&T's Unix System Laboratories subsidiary, then the owners of the System V copyright and the UNIX trademark. The *USL v. BSDi* lawsuit was filed in 1992 and led to an injunction on the distribution of Net/2 until the validity of USL's copyright claims on the source could be determined.

The lawsuit slowed development of the free-software descendants of BSD for nearly two years while their legal status was in question, and as a result systems based on the Linux kernel, which did not have such legal ambiguity, gained greater support. Linux and 386BSD began development at about the same time, and Linus Torvalds has said that if 386BSD had been available at the time, he would probably not have created Linux.

4.4BSD and descendants

The lawsuit was settled in January 1994, largely in Berkeley's favor. Of the 18,000 files in the Berkeley distribution, only 3 had to be removed and 70 modified to show USL copyright notices. A further condition of the settlement was that USL would not file further lawsuits against users and distributors of the Berkeley-owned code in the upcoming 4.4BSD release.

In June 1994, **4.4BSD** was released in two forms : the freely distributable **4.4BSD-Lite** contained no AT&T source, whereas **4.4BSD-Encumbered** was available, as earlier releases had been, only to AT&T licensees.

The final release from Berkeley was 1995's **4.4BSD-Lite Release 2**, after which the CSRG was dissolved and development of BSD at Berkeley ceased. Since then, several variants based directly or indirectly on 4.4BSD-Lite (such as FreeBSD, NetBSD, DragonflyBSD and OpenBSD) have been maintained.

In addition, the permissive nature of the BSD license has allowed many other operating systems, both free and proprietary, to incorporate BSD code. For example, Microsoft Windows has used BSD-derived code in its implementation of TCP/IP and bundles recompiled versions of BSD's command line networking tools with its current releases.[3] Also Darwin, the system on which Apple's Mac OS X is built, is partly derived from FreeBSD 5. Various commercial UNIXes, such as Solaris, also contain varying amounts of BSD code.

3. Technology

BSD pioneered many of the advances of modern computing. Berkeley's Unix was the first Unix to include libraries supporting the Internet Protocol stacks : *Berkeley sockets.* By integrating sockets with the Unix operating system's file descriptors, it became almost as easy to read and write data across a network as it was to access a disk. The AT&T laboratory eventually released their own STREAMS library, which incorporated much of the same functionality in a software stack with a better architecture, but the wide distribution of the existing sockets library, together with the unfortunate omission of a function call for polling a set of open socket's equivalent to the select call in the Berkeley library, reduced the impact of the new API.

Today, BSD continues to be used as a tested for technology by academic organizations, as well as finding uses in a lot of commercial and free products and, increasingly, in embedded devices. The general quality of its source code, as well as its documentation (especially reference manual pages, commonly referred to as *man pages*), make it well-suited for many purposes.

The permissive nature of the BSD license allows companies to distribute derived products as proprietary software without exposing source code and sometimes intellectual property to competitors. Searching for strings containing "University of California, Berkeley" in the documentation of products, in the static data sections of binaries and ROMs, or as part of other information about a software program, will often show BSD code has been used. This permissiveness also makes BSD code suitable for use in open source products, and the license is compatible with many other open source licenses.

BSD operating systems can run much native software of several other operating systems on the same architecture, using a binary compatibility layer. Much simpler and faster than emulation, this allows, for instance, applications intended for Linux to be run at effectively full speed. This makes BSDs not only suitable for server environments, but also for workstation ones, given the increasing availability of commercial or closed-source software for Linux only. This also allows administrators to migrate legacy commercial applications, which may have only supported commercial Unix variants, to a more modern operating system, retaining the functionality of such applications until they can be replaced by a better alternative.

Current BSD operating system variants support many of the common IEEE, ANSI, ISO, and POSIX standards, while retaining most of the traditional BSD behavior. Like AT&T Unix, the BSD kernel is monolithic, meaning that device drivers in the kernel run in privileged mode, as part of the core of the operating system. Early versions of BSD were used to form Sun Microsystems' SunOS, founding the first wave of popular Unix workstations.

4. Significant BSD Descendants

BSD has been the base of a large number of operating systems. Most notable among these today is perhaps the major open source BSDs, FreeBSD, NetBSD and OpenBSD—sometimes known as *the BSDs*—which have themselves spawned a number of children, including Dragonfly BSD, FreeSBIE, MirOS BSD, DesktopBSD, and PC-BSD. They are targeted at an array of systems for different purposes and are common in government facilities, universities and in commercial use. A number of commercial operating systems are also partly or wholly based on BSD or its descendants, including Sun's SunOS and Apple Inc.'s Mac OS X. A selection of significant Unix versions and Unix-like operating systems that descend from BSD includes :

- FreeBSD, a major open source effort focusing on performance and the x86 platform.
- NetBSD, an open source BSD with an emphasis on portability and clean design.
- OpenBSD, a 1995 fork of NetBSD, focuses on portability, standardization, correctness, proactive security and integrated cryptography.
- DragonFly BSD, a fork of FreeBSD to follow an alternative design, particularly related to SMP.
- PC-BSD and DesktopBSD, distributions of FreeBSD with emphasis on ease of use and user friendly interfaces for the desktop/laptop PC user.
- Tru64 UNIX (formerly DEC OSF/1 AXP or Digital UNIX), the port of OSF/1 for DEC Alpha-based systems from DEC, Compaq and HP.
- Juniper Networks JunOS, the operating system for Juniper routers, a customized version of FreeBSD, and a variety of other embedded operating systems.
- Apple Inc.'s Darwin, the core of Mac OS X; built on the XNU kernel (part Mach, part FreeBSD, part Apple-derived code) and a userland much of which comes from FreeBSD.
- Early versions of Sun Microsystems SunOS (up to SunOS 4.1.4), an enhanced version of 4BSD for the Sun Motorola 68k-based Sun-2 and Sun-3 systems, SPARC-based systems, and x86-based Sun386i systems.
- DEC's Ultrix, the official version of Unix for its PDP-11, VAX, and DECstation systems.
- OSF/1, a microkernel-based UNIX developed by the Open Software Foundation, incorporating the Mach kernel and parts of 4BSD.
- DEMOS, a Soviet BSD clone.
- NeXT NEXTSTEP and OPENSTEP, based on the Mach kernel and 4BSD; the ancestor of Mac OS X.
- 386BSD, the first open source BSD-based operating system and the ancestor of most current BSD systems.
- BSD/OS, a (now defunct) proprietary BSD for PCs.

BSD licenses represent a family of permissive free software licenses. The original was used for the Berkeley Software Distribution, a Unix-like operating system for which the license is named. The original owners of BSD were the Regents of the University of California because BSD was first written at the University of California, Berkeley. The first version of the license was revised, and the resulting licenses are more properly called modified BSD licenses. Permissive licenses, sometimes with important differences pertaining to license compatibility, are referred to as "BSD-style licenses". Several BSD-like licenses, including the New BSD license, have been vetted by the Open Source Initiative as meeting their definition of source. The licenses have few restrictions compared to other free software licenses such as the GNU General Public License or even the default restrictions provided by copyright, putting it relatively closer to the public domain. The BSD licenses have been referred to as *copycenter*, as a comparison to standard copyright and Copyleft free software : "Take it down to the copy center and make as many copies as you want."

3.3 LINUX

Linux	
Tux, the penguin, mascot of the Linux kernel	
OS family	Unix-like
Latest stable release	2.6.23.13 (Linux kernel) / 9 January 2008
Latest unstable release	2.6.24-rc7 (Linux kernel) / 6 January 2008
Kernel type	Monolithic kernel
License	GNU General Public License and others
Working state	Current

Linux (pronounced IPA variants exist) is a Unix-like computer operating system. Linux is one of the most prominent examples of free software and open source development; typically all underlying source code can be freely modified, used, and redistributed by anyone.

The Linux kernel was first released to the public on 17 September 1991, for the Intel x86 PC architecture. The kernel was augmented with system utilities and libraries from the GNU project to create a usable operating system, which led to an alternative term, **GNU/Linux**. Linux is packaged for different uses in Linux distributions, which contain the sometimes-modified kernel along with a variety of other software packages tailored to different requirements.

Predominantly known for its use in servers, Linux is supported by corporations such as Dell, Hewlett-Packard, IBM, Novell, Oracle Corporation, Red Hat, and Sun Microsystems. It is used as an operating system for a wide variety of computer hardware, including desktop computers, supercomputers, video game systems, such as PlayStation 2, 3, several arcade games, and embedded devices, such as mobile phones and routers.

In 1992, Linus Torvalds explained that he pronounces Linux as /'l ?n ?ks/, though other variations are common.

The Linux kernel is currently one of the most active, and most important, free and open source software development projects. In 1991, Linus Torvalds used the Internet to invite collaboration on his infant project to develop an operating system kernel sporting a system very much like Unix. He wanted a Unix-like operating system that would work on his computer, an early and expensive 386 machine, and was unsatisfied with anything available at an affordable cost, including academic teaching examples like Minix (from Professor Andrew Tannenbaum). Since then the Linux kernel has been used in multiple Linux system distributions that are currently supported by organizations like IBM, Novell, HP, many universities (*e.g.*, ETH-Zurich), Bell Labs, and Borland. The Linux kernel is the kernel used in the GNU/Linux operating system, and is currently in its 2nd major version release, and 6th minor version. The official home page of the Linux kernel project is kernel.org.

3.3.1 What is Linux and Why is it So Popular ?

Every desktop computer uses an **operating system**. The most popular operating systems in use today are :

- Windows
- Mac OS
- UNIX

Linux is a version of the **UNIX** operating system that has become very popular over the last several years.

Operating systems are computer programs. An operating system is the first piece of software that the computer executes when you turn the machine on. The operating system loads itself into memory and begins managing the resources available on the computer. It then provides those resources to other applications that the user wants to execute. Typical services that an operating system provides include :

- **A task scheduler.** The task scheduler is able to allocate the execution of the CPU to a number of different tasks. Some of those tasks are the different applications that the user is running, and some of them are operating system tasks. The task scheduler is the part of the operating system that lets you print a document from your word processor in one window while you are downloading a file in another window and recalculating a spreadsheet in a third window.
- **A memory manager.** The memory manager controls the system's RAM and normally creates a larger virtual memory space using a file on the hard disk. (See also this Question of the Day.)
- **A disk manager.** The disk manager creates and maintains the directories and files on the disk. When you request a file, the disk manager brings it in from the disk.
- **A network manager.** The network manager controls all data moving between the computer and the network.
- **Other I/O services manager.** The OS manages the keyboard, mouse, video display, printers, etc.
- **Security manager.** The OS maintains the security of the information in the computer's files and controls who can access the computer.

An operating system normally also provides the default user interface for the system. The standard "look" of Windows 98 includes the Start button, the task bar, etc. The Mac OS provides a completely different look and feel for Macintosh computers.

Linux is as much a phenomenon as it is an operating system. To understand why Linux has become so popular, it is helpful to know a little bit about its history. The first version of UNIX was originally developed several decades ago and was used primarily as a research operating system in universities. High-powered desktop workstations from companies like Sun proliferated in the 1980s, and they were all based on UNIX. A number of companies entered the workstation field to compete against Sun : HP, IBM, Silicon Graphics, Apollo, etc. Unfortunately, each one had its own version of UNIX and this made the sale of software difficult. Windows NT was Microsoft's answer to this marketplace. NT provides the same sort of features as UNIX operating systems—security, support for multiple CPUs, large-scale memory and disk management, etc.,—but it does it in a way that is compatible with most Windows applications.

The entry of Microsoft into the high-end workstation arena created a strange dynamic. The proprietary operating systems owned by separate companies and the lack of a central authority in the UNIX world weaken UNIX, but many people have personal problems with Microsoft. Linux stepped into this odd landscape and captured a lot of attention.

The Linux kernel, created by **Linus Torvalds**, was made available to the world for free. Torvalds then invited others to add to the kernel provided that they keep their contributions free. Thousands of programmers began working to enhance Linux, and the operating system grew rapidly. Because it is free and runs on PC platforms, it gained a sizeable audience among hard-core developers very quickly. Linux has a dedicated following and appeals to several different kinds of people :

- People who already know UNIX and want to run it on PC-type hardware.
- People who want to experiment with operating system principles.
- People who need or want a great deal of control over their operating system.
- People who have personal problems with Microsoft.

3.3.2 History

Unix

In order to understand the popularity of Linux, we need to travel back in time, about 30 years ago...Imagine computers as big as houses, even stadiums. While the sizes of those computers posed substantial problems, there was one thing that made this even worse : every computer had a different operating system. Software was always customized to serve a specific purpose, and software for one given system did not run on another system. Being able to work with one system did not automatically mean that you could work with another. It was difficult, both for the users and the system administrators. Computers were extremely expensive then, and sacrifices had to be made even after the original purchase just to get the users to understand how they worked. The total cost per unit of computing power was enormous. Technologically the world was not quite that advanced, so they had to live with the size for another decade. In 1969, a team of developers in the Bell Labs laboratories started working on a solution for the software problem, to address these compatibility issues. They developed a new operating system, which was

1. Simple and elegant.
2. Written in the C programming language instead of in assembly code.
3. Able to recycle code.

The Bell Labs developers named their project "UNIX." The code recycling features were very important. Until then, all commercially available computer systems were written in a code specifically developed for one system. UNIX on the other hand needed only a small piece of that special code, which is now commonly named the kernel. This kernel is the only piece of code that needs to be adapted for every specific system and forms the base of the UNIX system. The operating system and all other functions were built around this kernel and written in a higher programming language, C.

Linus and Linux

By the beginning of the 90s home PCs were finally powerful enough to run a full blown UNIX. Linus Torvalds, a young man studying computer science at the university of Helsinki, thought it would be a good idea to have some sort of freely available academic version of UNIX, and promptly started to code. He started to ask questions, looking for answers and solutions that would help him get UNIX on his PC.

Below is one of his first posts in comp.os.minix, dating from 1991 :

From : torvalds@klaava.Helsinki.FI (Linus Benedict Torvalds)

Newsgroups : comp.os.minix

Subject : Gcc-1.40 and a posix-question

Message-ID : <1991Jul3.100050.9886@klaava.Helsinki.FI>

Date : 3 Jul 91 10 : 00 : 50 GMT

Hello net landers,

Due to a project I'm working on (in minix), I'm interested in the posix

standard definition. Could somebody please point me to a (preferably)

machine-readable format of the latest posix rules ? Ftp-sites would be nice.

From the start, it was Linus' goal to have a free system that was completely compliant with the original UNIX. That is why he asked for POSIX standards, POSIX still being the standard for UNIX. In those days plug-and-play wasn't invented yet, but so many people were interested in having a UNIX system of their own, that this was only a small obstacle. New drivers became available for all kinds of new hardware, at a continuously rising speed. Almost as soon as a new piece of hardware became available, someone bought it and submitted it to the Linux test, as the system was gradually being called, releasing more free code for an ever wider range of hardware. These coders didn't stop at their PC's; every piece of hardware they could find was useful for Linux. Back then, those people were called "nerds" or "freaks", but it didn't matter to them, as long as the supported hardware list grew longer and longer. Thanks to these people, Linux is now not only ideal to run on new PC's, but is also the system of choice for old and exotic hardware that would be useless if Linux didn't exist. Two years after Linus' post, there were 12000 Linux users. The project, popular with hobbyists, grew steadily, all the while staying within the bounds of the POSIX standard. All the features of UNIX were added over the next couple of years, resulting in the mature operating system Linux has become today. Linux is a full UNIX clone, fit for use on workstations as well as on middle-range and high-end servers. Today, a lot of the important players on the hard- and software market each have their team of Linux developers; at your local dealer's you can even buy pre-installed Linux systems with official support - eventhough there is still a lot of hard-and software that is not supported, too.

3.3.3 Current Application of Linux Systems

Today Linux has joined the desktop market. Linux developers concentrated on networking and services in the beginning, and office applications have been the last barrier to be taken down. We don't like to admit that Microsoft is ruling this market, so plenty of alternatives have been started over the last couple of years to make Linux an acceptable choice as a workstation, providing an easy user interface and MS compatible office applications like word processors, spreadsheets, presentations and the like. On the server side, Linux is well-known as a stable and reliable platform, providing database and trading services for companies like Amazon, the well-known online bookshop, US Post Office, the German army and many others. Especially Internet providers and Internet service providers have grown fond of Linux as firewall, proxy- and web server, and you will find a Linux box within reach of every UNIX system administrator who appreciates a comfortable management station. Clusters of Linux machines are used in the creation of movies such as "Titanic", "Shrek" and others. In post offices, they are the nerve centers that route mail and in large search engine, clusters are used to perform internet searches.These are only a few of the thousands of heavy-duty jobs that Linux is performing day-to-day across the world.

It is also worth to note that modern Linux not only runs on workstations, mid- and high-end servers, but also on "gadgets" like PDA's, mobiles, a shipload of embedded applications and even on experimental wristwatches. This makes Linux the only operating system in the world covering such a wide range of hardware.

3.3.4 The User Interface

1. Is Linux Difficult ?

Whether Linux is difficult to learn depends on the person you're asking. Experienced UNIX users will say no, because Linux is an ideal operating system for power-users and programmers, because it has been and is being developed by such people. Everything a good programmer can wish for is available : compilers, libraries, development and debugging tools. These packages come with every standard Linux distribution. The C-compiler is included for free—as opposed to many UNIX distributions demanding licensing fees for this tool. All the documentation and manuals are there, and examples are often included to help you get started in no time. It feels like UNIX and switching between UNIX and Linux is a natural thing. In the early days of Linux, being an expert was kind of required to start using the system. Those who mastered Linux felt better than the rest of the "losers" who hadn't seen the light yet. It was common practice to tell a beginning user to "RTFM" (read the manuals). While the manuals were on every system, it was difficult to find the documentation, and even if someone did, explanations were in such technical terms that the new user became easily discouraged from learning the system. The Linux-using community started to realize that if Linux was ever to be an important player on the operating system market, there had to be some serious changes in the accessibility of the system.

2. *Linux for Non-experienced Users*

Companies such as RedHat, SuSE and Mandriva have sprung up, providing packaged Linux distributions suitable for mass consumption. They integrated a great deal of Graphical User Interfaces (GUIs), developed by the community, in order to ease management of programs and services. As a Linux user today you have all the means of getting to know your system inside out, but it is no longer necessary to have that knowledge in order to make the system comply to your requests. Nowadays you can log in graphically and start all required applications without even having to type a single character, while you still have the ability to access the core of the system if needed. Because of its structure, Linux allows a user to grow into the system : it equally fits new and experienced users. New users are not forced to do difficult things, while experienced users are not forced to work in the same way they did when they first started learning Linux. While development in the service area continues, great things are being done for desktop users, generally considered as the group least likely to know how a system works. Developers of desktop applications are making incredible efforts to make the most beautiful desktops you've ever seen, or to make your Linux machine look just like your former MS Windows or an Apple workstation. The latest developments also include 3D acceleration support and support for USB devices, single-click updates of system and packages, and so on. Linux has these, and tries to present all available services in a logical form that ordinary people can understand. Below is a short list containing some great examples; these sites have a lot of screenshots that will give you a glimpse of what Linux on the desktop can be like :

- http ://www.gnome.org
- http ://kde.org/screenshots/
- http ://www.openoffice.org
- http ://www.mozilla.org

3.3.5 Does Linux have a Future ?

1. *Open Source*

The idea behind Open Source software is rather simple : When programmers can read, distribute and change code, the code will mature. People can adapt it, fix it, debug it, and they can do it at a speed that dwarfs the performance of software developers at conventional companies. This software will be more flexible and of a better quality than software that has been developed using the conventional channels, because more people have tested it in more different conditions than the closed software developer ever can. The Open Source initiative started to make this clear to the commercial world, and very slowly, commercial vendors are starting to see the point. While lots of academics and technical people have already been convinced for 20 years now that this is the way to go, commercial vendors needed applications like the Internet to make them realize they can profit from Open Source. Now Linux has grown past the stage where it was almost exclusively an academic system, useful only to a handful of people with a technical background. Now Linux provides more than the operating system : there is an entire infrastructure supporting the chain of effort of creating an operating system, of making and testing programs for it, of bringing everything to the users, of supplying maintenance, updates and support and customizations, etcetera. Today, Linux is ready to accept the challenge of a fast-changing world.

2. Ten Years of Experience at Your Service

While Linux is probably the most well-known Open Source initiative, there is another project that contributed enormously to the popularity of the Linux operating system. This project is called SAMBA, and its achievement is the reverse engineering of the Server Message Block (SMB)/Common Internet File System (CIFS) protocol used for file- and print-serving on PC-related machines, natively supported by MS Windows NT and OS/2, and Linux. Packages are now available for almost every system and provide interconnection solutions in mixed environments using MS Windows protocols : Windows-compatible (up to and includingWinXP) file- and print-servers. Maybe even more successful than the SAMBA project is the Apache HTTP server project. The server runs on UNIX, Windows NT and many other operating systems. Originally known as "A PAtCHy server", based on existing code and a series of "patch files", the name for the matured code deserves to be connoted with the native American tribe of the Apache, well-known for their superior skills in warfare strategy and inexhaustible endurance. Apache has been shown to be substantially faster, more stable and more feature-full than many other web servers. Apache is run on sites that get millions of visitors per day, and while no official support is provided by the developers, the Apache user community provides answers to all your questions. Commercial support is now being provided by a number of third parties.

In the category of office applications, a choice of MS Office suite clones is available, ranging from partial to full implementations of the applications available on MS Windows workstations. These initiatives helped a great deal to make Linux acceptable for the desktop market, because the users don't need extra training to learn how to work with new systems. With the desktop comes the praise of the common users, and not only their praise, but also their specific requirements, which are growing more intricate and demanding by the day. The Open Source community, consisting largely of people who have been contributing for over half a decade, assures Linux' position as an important player on the desktop market as well as in general IT application. Paid employees and volunteers alike are working diligently so that Linux can maintain a position in the market. The more users, the more questions. The Open Source community makes sure answers keep coming, and watches the quality of the answers with a suspicious eye, resulting in ever more stability and accessibility. Listing all the available Linux software is beyond the scope of this guide, as there are tens of thousands of packages. Throughout this course we will present you with the most common packages, which are almost all freely available. In order to take away some of the fear of the beginning user, here's a screenshot of one of your most-wanted programs. You can see for yourself that no effort has been spared to make users who are switching from Windows feel at home :

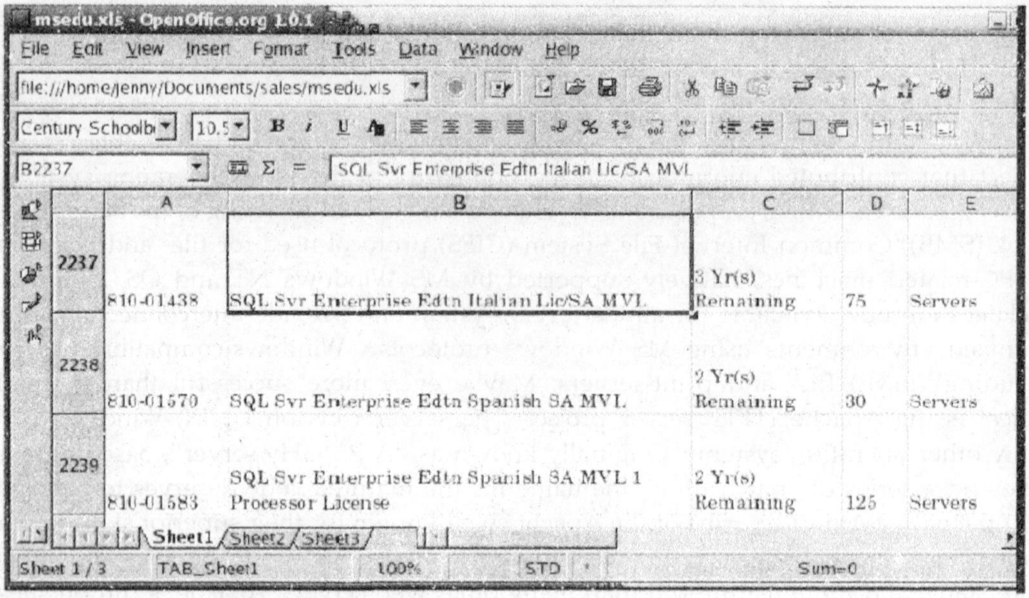

Fig. 3.1. Open Office MS-compatible Spreadsheet.

3.3.6 Properties of Linux

1. Linux Pros

A lot of the advantages of Linux are a consequence of Linux' origins, deeply rooted in UNIX, except for the first advantage, of course :

- **Linux is free**

  As in free beer, they say. If you want to spend absolutely nothing, you don't even have to pay the price of a CD. Linux can be downloaded in its entirety from the Internet completely for free. No registration fees, no costs per user, free updates, and freely available source code in case you want to change the behaviour of your system.

  Most of all, Linux is free as in free speech :

  The license commonly used is the GNU Public License (GPL). The license says that anybody who may want to do so, has the right to change Linux and eventually to redistribute a changed version, on the one condition that the code is still available after redistribution. In practice, you are free to grab a kernel image, for instance to add support for teletransportation machines or time travel and sell your new code, as long as your customers can still have a copy of that code.

- **Linux is portable to any hardware platform**

  A vendor who wants to sell a new type of computer and who doesn't know what kind of OS his new machine will run (say the CPU in your car or washing machine), can take a Linux kernel and make it work on his hardware, because documentation related to this activity is freely available.

- **Linux was made to keep on running**

  As with UNIX, a Linux system expects to run without rebooting all the time. That is why a lot of tasks are being executed at night or scheduled automatically for other calm moments, resulting in higher availability during busier periods and a more balanced use of the hardware. This property allows for Linux to be applicable also in environments where people don't have the time or the possibility to control their systems night and day.

- **Linux is secure and versatile**

  The security model used in Linux is based on the UNIX idea of security, which is known to be robust and of proven quality. But Linux is not only fit for use as a fort against enemy attacks from the Internet : it will adapt equally to other situations, utilizing the same high standards for security. Your development machine or control station will be as secure as your firewall.

- **Linux is scalable**

  From a Palmtop with 2 MB of memory to a petabyte storage cluster with hundreds of nodes : add or remove the appropriate packages and Linux fits all. You don't need a supercomputer anymore, because you can use Linux to do big things using the building blocks provided with the system. If you want to do little things, such as making an operating system for an embedded processor or just recycling your old 486, Linux will do that as well.

- **The Linux OS and most Linux applications have very short debug-times**

  Because Linux has been developed and tested by thousands of people, both errors and people to fix them are usually found rather quickly. It sometimes happens that there are only a couple of hours between discovery and fixing of a bug.

2. Linux Cons

- **There are far too many different distributions**

  "Quot capites, tot rationes", as the Romans already said : the more people, the more opinions. At first glance, the amount of Linux distributions can be frightening, or ridiculous, depending on your point of view. But it also means that everyone will find what he or she needs. You don't need to be an expert to find a suitable release. When asked, generally every Linux user will say that the best distribution is the specific version he is using. So which one should you choose ? Don't worry too much about that : all releases contain more or less the same set of basic packages. On top of the basics, special third party software is added making, for example, TurboLinux more suitable for the small and medium enterprise, RedHat for servers and SuSE for workstations. However, the differences are likely to be very superficial. The best strategy is to test a couple of distributions; unfortunately not everybody has the time for this. Luckily, there is plenty of advice on the subject of choosing your Linux. A quick search on Google, using the keywords "choosing your distribution" brings up tens of links to good advise. The Installation HOWTO also discusses choosing your distribution.

- **Linux is not very user friendly and confusing for beginners**

  It must be said that Linux, at least the core system, is less user friendly to use than MS Windows and certainly more difficult than MacOS, but... In light of its popularity, considerable effort has been made to make Linux even easier to use, especially for new users. More information is being released daily, such as this guide, to help fill the gap for documentation available to users at all levels.

- **Is an Open Source product trustworthy ?**

  How can something that is free also be reliable ? Linux users have the choice whether to use Linux or not, which gives them an enormous advantage compared to users of proprietary software, who don't have that kind of freedom. After long periods of testing, most Linux users come to the conclusion that Linux is not only as good, but in many cases better and faster then the traditional solutions. If Linux were not trustworthy, it would have been long gone, never knowing the popularity it has now, with millions of users. Now users can influence their systems and share their remarks with the community, so the system gets better and better every day. It is a project that is never finished, that is true, but in an ever changing environment, Linux is also a project that continues to strive for perfection.

3.3.7 Linux Flavors

1. Linux and GNU

Although there are a large number of Linux implementations, you will find a lot of similarities in the different distributions, if only because every Linux machine is a box with building blocks that you may put together following your own needs and views. Installing the system is only the beginning of a longterm relationship. Just when you think you have a nice running system, Linux will stimulate your imagination and creativeness, and the more you realize what power the system can give you, the more you will try to redefine its limits. Linux may appear different depending on the distribution, your hardware and personal taste, but the fundamentals on which all graphical and other interfaces are built, remain the same. The Linux system is based on GNU tools (Gnu's Not UNIX), which provide a set of standard ways to handle and use the system. All GNU tools are open source, so they can be installed on any system. Most distributions offer pre-compiled packages of most common tools, such as RPM packages on RedHat and Debian packages (also called deb or dpkg) on Debian, so you needn't be a programmer to install a package on your system. However, if you are and like doing things yourself, you will enjoy Linux all the better, since most distributions come with a complete set of development tools, allowing installation of new software purely from source code. This setup also allows you to install software even if it does not exist in a pre-packaged form suitable for your system.

A list of common GNU software :

- Bash : The GNU shell.
- GCC : The GNU C Compiler.
- GDB : The GNU Debugger.
- Coreutils : a set of basic UNIX-style utilities, such as **ls, cat** and **chmod.**

- Findutils : to search and find files.
- Fontutils : to convert fonts from one format to another or make new fonts.
- The Gimp : GNU Image Manipulation Program.
- Gnome : the GNU desktop environment.
- Emacs : a very powerful editor.
- Ghostscript and Ghostview : interpreter and graphical frontend for Post Script files.
- GNU Photo : software for interaction with digital cameras.
- Octave : a programming language, primarily intended to perform numerical computations and image processing.
- GNU SQL : relational database system.
- Radius : a remote authentication and accounting server.

Many commercial applications are available for Linux, and for more information about these packages we refer to their specific documentation. Throughout this guide we will only discuss freely available software, which comes (in most cases) with a GNU license.

To install missing or new packages, you will need some form of software management. The most common implementations include RPM and dpkg. RPM is the RedHat Package Manager, which is used on a variety of Linux systems, eventhough the name does not suggest this. Dpkg is the Debian package management system, which uses an interface called *apt-get*, that can manage RPM packages as well. Novell Ximian Red Carpet is a third party implementation of RPM with a graphical front-end. Other third party software vendors may have their own installation procedures, sometimes resembling the InstallShield and such, as known on MS Windows and other platforms. As you advance into Linux, you will likely get in touch with one or more of these programs.

2. GNU/Linux

The Linux kernel (the *bones* of your system) is not part of the GNU project but uses the same license as GNU software. A great majority of utilities and development tools (the *meat* of your system), which are not Linux-specific, are taken from the GNU project. Because any usable system must contain both the kernel and at least a minimal set of utilities, some people argue that such a system should be called a *GNU/Linux* system. In order to obtain the highest possible degree of independence between distributions, this is the sort of Linux that we will discuss throughout this course. If we are not talking about a GNU/Linux system, the specific distribution, version or program name will be mentioned.

3. Which distribution should we install ?

Prior to installation, the most important factor is your hardware. Since every Linux distribution contains the basic packages and can be built to meet almost any requirement (because they all use the Linux kernel), you only need to consider if the distribution will run on your hardware. LinuxPPC for example has been made to run on Apple and other PowerPCs and does not run on an ordinary x86 based PC. LinuxPPC does run on the new Macs, but you can't use it for some of the older ones with ancient bus technology. Another tricky case is Sun hardware, which could be an old SPARC CPU or a newer UltraSparc, both requiring different versions of Linux. Some Linux distributions are optimized for certain processors, such as Athlon CPUs, while they will at the same time run decent enough on the standard

486, 586 and 686 Intel processors. Sometimes distributions for special CPUs are not as reliable, since they are tested by fewer people. Most Linux distributions offer a set of programs for generic PCs with special packages containing optimized kernels for the x86 Intel based CPUs. These distributions are well-tested and maintained on a regular basis, focusing on related server implementation and easy installation and update procedures. Examples are Debian, Ubuntu, Fedora, SuSE and Mandriva, which are by far the most popular Linux systems and generally considered easy to handle for the beginning user, while not blocking professionals from getting the most out of their Linux machines. Linux also runs decently on laptops and middle-range servers. Drivers for new hardware are included only after extensive testing, which adds to the stability of a system. While the standard desktop might be Gnome on one system, another might offer KDE by default. Generally, both Gnome and KDE are available for all major Linux distributions. Other window and desktop managers are available for more advanced users. The standard installation process allows users to choose between different basic setups, such as a workstation, where all packages needed for everyday use and development are installed, or a server installation, where different network services can be selected. Expert users can install every combination of packages they want during the initial installation process. The goal of this guide is to apply to all Linux distributions. For your own convenience, however, it is strongly advised that beginners stick to a mainstream distribution, supporting all common hardware and applications by default. The following are very good choices for novices :

- Fedora Core
- Debian
- SuSE Linux
- Mandriva (former MandrakeSoft)
- Knoppix : an operating system that runs from your CD-ROM, you don't need to install anything.

Downloadable ISO-images can be obtained from LinuxISO.org. The main distributions can be purchased in any decent computer shop.

3.3.8 Basic Linux Commands

1. mkdir - make directories

Options

Create the DIRECTORY(ies), if they do not already exist. Mandatory arguments to long options are mandatory for short options too.

Usage

-m, mode=MODE set permission mode (as in chmod), not rwxrwxrwx - umask

-p, parents no error if existing, make parent directories as needed

-v, verbose print a message for each created directory

-help display this help and exit

-version output version information and exit

2. **cd - change directories**

   Use cd to change directories. Type cd followed by the name of a directory to access that directory. Keep in mind that you are always in a directory and can navigate to directories hierarchically above or below.

3. **mv- change the name of a directory**

   Type mv followed by the current name of a directory and the new name of the directory.

   Ex : mv testdir newnamedir

4. **pwd - print working directory**

   will show you the full path to the directory you are currently in. This is very handy to use, especially when performing some of the other commands on this page.

5. **rmdir - Remove an existing directory**

   rm -r Removes directories and files within the directories recursively.

6. **chown - change file owner and group**

   Usage

   chown [OPTION] OWNER[:[GROUP]] FILE

   chown [OPTION] :GROUP FILE

   chown [OPTION] —reference=RFILE FILE

   Options

   Change the owner and/or group of each FILE to OWNER and/or GROUP. With —reference, change the owner and group of each FILE to those of RFILE.

   -c, changes like verbose but report only when a change is made

   -dereference affect the referent of each symbolic link, rather than the symbolic link itself

   -h, no-dereference affect each symbolic link instead of any referenced file (useful only on systems that can change the ownership of a symlink)

   -from=CURRENT_OWNER :CURRENT_GROUP

   change the owner and/or group of each file only if its current owner and/or group match those specified here. Either may be omitted, in which case a match is not required for the omitted attribute.

   -no-preserve-root do not treat '/' specially (the default)

   -preserve-root fail to operate recursively on '/'

   -f, -silent, -quiet suppress most error messages

   -reference=RFILE use RFILE's owner and group rather than the specifying

   OWNER : GROUP values

   -R, -recursive operate on files and directories recursively

   -v, -verbose output a diagnostic for every file processed

   The following options modify how a hierarchy is traversed when the -R option is also specified. If more than one is specified, only the final one takes effect.

-H if a commlland line argument is a symbolic link to a directory, traverse it

-L traverse every symbolic link to a directory encountered

-P do not traverse any symbolic links (default)

7. **chmod - change <u>file access</u> permissions**

Usage

chmod [-r] permissions filenames

r Change the permission on files that are in the subdirectories of the directory that you are currently in permission Specifies the rights that are being granted. Below is the different rights that you can grant in an alpha numeric format filenames. File or directory that you are associating the rights with Permissions.

u - User who owns the file.

g - Group that owns the file.

o - Other.

a - All.

r - Read the file.

w - Write or edit the file.

x - Execute or run the file as a program.

Numeric Permissions :

CHMOD can also to attributed by using Numeric Permissions :

400 read by owner

040 read by group

004 read by anybody (other)

200 write by owner

020 write by group

002 write by anybody

100 execute by owner

010 execute by group

001 execute by anybody

8. **ls - Short listing of directory contents**

-a list hidden files

-d list the name of the current directory

-F show directories with a trailing '/'
executable files with a trailing '*'

-g show group ownership of file in long listing

-i print the inode number of each file

-l long listing giving details about files and directories

-R list all subdirectories encountered

-t sort by time modified instead of name

9. cp - Copy files l

cp myfile yourfile

Copy the files "myfile" to the file "yourfile" in the current working directory. This command will create the file "yourfile" if it doesn't exist. It will normally overwrite it without warning if it exists.

cp -i myfile yourfile

With the "-i" option, if the file "yourfile" exists, you will be prompted before it is overwritten.

cp -i /data/myfile

Copy the file "/data/myfile" to the current working directory and name it "myfile". Prompt before overwriting the file.

cp -dpr srcdir destdir

Copy all files from the directory "srcdir" to the directory "destdir" preserving links (-poption), file attributes (-p option), and copy recursively (-r option). With these options, a directory and all it contents can be copied to another dir.

10. ln - Creates a symbolic link to a file.

ln -s test symlink

Creates a symbolic link named symlink that points to the file test Typing "ls -i test symlink" will show the two files are different with different inodes. Typing "ls -l test symlink" will show that symlink points to the file test.

11. locate - A fast database driven file locator.

12. slocate -u

This command builds the slocate database. It will take several minutes to complete this command. This command must be used before searching for files, however cron runs this command periodically on most systems.locate whereis Lists all files whose names contain the string "whereis". directory.

more - Allows file contents or piped output to be sent to the screen one page at a time.

13. less - Opposite of the more command

14. cat - Sends file contents to standard output. This is a way to list the contents of short files to the screen. It works well with piping.

15. whereis - Report all known instances of a command

16. wc - Print byte, word, and line counts

17. bg

bg jobs Places the current job (or, by using the alternative form, the specified jobs) in the background, suspending its execution so that a new user prompt appears immediately. Use the jobs command to discover the identities of background jobs.

18. cal month year - Prints a calendar for the specified month of the specified year.

19. cat files - Prints the contents of the specified files.

20. clear - Clears the terminal screen.

21. **cmp file1 file2 -** Compares two files, reporting all discrepancies. Similar to the diff command, though the output format differs.
22. **diff file1 file2** - Compares two files, reporting all discrepancies. Similar to the cmp command, though the output format differs.
23. **dmesg -** Prints the messages resulting from the most recent system boot.
24. **fg**

    fg jobs - Brings the current job (or the specified jobs) to the foreground.
25. **file files -** Determines and prints a description of the type of each specified file.
26. **find path -name pattern -print**

    Searches the specified path for files with names matching the specified pattern (usually enclosed in single quotes) and prints their names. The find command has many other arguments and functions; see the online documentation.
27. **finger users -** Prints descriptions of the specified users.
28. **free -** Displays the amount of used and free system memory.
29. **ftp hostname**

    Opens an FTP connection to the specified host, allowing files to be transferred. The FTP program provides subcommands for accomplishing file transfers; see the online documentation.
30. **head files -** Prints the first several lines of each specified file.
31. **ispell files -** Checks the spelling of the contents of the specified files.
32. **kill process_ids**

    kill - signal process_ids

    kill -l

    Kills the specified processes, sends the specified processes the specified signal (given as a number or name), or prints a list of available signals.
33. **all program**

    killall - signal program

    Kills all processes that are instances of the specified program or sends the specified signal to all processes that are instances of the specified program.
34. **mail -** Launches a simple mail client that permits sending and receiving e-mail messages.
35. **man title**

    man section title - Prints the specified man page.
36. **host** - Sends an echo request via TCP/IP to the specified host. A response confirms that the host is operational.
37. **reboot** - Reboots the system (requires root privileges).
38. **shutdown minutes**

    shutdown -r minutes

    Shuts down the system after the specified number of minutes elapses (requires root privileges). The -r option causes the system to be rebooted once it has shut down.

39. **sleep time** - Causes the command interpreter to pause for the specified number of seconds.
40. **sort files** - Sorts the specified files. The command has many useful arguments; see the online documentation.
41. **split file** - Splits a file into several smaller files. The command has many arguments; see the online documentation.
42. **sync** - Completes all pending input/output operations (requires root privileges).
43. **telnet host** - Opens a login session on the specified host.
44. **top** - Prints a display of system processes that's continually updated until the user presses the q key.
45. **traceroute host** - Uses echo requests to determine and print a network path to the host.
46. **uptime** - Prints the system uptime.
47. **w** - Prints the current system users.
48. **wall** - Prints a message to each user except those who've disabled message reception. Type **Ctrl-D** to end the message.

3.4 MOZILLA FIREFOX

Mozilla Firefox is a web browser project descended from the Mozilla application suite, managed by the Mozilla Corporation. Firefox had 16.80% of the recorded market share in Web browsers as of December 2007, making it the second-most-popular browser in current use worldwide.

Firefox uses the open source Gecko layout engine, which implements current Web standards plus a few features which are intended to anticipate likely additions to the standards.

Firefox includes tabbed browsing, a spell checker, incremental find, live bookmarking, a download manager, and a search system that includes Google. Functions can be added through more than 2,000 add-ons created by third party developers; the most popular include FoxyTunes (controls music players), Adblock Plus (ad blocker), StumbleUpon (website discovery), DownThemAll! (download functions) and Web Developer (web tools).

Firefox runs on various versions of Microsoft Windows, Mac OS X and Linux. Its current stable release is version 2.0.0.11, released on 30 November 2007. Firefox's source code is under the terms of the Mozilla tri-license as free and open source software.

Mozilla was the official, public, original name of Mozilla Application Suite by the Mozilla Foundation, currently known as Sea Monkey suite.

In informal use it has been used in a number of ways and in combination with other phrases, though all of them have been related to the now-defunct Netscape Communications Corporation and its related application software.

Only three things have ever formally used the term "Mozilla" alone :

- the codename for the Netscape Navigator software project.

- the official name of what was re-named Mozilla Application Suite.
- The Mascot of Netscape.

3.4.1 Mozilla Project

1. Mozilla Foundation

"Mozilla" is sometimes used to refer to the free software/open source project that was founded in order to create the next-generation Internet suite for Netscape. The Mozilla Organization was founded in 1998 to create the new suite. On July 15, 2003, the organization was formally registered as a non-profit organization, and became Mozilla Foundation. The foundation now creates and maintains the Mozilla Firefox browser and Mozilla Thunderbird e-mail application, among other software. The Mozilla trademark is held by the Mozilla Foundation as of 2006.

2. Mozilla Corporation

On August 3, 2005, Mozilla Foundation announced the creation of Mozilla Corporation, a wholly owned for-profit taxable subsidiary of Mozilla Foundation, that primarily focuses on delivering Firefox to end users. It will also oversee marketing and sponsorship of the products.

3. Mozilla Messaging

On February 19, 2008, Mozilla Messaging was announced, which like Mozilla Corporation is a for-profit subsidiary of Mozilla Foundation. Its focus will be on Thunderbird and possibly developing software related to other internet communication media.

3.4.2 Mozilla Software

- Firefox
- Thunderbird
- SeaMonkey
- Bugzilla
- Camino
- Sunbird
- Minimo

3.4.3 History

Dave Hyatt and Blake Ross began working on the Firefox project as an experimental branch of the Mozilla project. They believed the commercial requirements of Netscape's sponsorship and developer-driven feature creep compromised the utility of the Mozilla browser. To combat what they saw as the Mozilla Suite's software bloat, they created a stand-alone browser, with which they intended to replace the Mozilla Suite. On April 3, 2003, the Mozilla Organization announced that they planned to change their focus from the Mozilla Suite to Firefox and Thunderbird.

The Firefox project has undergone several name changes. Originally titled *Phoenix*, it was renamed because of trademark issues with Phoenix Technologies. The replacement name, *Firebird,* provoked an intense response from the Firebird free database software project. In response, the Mozilla Foundation stated that the browser should always bear the name *Mozilla Firebird* to avoid confusion with the database software. Continuing pressure from the database server's development community forced another change; on February 9, 2004, Mozilla Firebird became *Mozilla Firefox,* often referred to as simply *Firefox* and sometimes abbreviated as *Fx* or *fx.*

The Firefox project went through many versions before 1.0 was released on November 9, 2004. In addition to stability and security fixes, the Mozilla Foundation released its first major update to Firefox version 1.5 on November 29, 2005. On October 24, 2006, Mozilla released Firefox 2. This version includes updates to the tabbed browsing environment, the extensions manager, the GUI, and the find, search and software update engines; a new session restore feature; inline spell checking; and an antiphishing feature which was implemented by Google as an extension, and later merged into the program itself. In January 2008, Firefox Live Chat was launched. It is run by volunteers through a system powered by Jive Software. Anyone can ask a question, and get response within the hours of operation guaranteed. Outside or after hours, there is still a possibility of getting a live chat with an agent for assistance.

3.4.4 Features

Features included with Firefox are tabbed browsing, spell checker, incremental find, live bookmarking, an integrated download manager, and a search system that includes Google. The developers of Firefox aimed to produce a browser that "just surfs the web" and delivers the "best possible browsing experience to the widest possible set of people."

Users can customize Firefox with extensions and themes. Mozilla maintains an add-on repository at addons.mozilla.org with nearly 2000 add-ons in it as of September 2007. Firefox provides an environment for web developers in which they can use built-in tools, such as the Error Console or the DOM Inspector, or extensions, such as Firebug.

Mozilla Firefox supports many web standards, including HTML, XML, XHTML, SVG 1.1 (partial), CSS, ECMAScript (JavaScript), DOM, MathML, DTD, XSLT, XPath, and PNG images with alpha transparency. Firefox also supports standards proposals created by the WHATWG such as client-side storage, and canvas element.

Although Firefox 2 does not pass the Acid2 standards-compliance test, Firefox 3 Beta 2 does.

3.4.5 Security

Firefox uses a sandbox security model, and limits scripts from accessing data from other websites based on the same origin policy. It uses SSL/TLS to protect communications with web servers using strong cryptography when using the https protocol. It also provides support for web applications to use smartcards for authentication purposes.

The Mozilla Foundation offers a "bug bounty" to researchers who discover severe security holes in Firefox. Official guidelines for handling security vulnerabilities discourage early disclosure of vulnerabilities so as not to give potential attackers an advantage in creating exploits.

Because Firefox has fewer and less severe publicly known unpatched security vulnerabilities than Internet Explorer (see *Comparison of web browsers*), improved security is often cited as a reason to switch from Internet Explorer to Firefox. *The Washington Post* reports that exploit code for critical unpatched security vulnerabilities in Internet Explorer was available for 284 days in 2006. In comparison, exploit code for critical security vulnerabilities in Firefox was available for 9 days before Mozilla shipped a patch to remedy the problem.

A 2006 Symantec study showed that although Firefox had surpassed other browsers in the number of vendor-confirmed vulnerabilities that year through September, these vulnerabilities were patched far more quickly than those found in other browsers. Symantec later clarified their statement, saying that Firefox still had fewer security vulnerabilities than Internet Explorer, as counted by security researchers. As of January 07, 2008, Firefox 2 has five security vulnerabilities unpatched, the most severe of which was rated "less critical" by Secunia. Internet Explorer has seven security vulnerabilities unpatched, the most severe of which was rated "Moderately critical" by Secunia.

3.4.6 Licensing

Firefox is free and open source software, and is tri-licensed under the Mozilla Public License (MPL), GNU General Public License (GPL), and the GNU Lesser General Public License (LGPL). These licenses permit anyone to view, modify and/or redistribute the source code, and several publicly released applications have been built on it; for example, Netscape, Flock and Songbird make use of code from Firefox.

The official end-user builds of Firefox distributed from mozilla.com are licensed under the Mozilla EULA. Several elements do not fall under the scope of the tri-license and have their use restricted by the EULA, including the trademarked Firefox name and artwork, and the proprietary Talkback crash reporter. Because of this and the clickwrap agreement included in the Windows version, the Free Software Foundation (FSF) consider these builds proprietary software.

In the past, Firefox was licensed solely under the MPL, which the FSF criticizes for being weak copyleft; the license permits, in limited ways, proprietary derivative works. Additionally, code under the MPL cannot legally be linked with code under the GPL or the LGPL. To address these concerns, Mozilla re-licensed Firefox under the tri-license scheme of MPL, GPL, and LGPL. Since the re-licensing, developers have been free to choose the license under which they will receive the code, to suit their intended use : GPL or LGPL linking and derivative works when one of those licenses is chosen, or MPL use (including the possibility of proprietary derivative works) if they choose the MPL.

3.5 WIKIPEDIA

3.5.1 7 Things You Should Know About...

1. What is it ?

Wikipedia is a free online encyclopedia that anyone can add to or edit. The site was launched in early 2001 and has since grown to include millions of articles in dozens of languages. Despite concerns about the quality of openly editable information, Wikipedia has become one of the most popular online resources—statistics put Wikipedia as the eighth most-visited Web site in the United States, behind sites such as Yahoo, Google, MySpace, and eBay. Article topics range from the very broad to the highly specific, and the site offers tools to organize information into various content areas—such as "academic disciplines" and "glossaries"—with numerous topic breakdowns within each category. Each article contains any number of links to other Wikipedia articles or to external resources.

2. Whose doing it ?

Use of the site is pervasive, both within and outside the academic community. Wikipedia has become a primary research tool of college students—many students begin researching a topic at Google, and Wikipedia articles are often one of the first search results. At the same time, faculty and researchers increasingly turn to the site, though perhaps with a more critical eye. At some institutions, steps have been taken to limit the use of the site—after several students repeated the same inaccurate data from a Wikipedia article, the history department at Middlebury College banned Wikipedia citations in papers or on tests. Meanwhile, some academics have embraced the site as an educational tool. Faculty at Oberlin College and Columbia University, among others, have created assignments in which students create or edit Wikipedia articles to learn how to write neutral, expository text and to experience the process of peer review and revision.

3. How does it work ?

Through keyword searches, users locate and read articles, access photos and other graphics, and follow hyperlinks to resources related to the topic at hand. On certain Wikipedia pages, flags indicate if an article is out-of-date, for example, or contains no references, alerting users that the content might be less trustworthy than material on unflagged pages. The site also invites anyone to be a contributor. Although Wikipedia encourages contributors to create accounts, registration is not required. Users can edit or create entire articles, make changes to individual sections of articles, change the structure of an article, add images or links—all with the understanding that everything in Wikipedia can be changed by other users. The exceptions are articles that are "protected," a status assigned to entries that are targets of vandalism (intentionally posting inaccurate or defamatory information) or that frequently spawn ongoing disagreements among contributors. Pages that fall under protection include "Al Gore" and "Darfur conflict," but topics including "Mark Twain," "frog," and "Chevrolet" are also protected. Wikipedia users with administrator rights have the authority to assign or remove protection status, delete pages, and block individual users from editing articles. Protected (and semi-protected) pages require users to meet certain conditions to make edits. To change a semi-protected page, for example, a user must have been registered for at least four days.

A Discussion tab for each article provides a venue for users to discuss that article, its history and structure, and ways to improve it. Many articles (or sections of articles) are inherently contentious, and the Discussion tab is a place where users can have a side bar conversation about why certain edits to the article have been made or what information might expand an article's value without expressing a bias. The Discussion tab serves to fill a gap that necessarily exists given that contributors are disconnected from one another.

4. Why is it significant ?

Wikipedia puts control into the hands of users, who decide what topics are covered and at what depth. An emergent term or an obscure idea not found in a dictionary or a traditional encyclopedia can easily show up in Wikipedia, and the length of an article indicates community interest in the topic. For any wiki to be worth while the community of participants must work on a foundation of trust and openness; Wikipedia is an example of what can be accomplished by a disparate group of individuals, with a shared interest in a topic, working on such a foundation. Wikipedia offers extremely timely and always changing information—the site can reflect the current scholarship on a topic or, as in the case of the 2004 Indian Ocean tsunami, can present a nearly up-to-the-minute account of an unfolding event. In higher education, wikis have been put to use in courses ranging from humanities to science to business. With Wikipedia, students can take part in a collaborative process of creating and revising content in a global context, moving the opportunities for learning beyond the walls of the classroom or the university. An important part of academic training is seeing how knowledge is created and understanding that it is dynamic, evolving over-time based on the contributions of many individuals. Wikipedia provides a considerable measure of transparency about the provenance of information, allowing students to witness and take part in this evolution.

5. What are the downsides ?

Traditional encyclopedias undergo stringent review. Wikipedia forgoes the review requirement in favor of timeliness and the ability to include anyone who wants to contribute. As a result, every article is only as good as those who have taken the time to write or edit it, and quality across the site is uneven. Topic selection and coverage more accurately reflect community interest than academic value. In some cases, for example, single episodes of popular sitcoms are the subjects of Wikipedia entries, and the article on J. R. R. Tolkien's fictional Middle-earth is longer than the articles for many real nations. Although Wikipedia's ability to evolve as information changes is beneficial on one level, it also means that even if an article is deemed reliable, citing it as a source is problematic because it could change at any time.

6. Where is it going ?

Unlike any medium that preceded it, the Internet facilitates user created content, and Wikipedia demonstrates that such content has the potential to be substantive and valuable to the community at large. Due at least in part to the success of Wikipedia, numerous other wiki-based projects have appeared, reflecting burgeoning demand among creators and consumers for user-created content. At the same time, even as Wikipedia's content and usage grow, organizers of the site continue to address questions about accuracy and neutrality. Concerns about the quality of content prompted Larry Sanger, one of Wikipedia's cofounders, to launch Citizendium, designed, according to the site, to "improve on the Wikipedia model by adding 'gentle expert oversight' and requiring contributors to use their real names."

7. What are the implications for teaching and learning ?

Wikipedia blurs the line between consumption and creation of knowledge, giving motivated students the opportunity not only to use but also to generate knowledge and see themselves as members of a community of learners. Wikipedia offers students an opportunity to improve their research skills—by evaluating its content against other information sources—and to engage in a global community of collaborative content development. Students can see how knowledge is created, participate in that process, and understand when their comprehension of a topic is sufficient to make a valuable contribution. Some learning theorists contend that content creation and analysis is a necessary component of learning. Wikipedia can encourage students to analyze what they read, ask questions, and engage in reflective, creative learning.

3.6 JOOMLA!

Joomla! is an award-winning Content Management System (CMS) that will help you build websites and other powerful online applications. Best of all, Joomla! Is an open source solution that is freely available to everybody.

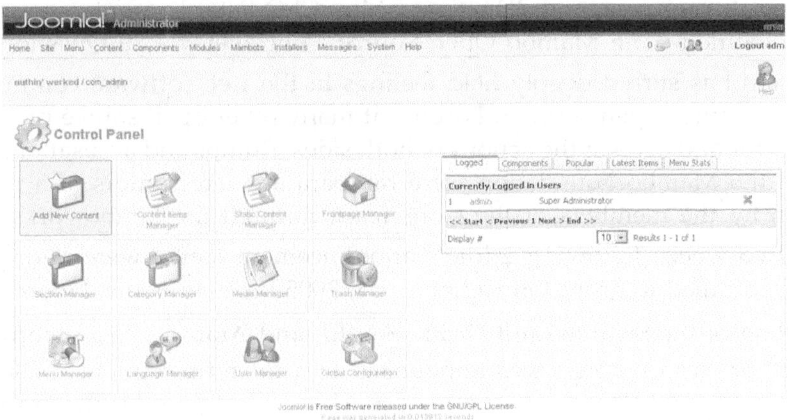

Fig. 3.2. Joomla! 1.0 screenshot of Admin page.

Developed by	The OSM Development Team
Latest release	1.5.1 / February 8, 2008
OS	Cross-platform
Genre	Content Management System
License	GPL
Website	http ://www.joomla.org/

Joomla! is a free, open source content management system for publishing content on the world wide web and intranets. Joomla! includes features such as page caching to improve performance, RSS feeds, printable versions of pages, news flashes, blogs, polls, website searching, and language internationalization. Joomla! Is licensed under the GPL, and is the result of a fork of Mambo. It is written with the PHP programming language and uses the MySQL database by default.

3.6.1 History

Joomla came into being as the result of a fork of Mambo by all of its then-core developers on August 17, 2005. At that time, the Mambo name was trademarked by Miro International

Pvt. Ltd, who formed a non-profit foundation with the stated purpose to fund the project and protect it from lawsuits. The development team claimed that many of the provisions of the foundation structure went against previous agreements made by the elected Mambo Steering Committee, lacked the necessary consultation with key stake holders, and included provisions that violated core open source values.

The development team created a website called OpenSourceMatters to distribute information to users, developers, web designers, and the community in general. The project team leader at the time Andrew Eddie, A.K.A. "MasterChief" (who rejoined the team as of 15 August, 2007), wrote an open letter to the community which appeared on the announcements section of the public forum at mamboserver.com.

A thousand people had joined the opensourcematters.org website within a day, most posting words of encouragement and support for the actions of the development team. The website received the Slashdot effect and news articles regarding the event appeared at newsforge.com, eweek.com, and ZDnet.com. Miro CEO Peter Lamont gave a public response in an article entitled "The Mambo Open Source Controversy - 20 Questions With Miro".

This event has stirred deeply held feelings in the free software community regarding what shall constitute "open source". Forums at many other open source projects were active with postings for and against the actions of both sides. Rumor and accusations of wrongdoing by Miro and the Mambo Foundation were rampant as were rumors of a potential venture capitalization by the members of the Core Team through the Jamboworks brand.

In the two weeks following Eddie's announcement teams were re-organized and the community continued to grow. On September 1, 2005 the new name, "Joomla", which is the English spelling of the Swahili (and Urdu : لمج □ and Arabic : لمج) word *jumla* meaning "all together" or "as a whole", was announced to a mixed reception of 3000+ followers of the Development Team. It was chosen by a marketing body under the employ of the Core Team prior to the name being announced to the wider open source community. The name did not actually appear in any community related polling for the software package during the initial stages towards forking and as such did not accurately reflect community involvement in the project. This was a key piece of marketing to the wider community by the Development Team as trademark records show that Joomla has a meaning of "minister" in Arabic. As this trademark for the name was initially finalized on the day of the release of the new name, it would be expected that the name would have been developed weeks or months earlier.

The first release of Joomla (Joomla 1.0.0) was announced on September 16, 2005. This was a re-branded release of Mambo 4.5.2.3 combined with other bug and moderate-level security fixes. In the project's roadmap, the core developers say Joomla 1.5 will be a completely re-written code base built with PHP 5. It was announced in 2005 and has been nominated for the Wired Vaporware Award in 2007, but since a third release candidate has been published on 6 October, 2007 (RC3), supporters expect a final product within the next years. Information about the development status of Joomla 1.5 can be found in the Joomla Team Blog. Joomla won the Packet Publishing Open Source Content Management System Award in 2006 and 2007.

3.6.2 Features

The Joomla package consists of many different parts, which are built to be as modular as possible, allowing extensions and integrations to be made easily. Examples of such are extensions called "Plugins". (Previously known as "Mambots".) Plugins are background extensions that extend Joomla with new functionality. The WikiBot, for example, allows the author of Joomla content to use "Wikitags" in Joomla articles which will auto-create dynamic hyperlinks to Wikipedia articles when displayed. There are over 2,500 extensions for Joomla available via the Extensions Directory, a site that Open Source Matters runs as an official directory of extensions.

In addition to Plug-in, more comprehensive extensions are available. "Components" allow webmasters to perform such tasks as build a community by expanding user features, backup a website, translate content and create URLs that are friendlier to search engines. "Modules" perform such tasks as displaying a calendar or allowing custom code like Google Ad Sense etc., to be inserted within the base Joomla code.

3.6.3 Community

Joomla has an official and many unofficial communities. As of December 2007, the official Joomla forum has more than 220,000 threads and over 1.1 million posts from over 150,000 registered members in 40 languages.[11] Unofficial sites are published in many languages, often with Joomla extensions that are region specific. Bi-directional text support for the Hebrew and Arabic languages, for example, can be found on 3rd party community portals. Unofficial web developers also build extensions and web templates for commercial sale and offer freelance customization services. Usually a template is distributed as a zip file which can be installed using the Joomla installer.

3.6.4 Joomla! in Action

Joomla! is used all over the world to power everything from simple, personal homepages to complex corporate web applications. Here are just some of the ways people use our software :

- Corporate websites or portals
- Online commerce
- Small business websites
- Non-profit and organizational websites
- Government applications
- Corporate intranets and extranets
- School and church websites
- Personal or family homepages
- Community-based portals
- Magazines and newspapers
- The possibilities are limitless...

Joomla! Can be used to easily manage every aspect of your website, from adding content and images to updating a product catalog or taking online reservations.

3.6.5 Joomla! for End Users

The basic Joomla! Package is designed to be easy to install, even for non-programmers. Most people have no trouble getting our software up and running, and there is plenty of support available for newbie's. We have a growing, active community of more than 150,000 friendly users and developers on our forums eager to help.

Once Joomla! is installed and running, it is simple for even non-technical users to add or edit content, update images, and to manage the critical data that makes your company or organization go. Anybody with basic word processing skills can easily learn to manage a Joomla! Site.

Via a simple, browser-based interface you will be able to easily add new press releases or news items, manage staff pages, job listings, product images, and create an unlimited amount of sections or content pages on your site. You can try our simple demo to get quick taste of what Joomla! is all about.

3.6.6 Taking Joomla! to the Next Level

Out of the box, Joomla! does a great job of managing the content needed to make your website sing. But for many people, the true power of Joomla! lies in the application framework that makes it possible for thousands of developers around the world to create powerful add-ons and extensions. Here are just some examples of the hundreds of available extensions :

- Dynamic form builders
- Business or organizational directories
- Document management
- Image and multimedia galleries
- E-commerce and shopping cart engines
- Forums and chat software
- Calendars
- Blogging software
- Directory services
- E-mail newsletters
- Data collection and reporting tools
- Banner advertising systems
- Subscription services
- and many, many more...

You can find more examples over at our growing Joomla! Extensions Directory. Prepare to be amazed at the amount of exciting work produced by our active developer community!

3.6.7 Joomla! for Developers

Many companies or organizations have requirements that go beyond what is available in the basic Joomla! package or in a freely available extension.

Thankfully, Joomla! offers a powerful application framework that makes it easy for developers to create sophisticated add-ons that extend the power of Joomla! into virtually unlimited directions.

Using the core framework, developers can easily build :

- Integrated e-commerce systems
- Inventory control systems
- Data reporting tools
- Custom product catalogs
- Complex business directories
- Reservation systems
- Communication tools
- Application bridges
- or any kind of application to suit a unique need...

If your company or organization hires a third party Joomla! developer or builds in-house software using the Joomla! Framework, you are building on an open platform that does not tie you to anyone developer or to a proprietary, closed application.

You can learn more about developing on the Joomla! framework over at our developer's network. The beauty of Joomla! is that you can leverage our framework and user interface to deliver applications to your end users in a familiar, powerful environment.

So What's the Catch ?

There is no catch. Joomla! is free, open, and available to all under the GPL license. We don't claim to be perfect, and can't promise to meet every requirement in the world. But for many web applications, our software is perfectly suited for the job. We are adding great new features with each release, and with the help and advice of our incredible user community we plan on delivering award-winning software for years to come.

3.7 GNU COMPILER COLLECTION

GNU COMPILER COLLECTION

Developed by	GNU Project
Latest release	4.2.3 / 1 February, 2008
OS	Cross-platform
Platform	GNU
Genre	Compiler
License	GNU General Public License, GNU Lesser General Public License
Website	http ://gcc.gnu.org/

Fig. 3.3.

The **GNU Compiler Collection** (usually shortened to **GCC**) is a set of compilers produced for various programming languages by the GNU Project. GCC is a key component of the GNU toolchain. As well as being the official compiler of the GNU system, GCC has been adopted as the standard compiler by most other modern Unix-like computer operating systems, including Linux, the BSD family and Mac OS X. GCC has been ported to a wide variety of computer architectures, and is widely deployed as a tool in commercial, proprietary and closed source software development environments. GCC is also used in popular embedded platforms like Symbian, Playstation and Sega Dreamcast.

Originally named the **GNU C Compiler**, because it only handled the C programming language, GCC 1.0 was released in 1987, and the compiler was extended to compile C++ in December of that year. Front ends were later developed for Fortran, Pascal, Objective C, Java, and Ada, among others.

Distributed by the Free Software Foundation (FSF) under the terms of the GNU General Public License (GNU GPL) and the GNU Lesser General Public License (GNU LGPL), GCC is free software.

3.7.1 History

GCC was started by Richard Stallman in 1985. He extended an existing compiler to compile C. The compiler originally compiled Pastel, an extended, nonportable dialect of Pascal, and was written in Pastel. It was re-written in C by Len Tower and Stallman, and released in 1987 as the compiler for the GNU Project, in order to have a compiler available that was free software. Its development was supervised by the Free Software Foundation.

In 1997, a group of developers, dissatisfied with the slow pace and closed nature of official GCC development, formed a project called EGCS (Experimental/Enhanced GNU Compiler System), which merged several experimental forks into a single project forked from GCC. EGCS development subsequently proved more vigorous than GCC development, and EGCS was eventually "blessed" as the official version of GCC in April 1999.

GCC is now maintained by a varied group of programmers from around the world. It has been ported to more kinds of processors and operating systems than any other compiler.

GCC is often the compiler of choice for developing software that is required to execute on a wide variety of hardware. Differences in native compilers lead to difficulties in developing code that will compile correctly on all the compilers and build scripts that will run for all the platforms. By using GCC, the same parser is used for all platforms, so if the code compiles on one, chances are high that it compiles on all.

3.7.2 Languages

The standard compiler release 4.2 includes front ends for : C, C++ (*G++*), Java (*GCJ*), Ada (*GNAT*), Objective-C, Objective-C++, and Fortran (*GFortran*). Also available, but not in standard are : Modula-2, Modula-3, Pascal, PL/I, D (*dgcc*), Mercury, VHDL (*GHDL*).

The Fortran front end was g77 before version 4.0, which only supports Fortran 77. In newer versions, g77 was dropped in favor of the new GFortran front end that supports Fortran 95. A front end for CHILL was previously included, but has been dropped owing to a lack of maintenance.

3.7.3 Architectures

GCC target processors as of version 4.1 include :

- Alpha
- ARM
- Atmel AVR
- BlackfinHC12
- H8/300
- IA-32 (x86)
- x86-64IA-64
- MorphoSys
- Motorola 68000MIPS
- PA-RISC
- PDP-11
- PowerPCR8C/M16C/M32C
- System/390/zSeries
- SuperH
- SPARC
- VAX

Lesser-known target processors supported in the standard release have included :

- A29K
- ARC
- C4x
- ETRAX CRISD30V
- DSP16xx
- FR-30
- FR-VIntel i960
- IP2000
- M32R
- 68HC11MCORE
- MMIX
- MN10200
- MN10300Motorola 88000
- NS32K
- ROMPStormy16
- V850
- Xtensa
- AVR32

Additional processors have been supported by GCC versions maintained separately from the FSF version :

- D10V
- MePMicroBlaze
- Z8000
- MSP430Nios II and NiosPDP-10TIGCC (Motorola 68000 variation).

When retargeting GCC to a new platform, bootstrapping is often used.

3.7.4 Structure

GCC's external interface is generally standard for a Unix compiler. Users invoke a driver program named gcc, which interprets command arguments, decides which language compilers to use for each input file, runs the assembler on their output, and then possibly runs the linker to produce a complete executable binary.

Each of the language compilers is a separate program that takes in source code and produces assembly language. All have a common internal structure. A per-language front end parses the source code in that language and produces an abstract syntax tree ("tree" for short), and a back end converts the trees to GCC's Register Transfer Language (RTL). Compiler optimizations and static code analysis techniques (such as FORTIFY_SOURCE, a compiler directive which attempts to discover some buffer overflows) are applied to the code. Finally, assembly language is produced using architecture-specific pattern matching originally based on an algorithm of Jack Davidson and Chris Fraser.

Nearly all of GCC is written in C with the exception of the Ada frontend; much of the Ada frontend is written in Ada.

3.7.5 Front Ends

Frontends vary internally, having to produce trees that can be handled by the backend. The parsers are hand-coded recursive descent parsers.

Until recently, the tree representation of the program was not fully independent of the processor being targeted. Confusingly, the meaning of a tree was somewhat different for different language front-ends, and front-ends could provide their own tree codes.

In 2005, two new forms of language-independent trees were introduced. These new tree formats are called GENERIC and GIMPLE. Parsing is now done by creating temporary language-dependent trees, and converting them to GENERIC. The so-called "gimplifier" then lowers this more complex form into the simpler SSA-based GIMPLE form which is the common language for a large number of new powerful language- and architecture-independent global (function scope) optimizations.

3.7.6 Optimization

Optimization on trees does not generally fit into what most compiler developers would consider a front end task, as it is not language dependent and does not involve parsing. GCC developers have given this part of the compiler the somewhat contradictory name the "middle end." These optimizations include dead code elimination, partial redundancy elimination, global value numbering, sparse conditional constant propagation, and scalar replacement of aggregates. Array dependence based optimizations such as automatic vectorization are currently being developed.

3.7.7 Back end

The behavior of the GCC back end is partly specified by preprocessor macros and functions specific to a target architecture, for instance to define the endianness, word size, and calling conventions. The front part of the back end uses these to help decide RTL generation, so although GCC's RTL is nominally processor-independent, the initial sequence of abstract instructions is already adapted to the target.

The exact set of GCC optimizations varies from release to release as it develops, but includes the standard algorithms, such as loop optimization, jump threading, common subexpression elimination, instruction scheduling, and so forth. The RTL optimizations are of less importance with the recent addition of global SSA-based optimizations on GIMPLE trees, as RTL optimizations have a much more limited scope, and have less high-level information.

A "reloading" phase changes abstract (pseudo-) registers into real machine registers, using data collected from the patterns describing the target's instruction set. This is a somewhat complicated phase, because it must account for the vagaries of all of GCC's targets.

The final phase is somewhat anticlimactic, since the patterns to match were generally chosen during reloading, and so the assembly code is simply built by running substitutions of registers and addresses into the strings specifying the instructions.

3.7.8 Debugging GCC Programs

The primary tool for debugging GCC code is the GNU Debugger (gdb). Among more specialized tools are Valgrind for finding memory errors and leaks. The GNU Profiler (gprof) can be used to find out how much time is spent in which routines, and how often they are called; this requires compiling programs with special *profiling* options.

3.7.9 License

"GCC 4.2.1 will be the last release of GCC covered by version 2 of the GNU General Public License. All future releases will be released under GPL version 3."

3.8 OPENOFFICE

Developed by	Sun Microsystems in collaboration with the community
Latest release	2.3.1 / December 4, 2007 , 81 days ago
OS	Cross-platform
Genre	Office suite
License	GNU Lesser General Public License
Website	http ://www.openoffice.org/

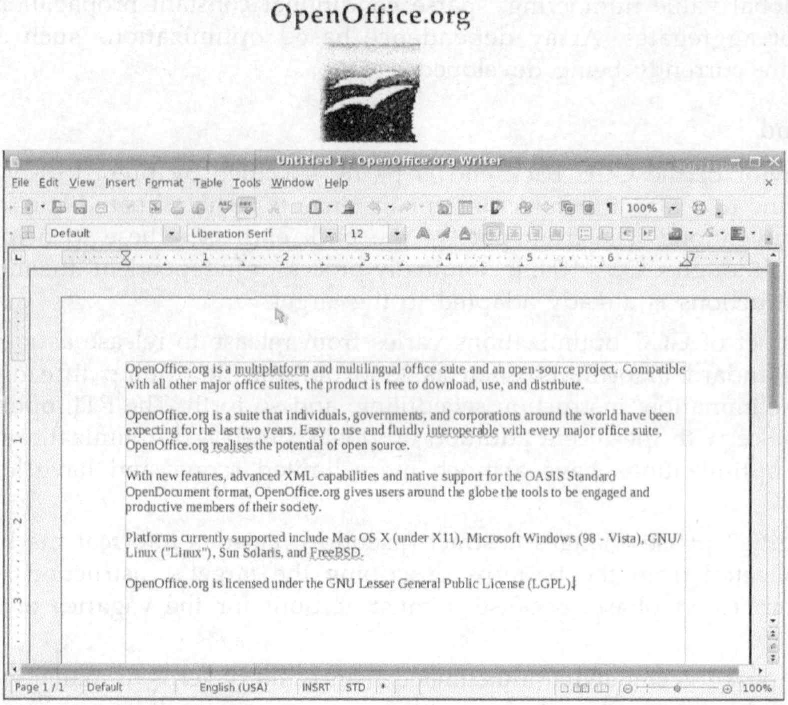

Fig. 3.4. OpenOffice.org Writer editing a text document under Ubuntu.

OpenOffice.org (**OO.o** or **OOo**) is an office application suite available for a number of different computer operating systems. It supports the OpenDocument standard for data interchange as its default file formats, as well as Microsoft Office '97-2003 formats, among many others.

OpenOffice.org is based on StarOffice, an office suite developed by StarDivision and acquired by Sun Microsystems in August 1999. The source code of the suite was released in July 2000 with the aim of reducing the dominant market share of Microsoft Office by providing a free, open and high-quality alternative. OpenOffice.org is free software, available under the GNU Lesser General Public License (LGPL).

The project and software are informally referred to as *OpenOffice*, but this term is a trademark held by another party, requiring the project to adopt *OpenOffice.org* as its formal name.

3.8.1 Features

According to its mission statement, the OpenOffice.org project aims *"To create, as a community, the leading international office suite that will run on all major platforms and provide access to all functionality and data through open-component based APIs and an XML-based file format."*

OpenOffice.org aims to compete with Microsoft Office and emulate its look and feel where suitable. It can read and write most of the file formats found in Microsoft Office, and many other applications; an essential feature of the suite for many users. OpenOffice.org has been found to be able to open files of older versions of Microsoft Office and damaged files that newer versions of Microsoft Office itself cannot open. However, it cannot open older Word for Macintosh (MCW) files.

3.8.2 Platforms

Platforms for which OO.o is available include Microsoft Windows, Linux, Solaris, BSD, OpenVMS, OS/2 and IRIX. The current primary development platforms are Microsoft Windows, Linux and Solaris.

A port for Mac OS X exists for OS X machines which have the X Window System component installed. A port to OS X's native Aqua user interface is in progress, and is scheduled for completion for the 3.0 milestone. NeoOffice is an independent fork of OpenOffice, specially adapted for Mac OS X.

3.8.3 Components

OpenOffice.org is a collection of applications that work together closely to provide the features expected from a modern office suite. Many of the components are designed to mirror those available in Microsoft Office. The components available include :

- **Writer**

  A word processor similar in look and feel to Microsoft Word and offering a comparable range of functions and tools. It also includes the ability to export Portable Document Format (PDF) files with no additional software, and can also function as a WYSIWYG editor for creating and editing web pages. One important difference between Writer and Microsoft Word is that in Writer, many functions and number formats from Calc (below) are available in Writer's tables.

- **Calc**

  A spreadsheet similar to Microsoft Excel with a roughly equivalent range of features. Calc provides a number of features not present in Excel, including a system which automatically defines series for graphing, based on the layout of the user's data. Calc is also capable of writing spreadsheets directly as a PDF file.

- **Impress**

  A presentation program similar to Microsoft PowerPoint. It can export presentations to Adobe Flash (SWF) files allowing them to be played on any computer with the Flash player installed. It also includes the ability to create PDF files, and the ability to read Microsoft PowerPoint's .ppt format. Impress suffers from a lack of ready-made presentation designs. However, templates are readily available on the Internet.

- **Base**

  A database program similar to Microsoft Access. Base allows the creation and manipulation of databases, and the building of forms and reports to provide easy access to data for end-users. As with Access, Base may be used as a front-end to a number of different database systems, including Access databases (JET), ODBC data sources and MySQL/PostgreSQL. Base became part of the suite starting with version 2.0. Native to the OpenOffice.org suite is an adaptation of HSQL. While ooBase can be a front-end for any of the databases listed, there is no need for any of them to be installed.

- **Draw**

  A vector graphics editor comparable in features to early versions of CorelDRAW. It features versatile "connectors" between shapes, which are available in a range of line styles and facilitate building drawings such as flowcharts. It has similar features to Desktop publishing software such as Scribus and Microsoft Publisher.

- **Math**

  A tool for creating and editing mathematical formulae, similar to Microsoft Equation Editor. Formulae can be embedded inside other OpenOffice.org documents, such as those created by Writer. It supports multiple fonts and can export to PDF.

- **QuickStarter**

  A small program for Windows and Linux that runs when the computer starts for the first time. It loads the core files and libraries for OpenOffice.org during computer startup and allows the suite applications to start more quickly when selected later. The amount of time it takes to open OpenOffice.org applications was a common complaint in version 1.0 of the suite, and Quickstarter was a solution of sorts. Substantial improvements were made in this area for version 2.2.

- **The macro recorder**

  Is used to record user actions and replay them later to help with automating tasks, using OOoBasic.

It is not possible to download these components individually on Windows, though they can be installed separately. Most Linux distributions break the components into individual packages which may be downloaded and installed separately.

OpenOffice.org Basic

OpenOffice.org Basic is a programming language similar to Microsoft Visual Basic for Applications (VBA) based on StarOffice Basic. In addition to the macros, the upcoming Novell edition of OpenOffice.org 2.0 supports running Microsoft VBA macros, a feature expected to be incorporated into the mainstream version soon.

OpenOffice.org Basic is available in the Writer and Calc applications. It is written in functions called subroutines or macros, with each macro performing a different task, such as counting the words in a paragraph. OpenOffice.org Basic is especially useful in doing repetitive tasks that have not been integrated in the program.

As the OpenOffice.org database, called "Base", uses documents created under the Writer application for reports and forms, one could say that Base can also be programmed with OpenOffice.org Basic.

3.8.4 File Formats

OpenOffice.org pioneered the ISO/IEC standard OpenDocument file formats (ODF), which it uses natively, by default. It also supports reading (and in some cases writing) a large number of legacy proprietary file formats (*e.g.*, : WordPerfect, StarOffice, Lotus software, MS Works, Rich Text Format), most notably including Microsoft Office formats after which the OpenDocument specification was "approved for release as an ISO and IEC International Standard" under the name ISO/IEC 26300 : 2006.

3.8.5 Microsoft Office Interoperability

In response to Microsoft's recent movement towards using the Office Open XML format in Microsoft Office 2007, Novell has released an Office Open XML converter for OOo under a liberal BSD license (along with GNU GPL and LGPL licensed libraries), that will be submitted for inclusion into the OpenOffice.org project. This allows OOo to read and write Microsoft OpenXML-formatted word processing documents (.docx) in OpenOffice.org. Currently it works only with the latest Novell edition of OpenOffice.org.

Sun Microsystems has developed an ODF plugin for Microsoft Office which enables users of Microsoft Office Word, Excel and PowerPoint to read and write ODF documents. The plugin currently works with Microsoft Office 2003, Microsoft Office XP and Microsoft Office 2000. Support for Microsoft Office 2007 is only available in combination with Microsoft Office 2007 SP1.

Several software companies (including Microsoft and Novell) are working on an add-in for Microsoft Office that allows reading and writing ODF files. Currently it works only for Microsoft Word 2007 / XP / 2003.

Microsoft provides a compatibility pack to read and write Office Open XML files with Office 2000, XP and 2003. The compatibility pack can also be used as a stand-alone converter with Microsoft Office 97. This might be helpful to convert older Microsoft Office files via Office Open XML to ODF if a direct conversion doesn't work as expected.

3.8.6 History

Originally developed as the proprietary software application suite StarOffice by the German company StarDivision, the code was purchased in 1999 by Sun Microsystems. In August 1999 version 5.2 of StarOffice was made available free of charge.

On July 19, 2000, Sun Microsystems announced that it was making the source code of StarOffice available for download under both the LGPL and the Sun Industry Standards Source License (SISSL) with the intention of building an open source development community around the software. The new project was known as OpenOffice.org, and its website went live on October 13, 2000.

Work on version 2.0 began in early 2003 with the following goals : better interoperability with Microsoft Office; better performance, with improved speed and lower memory usage; greater scripting capabilities; better integration, particularly with GNOME; an easier-to-find and use database front-end for creating reports, forms and queries; a new built-in SQL database; and improved usability. A beta version was released on March 4, 2005.

On September 2, 2005 Sun announced that it was retiring the SISSL. As a consequence, the OpenOffice.org Community Council announced that it would no longer dual license the office suite, and future versions would use only the LGPL.

On October 20, 2005, OpenOffice.org 2.0 was formally released to the public. Eight weeks after the release of Version 2.0, an update, OpenOffice.org 2.0.1, was released. It fixed minor bugs and introduced new features.

As of the 2.0.3 release, OpenOffice.org changed its release cycle from 18-months to releasing updates, feature enhancements and bug fixes every three months.

OpenOffice Versions

Version	*Release Date*	*Description*
Build 638c	October 2001	The first milestone release
1.0	May 1, 2002	
1.0.3.1	May 2, 2003	Recommended for Windows 95
1.1	September 2, 2003	
1.1.1	March 30, 2004	Bundled with The OpenCD
1.1.3	October 4, 2004	
1.1.4	December 22, 2004	
1.1.5	September 14, 2005	Last release for 1.x product line It can edit OpenOffice.org 2 files
1.1.5 secpatch	July 4, 2006	Security patch (macros)
2.0	October 20, 2005	Milestone
2.0.1	December 21, 2005	
2.0.2	March 8, 2006	
2.0.3	June 29, 2006	
2.0.4	October 13, 2006	
2.1.0	December 12, 2006	
2.2.0	March 28, 2007	Included a security update; Reintroduced font kerning[18]
2.2.1	June 12, 2007	
2.3.0	September 17, 2007	Updated charting component
2.3.1	December 4, 2007	Stability and security update

3.8.7 StarOffice

Sun subsidizes the development of OpenOffice.org in order to use it as a base for its commercial proprietary StarOffice application software. Releases of StarOffice since version 6.0 have been based on the OpenOffice.org source code, with some additional proprietary components, including :

- Additional bundled fonts (especially East Asian language fonts).
- Adabas D database.
- Additional document templates.
- Clip art.
- Sorting functionality for Asian versions.
- Additional file filters.
- Migration assessment tool (Enterprise Edition).
- Macro migration tool (Enterprise Edition).
- Configuration management tool (Enterprise Edition).

OpenOffice.org, therefore, inherited many features from the original StarOffice upon which it was based including the OpenOffice.org XML file format which it retained until version 2, when it was replaced by OpenDocument.

3.8.8 Development

Overview

The OpenOffice.org API is based on a component technology known as Universal Network Objects (UNO). It consists of a wide range of interfaces defined in a CORBA-like interface description language.

The document file format used is based on XML and several export and import filters. All external formats read by OpenOffice.org are converted back and forth from an internal XML representation. By using compression when saving XML to disk, files are generally smaller than the equivalent binary Microsoft Office documents. The native file format for storing documents in version 1.0 was used as the basis of the OASIS OpenDocument file format standard, which has become the default file format in version 2.0.

Development versions of the suite are released every few weeks on the developer zone of the OpenOffice.org website. The releases are meant for those who wish to test new features or are simply curious about forthcoming changes; they are not suitable for production use.

Native desktop integration

OpenOffice.org 1.0 was criticized for not having the look and feel of applications developed natively for the platforms on which it runs. Starting with version 2.0, OpenOffice.org uses native widget toolkit, icons, and font-rendering libraries across a variety of platforms, to better match native applications and provide a smoother experience for the user. There are projects underway to further improve this integration on both GNOME and KDE.

This issue has been particularly pronounced on Mac OS X, whose standard user interface looks noticeably different from either Windows or X11-based desktop environments and requires the use of programming toolkits unfamiliar to most OpenOffice.org developers. There are two implementations of OpenOffice.org available for OS X :

OpenOffice.org Mac OS X (X11)

This official implementation requires the installation of X11.app or XDarwin, and is a close port of the well-tested Unix version. It is functionally equivalent to the Unix version, and its user interface resembles the look and feel of that version; for example, the application uses its own menu bar instead of the OS X menu at the top of the screen. It also requires system fonts to be converted to X11 format for OpenOffice.org to use them (which can be done during application installation).

OpenOffice.org Aqua

After a first step (completed) using Carbon, OpenOffice.org Aqua switched for Cocoa technology, and an Aqua version (based on Cocoa) is also being developed under the aegis of OpenOffice.org, with an Alpha version currently available.[25] Sun Microsystems is collaborating with OOo to further development of the Aqua version of OpenOffice.org for Mac.

3.8.9 Graphical Presentation Version Wise

3.8.9.1 *OpenOffice.org 1.1 Features*

Introduction	
OpenOffice.org 1.1 - word processor, spreadsheet application, presentation tool and more	
• OpenOffice.org 1.1 is an open, feature-rich multi-platform office productivity suite. The user interface and the functionality is very similar to other products in the market like Microsoft Office or Lotus SmartSuite, but compared to these commercial products OpenOffice.org is absolutely free.	
Highlights	
Word Processor	
	OpenOffice.org Writer is a full-featured word processor. The powerful Navigator and Stylist tools make changing the formatting throughout a document a simple task.
Spreadsheet	
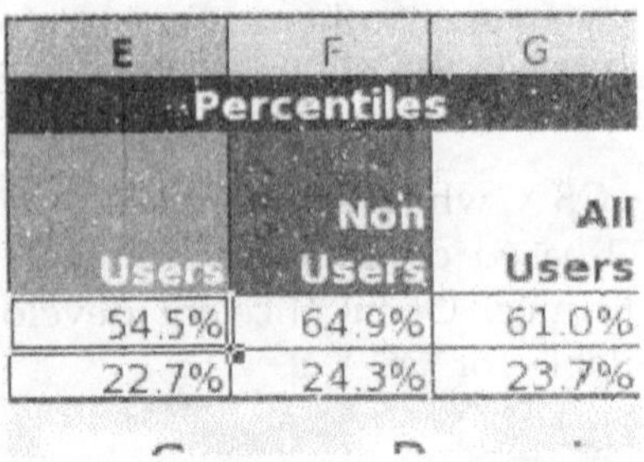	OpenOffice.org Calc provides full spreadsheet functionality incl. a huge number of statistical and scientific functions, pivot tables and charts.
Presentation Tool	
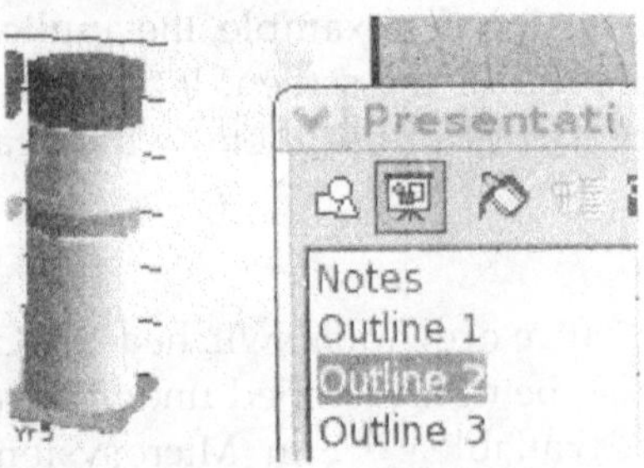	OpenOffice.org Impress is a full-featured presentation tool that allows to create and modify diagrams and pictures right within the application.

Drawings and Diagrams

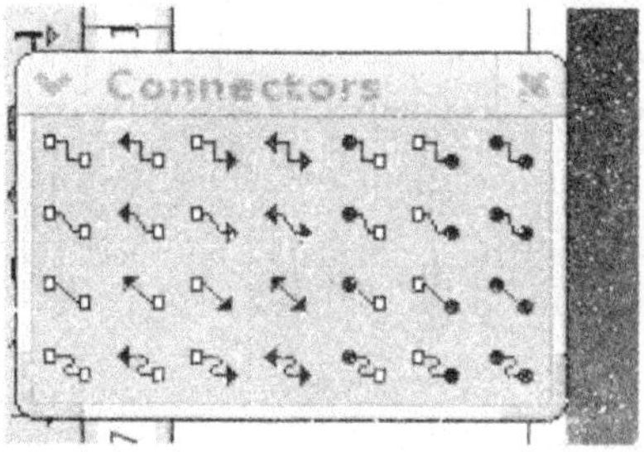

OpenOffice.org Draw is a drawing tool that supports both vector and bitmap images. The powerful Connectors allow to easily complex diagrams and org charts.

Database Access

With the database tools in OpenOffice.org users can easily access and analyze data, create complex reports or do a mail merge based on a customer database. Many open source and commercial database systems are supported.

Microsoft Office Compatibility

OpenOffice.org is able to read and write Microsoft Office files. This allows users to open and save Word, Excel and PowerPoint files on their preferred platform incl. Windows, Linux and Solaris.

One-click Export to PDF

OpenOffice.org 1.1 introduces the one-click PDF export feature that enables you to easily create PDF files without the need for any additional third party software. This feature makes exchanging documents in a standard "read-only" file format a trivial task. The creation of PDF files normally requires relatively expensive third party add-on tools. With OpenOffice.org this feature comes for free.

<table>
<tr><th colspan="2">Export to Flash (.SWF)</th></tr>
<tr><td></td><td>OpenOffice.org now can export presentations and drawings to the Macromedia Flash Format (SWF). Thus, it's now possible to view presentations in a simple web browser that has the Flash plugin installed. Recipients and users of Flash presentations don't have to install a special viewer anymore in order to view a presentation.</td></tr>
<tr><th colspan="2">Accessibility</th></tr>
<tr><td>
</td><td>OpenOffice.org 1.1 can now be used by handicapped people for example, people with sight problems. OpenOffice.org 1.1 provides a high contrast mode, and together with additional tools (see http ://www.sun.com/access/) it's even possible to use special entry devices.</td></tr>
<tr><th colspan="2">Support for many native languages</th></tr>
<tr><td>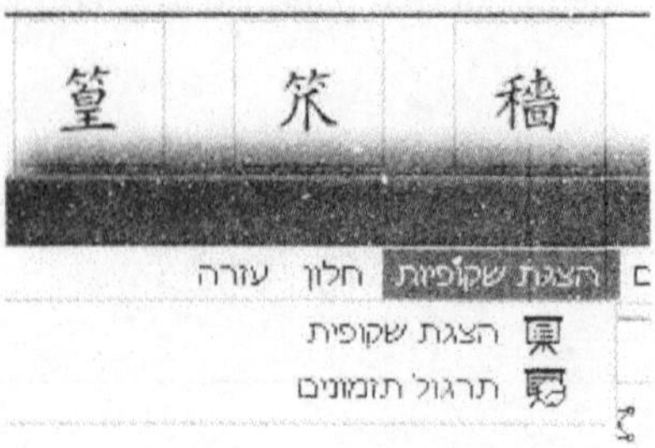</td><td>OpenOffice.org 1.1 introduces functionality like bi-directional and vertical writing that is required for many native languages. This allows OpenOffice.org 1.1 to be translated into Japanese, Hebrew and many other languages that have sophisticated text layout requirements. In addition the OpenOffice.org project has an increasing number of native-language projects where users can access OpenOffice.org information in their native language.</td></tr>
<tr><th colspan="2">Open XML File Format</th></tr>
<tr><td>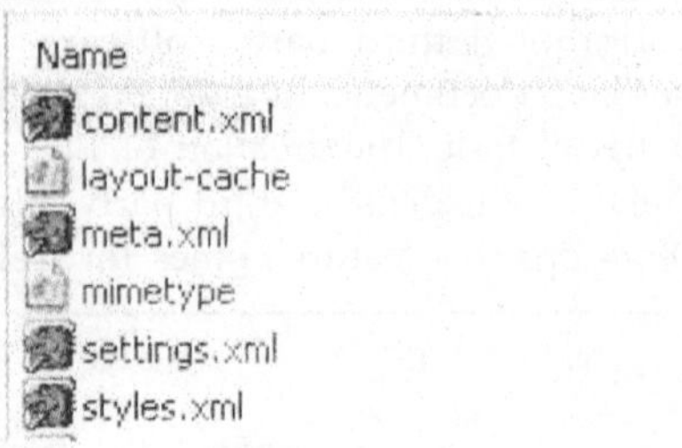
</td><td>The default file format in OpenOffice.org is an open XML file format defined in a 500-page specification document. Every OpenOffice.org file is a ZIP archive containing separate XML files for the content, styles, settings and meta data. OASIS is using the OpenOffice.org file format as the basis for the creation of a industry wide standard for an open office document file format. For ordinary end users this means that the content of documents can still be accessed and used even if OpenOffice.org would go away.</td></tr>
</table>

API and File Format Compatible with StarOffice 7[tm] Office Suite

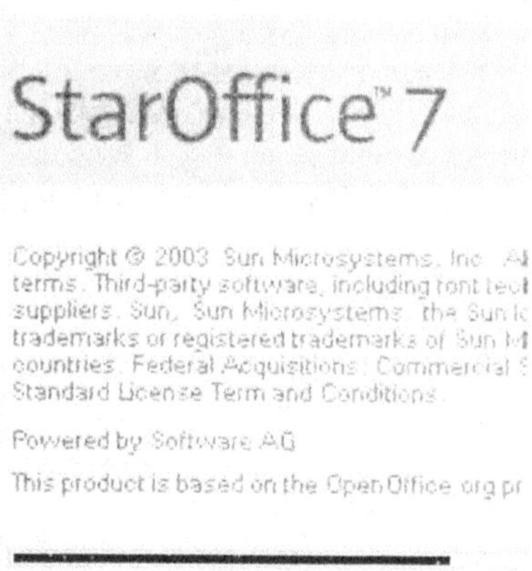

Since the StarOffice 7[tm] Office Suite is based on OpenOffice.org 1.1 both application suites are API and file format compatible. Sun Microsystems, Inc., the founder and main sponsor of the OpenOffice.org project, is providing support, training, enterprise tools and services for the StarOffice 7 Office Suite. More details about the relationship and the feature differences between OpenOffice.org and the StarOffice product can be found in a comparison document on the OpenOffice.org page at sun.com. Other office suites that are API and file format compatible with OpenOffice.org will soon be listed on the OpenOffice.org website. In order to get your OpenOffice.org based/compatible product included in that list please contact Erwin Tenhumberg or Louis Suarez-Potts.

Macro Recorder

The new macro recorder records and automates recurring tasks. For more sophisticated programming tasks the OpenOffice.org Software Development Kit (SDK) can be used. The SDK provides libraries, tools and documentation for the Java programming language, C++, Basic, OLE and XML. The SDK is a separate download.

3rd Party Add-ons

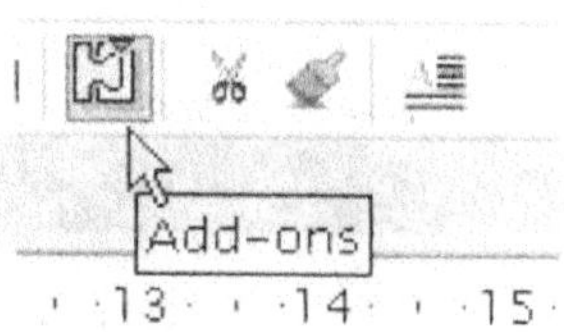

The new add-on framework and the new deployment tool (the "pkgchk" utility) allow developers to easily include new components and 3rd party add-ons into an existing OpenOffice.org installation.

XML File Filter Tool

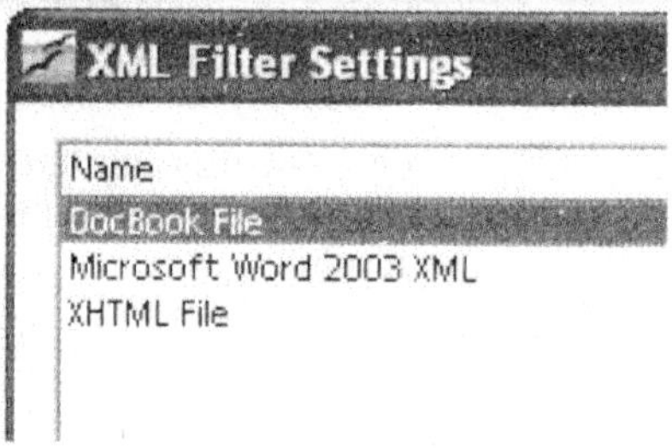

The new XML file filter tool makes it easy to integrate new import or export file filters that are based on XSL transformations. A popular use case for the XML filter tool is the support for the new Microsoft Office 2003 XML file formats.

ActiveX Control	
	OpenOffice.org 1.1 comes with an ActiveX control that allows users to view OpenOffice.org documents within a browser window (Internet Explorer) on the Windows platform. The ActiveX control can also be used within native applications developed in Microsoft VisualBasic or Borland Delphi.
Support for DocBook and PDA File Formats	
	OpenOffice.org allows users to export OpenOffice.org documents to popular file formats like DocBook or various small device file formats like AportisDoc. This gives users the possibility to carry their documents with them on their Palm Pilots and Pocket PC PDA's.
MYSQL Integration	
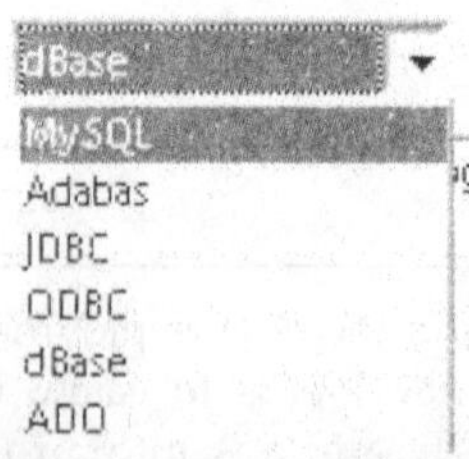	OpenOffice.org now has support for MySQL databases, *i.e.*, the open source database can be used for mail merge activities and the creation of reports. The combination of OpenOffice.org and MySQL (or another supported database) allows users to do tasks that many people used to solve by using products like Microsoft Access.
More Information	

3.8.9.2 OpenOffice.org 2.0 Features

Introduction
OpenOffice.org 2.0 - word processor, spreadsheet application, presentation tool and more
OpenOffice.org 2.0 is an open, feature-rich multi-platform office productivity suite. The user interface and the functionality is very similar to other products in the market like Microsoft Office or Lotus SmartSuite, but in contrast to these commercial products OpenOffice.org is absolutely free. A full description of the application can be found on the product pages at : • http ://www.openoffice.org/product/

A list of the features introduced in past versions of OpenOffice.org can be found at :

- http ://www.openoffice.org/dev_docs/features/1.1/index.html
- http ://www.openoffice.org/dev_docs/source/features.html

Highlights (Click on thumbnail images to see a larger picture!)

Open Standards XML File Format (OASIS OpenDocument)

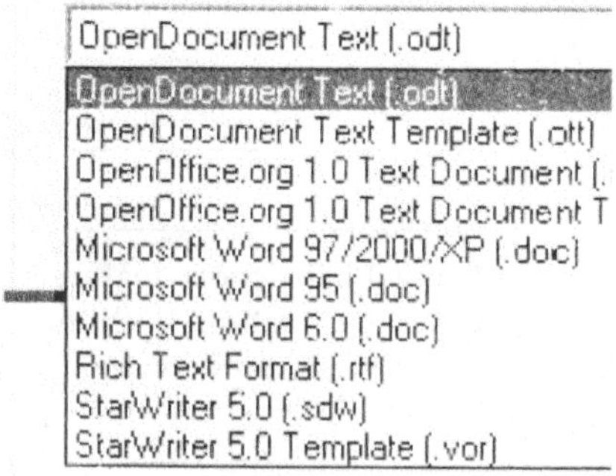

Beginning with version 2.0 OpenOffice.org uses the open standard OASIS OpenDocument XML format as the default file format. The OASIS OpenDocument format is a vendor and implementation independent file format, and thus guarantees freedom and independence.

In addition to OpenOffice.org itself, the open source office suite KOffice as well as OpenOffice.org derivatives like the StarOffice software support the OASIS OpenDocument file format. The OASIS OpenDocument file format is also one of the file formats recommended by the European Commission.

New Multi-pane View

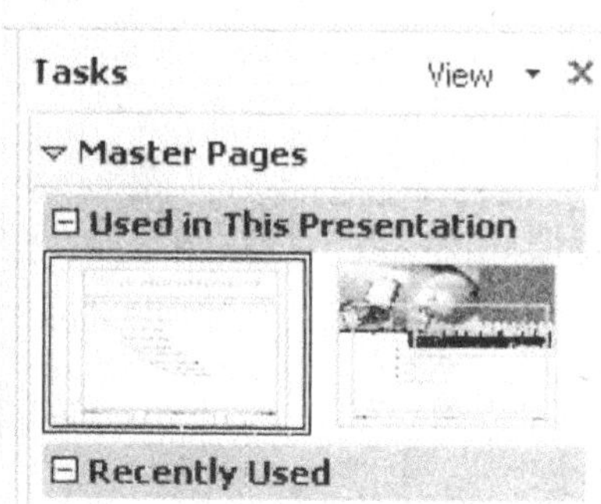

The new Multi-pane view increases the productivity and usability of OpenOffice.org. The Multi-pane view provides all important tools and windows through one coherent, integrated, and simple user interface. Former Microsoft PowerPoint users should find OpenOffice.org 2.0 easy to use.

New CustomShapes (compatible with Microsoft AutoShapes)

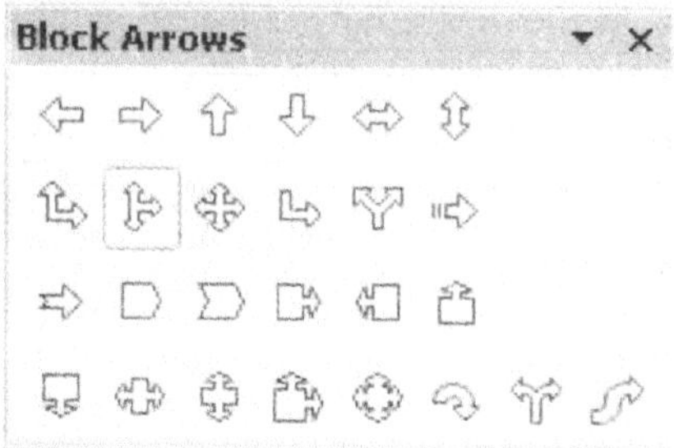

OpenOffice.org now supports CustomShapes, which are very similar to Microsoft's AutoShapes. As a consequence, AutoShapes are imported and displayed correctly. CustomShapes are shapes that can change not only their size but also their appearance.

More Slide Transitions and Animation Effects

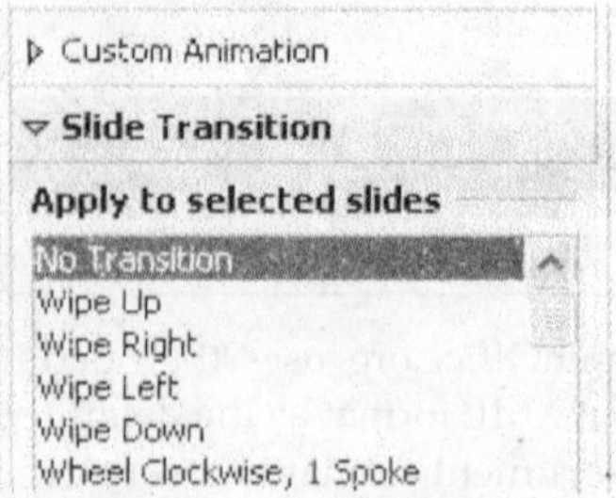

OpenOffice.org now supports many more animation effects and slide transitions. Now users have more options to give their presentations a professional appearance. In addition, the extended support for effects improves compatibility with Microsoft PowerPoint.

Enhanced PDF Export

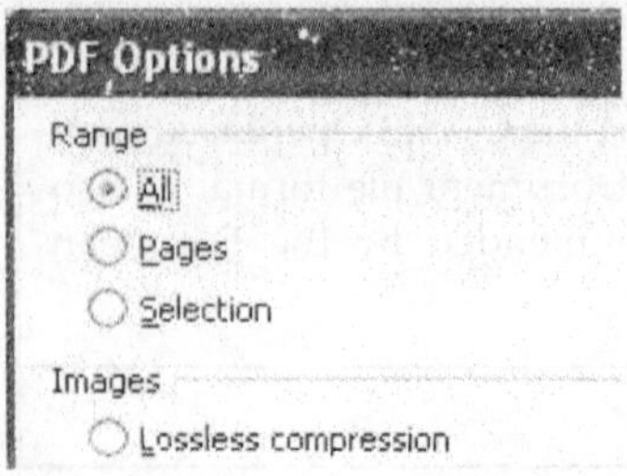

OpenOffice.org 1.1 introduced the PDF export feature. Version 2.0 now extends the basic export feature. With the new version it is possible to define the compression levels of embedded images. In addition, the PDF support now correctly handles thumbnail images and hyperlinks.

New enhanced Database Frontend

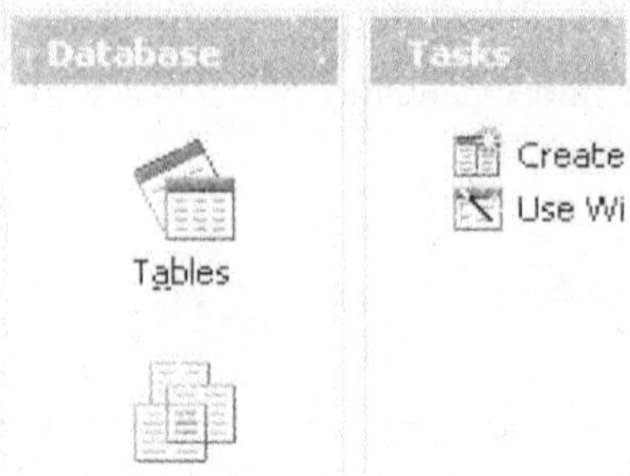

OpenOffice.org always had database front end tools, but in past versions they were very hidden. OpenOffice.org 2.0 starts to handle databases like any other application, *i.e.,* a new database can be created via the "File - New" menu. For novice users OpenOffice.org provides a new Table Wizard that allows creating database tables without any knowledge of databases or SQL. The new embedded HSQLDB database engine, based on Java technology, allows creating "database documents". These simple database files don't require a back end database server like MySQL or Adabas D. All information (table definitions, data, queries, forms, reports) is stored in one XML file.

Mail Merge Wizard

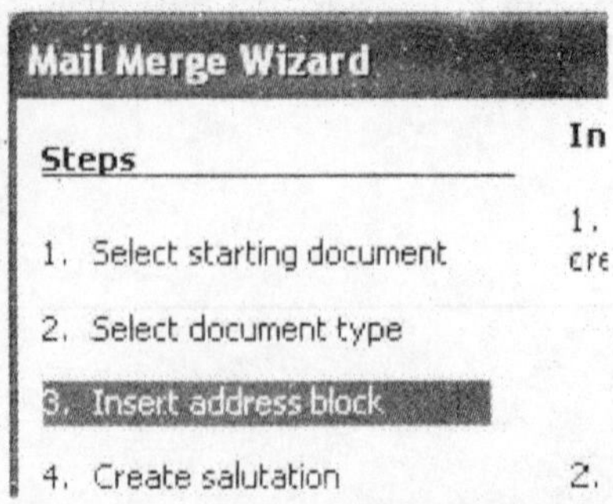

The new Mail Merge Wizard makes it very easy to do mailings to hundreds of recipients. The wizard guides users step by step through the process. Various data sources can be used for the address information.

<table>
<tr><td colspan="2">Enhanced Word Count Feature</td></tr>
<tr><td>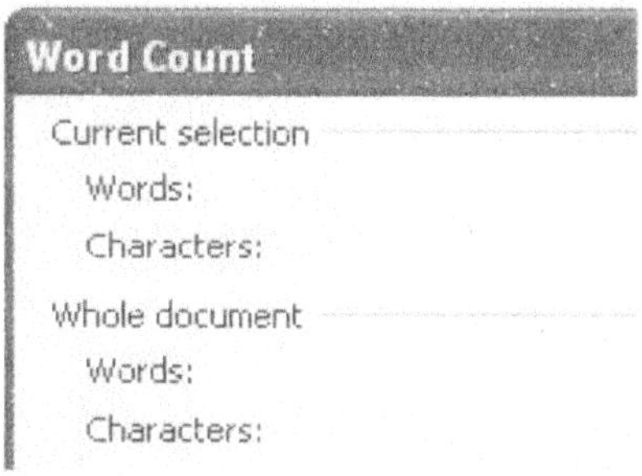
</td><td>In the past it was only possible to find document statistics under "File - Properties ...". It also was impossible to count the number of words in a selection. OpenOffice.org 2.0 eliminates this restriction. Now a new word count dialog can be found in the "Tools" menu.</td></tr>
<tr><td colspan="2">Support for Nested Tables</td></tr>
<tr><td>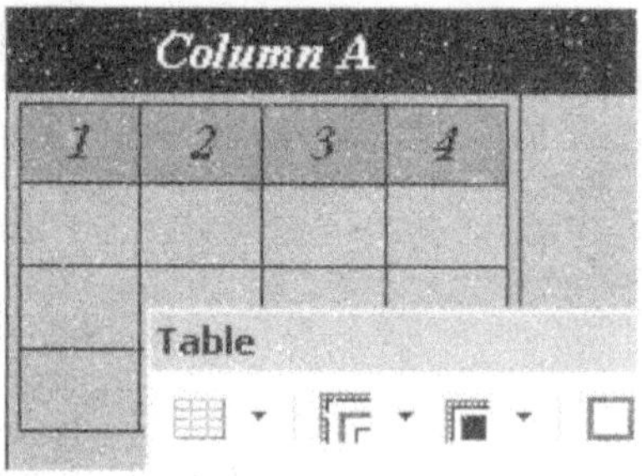
</td><td>With OpenOffice.org 2.0 it is now possible to create tables within tables (nested tables). This increases overall usability, and also improves compatibility with Microsoft Word.</td></tr>
<tr><td colspan="2">Digital Signatures Support</td></tr>
<tr><td>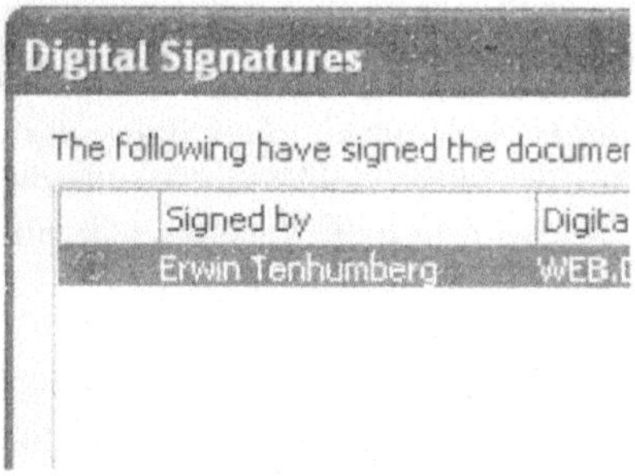
</td><td>Another new feature is the support of digital signatures. OpenOffice.org uses certificates stored in the regular repositories.</td></tr>
<tr><td colspan="2">XForms Support</td></tr>
<tr><td>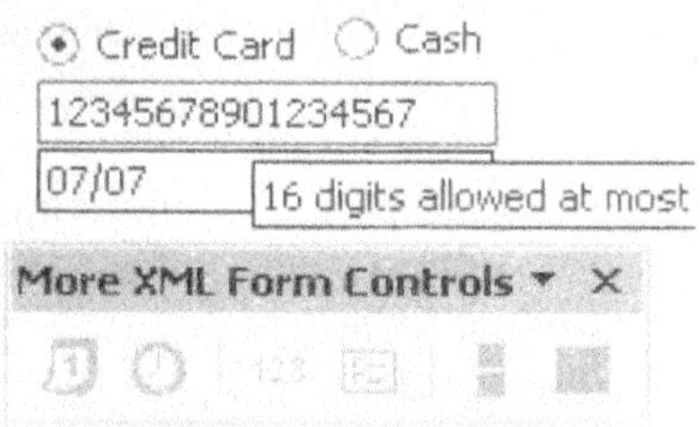
</td><td>OpenOffice.org 2.0 now allows creating forms based on the open W3C XForms standard. With XForms it is very easy to implement simple logic without any programming.</td></tr>
</table>

WordPerfect Filters

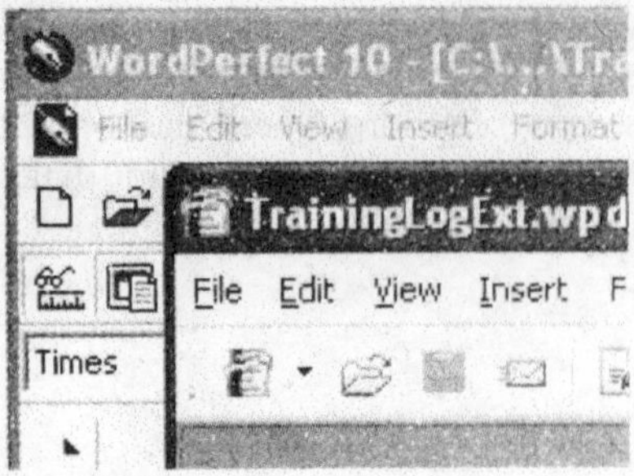

OpenOffice.org 2.0 includes a WordPerfect filter developed by the open source community. Developers are invited to contribute to this project.

65,536 Rows in Calc

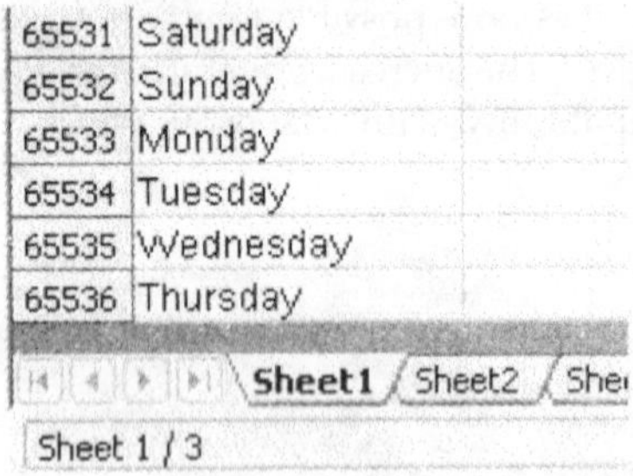

OpenOffice.org 1.1 supported only 32,768 rows in spreadsheet documents, which caused Microsoft Excel interoperability issues. The new version now takes OpenOffice.org to the same level as Microsoft Excel.

Enhanced PivotTable Support

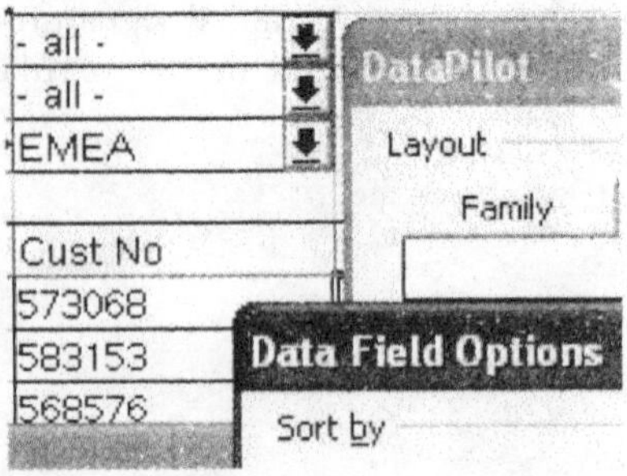

With the DataPilot in OpenOffice.org 2.0 (similar to Microsoft Excel's PivotTable feature) it is now possible to create new groups, filter data based on values, show differences and percentages instead of absolute values, etc. The new DataPilot features turn OpenOffice.org Calc into a very powerful tool for data analysis.

Native Installers

OpenOffice.org 2.0 supports native installation mechanisms. For example, .MSI and .CAB files are provided on Microsoft Windows; RPM files are available for Linux.

For users with more sophisticated management requirements, Sun provides configuration management tools as part of the StarOffice software. StarOffice 8 will also introduce Macro migration tools.

<table>
<tr><td colspan="2">Native Desktop Integration</td></tr>
<tr><td>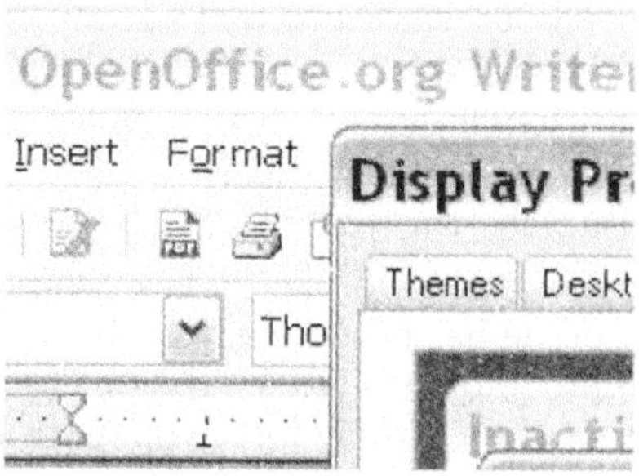
</td><td>The OpenOffice.org 2.0 applications integrate nicely into the desktop environment. Thus, OpenOffice.org looks and behaves like any other application on a given platform. On Windows XP it looks like a Windows application, and on Linux it uses the same UI widgets as GIMP or Evolution.</td></tr>
<tr><td colspan="2">Floating Toolbars</td></tr>
<tr><td>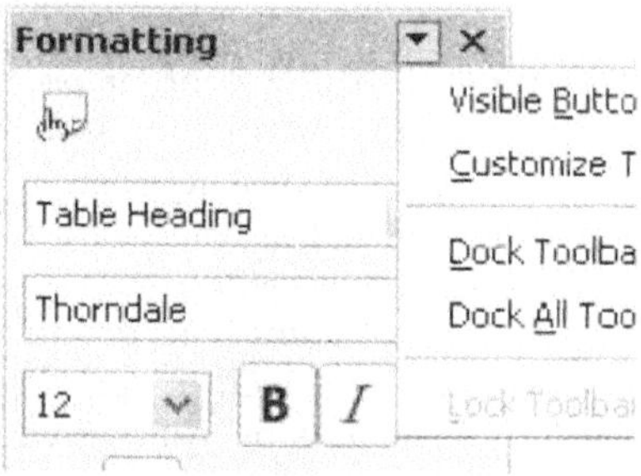
</td><td>Toolbars are much more flexible in OpenOffice.org 2.0. It is now very easy to move, attach, and detach toolbars, and to move them around and customize them.</td></tr>
<tr><td colspan="2">Support, Services and Solutions</td></tr>
<tr><td>
</td><td>An increasing number of companies provide support, services and solutions for OpenOffice.org.
More and more companies also offer derived versions of OpenOffice.org that include additional components like management tools (e.g., StarOffice).</td></tr>
</table>

SUMMARY

Apache

The *Apache License* (*Apache Software License* previous to version 2.0) is a free software license authored by the Apache Software Foundation (ASF). The Apache License (versions 1.0, 1.1, and 2.0) requires preservation of the copyright notice and disclaimer, but it is not a Copyleft license — it allows use of the source code for the development of free and open source software as well as proprietary and closed source software.

Berkeley Software Distribution (BSD), sometimes called *Berkeley Unix*, is the UNIX derivative distributed by the University of California, Berkeley, starting in the 1970s.

Linux (pronounced IPA : /□ 1 □ n □ ks/; variants exist) is a Unix-like computer operating system. Linux is one of the most prominent examples of free software and open source development; typically all underlying source code can be freely modified, used, and redistributed by anyone.

Mozilla Firefox is a web browser project descended from the Mozilla application suite, managed by the Mozilla Corporation. Firefox had 16.80% of the recorded market share in Web browsers as of December 2007, making it the second-most-popular browser in current use worldwide.

Wikipedia is a free online encyclopedia that anyone can add to or edit. The site was launched in early 2001 and has since grown to include millions of articles in dozens of languages. Despite concerns about the quality of openly editable information, Wikipedia has become one of the most popular online resources—statistics put Wikipedia as the eighth most-visited Web site in the United States, behind sites such as Yahoo, Google, MySpace, and eBay. Article topics range from the very broad to the highly specific, and the site offers tools to organize information into various content areas—such as "academic disciplines" and "glossaries"—with numerous topic breakdowns within each category. Each article contains any number of links to other Wikipedia articles or to external resources.

Joomla! is a free, open source content management system for publishing content on the world wide web and intranets. Joomla! includes features such as page caching to improve performance, RSS feeds, printable versions of pages, news flashes, blogs, polls, website searching, and language internationalization. Joomla! Is licensed under the GPL, and is the result of a fork of Mambo. It is written with the PHP programming language and uses the MySQL database by default. The *GNU Compiler Collection* (usually shortened to *GCC*) is a set of compilers produced for various programming languages by the GNU Project. GCC is a key component of the GNU toolchain. As well as being the official compiler of the GNU system, GCC has been adopted as the standard compiler by most other modern Unix-like computer operating systems, including Linux, the BSD family and Mac OS X. GCC has been ported to a wide variety of computer architectures, and is widely deployed as a tool in commercial, proprietary and closed source software development environments. GCC is also used in popular embedded platforms like Symbian, Playstation and Sega Dreamcast.

OpenOffice.org (*OO.o* or *OOo*) is an office application suite available for a number of different computer operating systems. It supports the OpenDocument standard for data interchange as its default file formats, as well as Microsoft Office '97–2003 formats, among many others.

REVIEW QUESTIONS

1. What source code will you be releasing, and how will it be licensed ?
2. How can you protect users from copyright infringement ?
3. Explain the working of "Apache ".
4. Explain the working of "BSD ".
5. Explain the working of "Linux ".
6. Explain the working of "GCC".
7. Explain the working of "Open Office".
8. Explain how you will install the Linux.
9. What is FTP server ? Why we use it ?
10. Why Open office is good ? Also explain the advantages of open office ?
11. Is it possible HTTP and HTTPS from the same server ?

□□□

Chapter **4**

OPEN SOURCE PROJECT

4.1 STARTING AND MAINTAINING AN OPEN SOURCE PROJECT

4.1.1 Getting Started

Vaporware is software that is 'floated' to see if there is interest. Many projects, if donated to the open source methodology would find usage, development and markets much quicker. Lost code might be resurrected and enhanced. More and more computer users are learning to use the excellent development tools created and enhanced by programmers. If you have a good idea, open source is a way of making it happen.

How do we start a project ?

- Create a new open source project.
- Download a project we have released.
- Explore the latest from the Google Summer of code, Wikipedia and Code guru.
- Watch open source developers talk about their craft.
- Learn about the latest technologies through Wikipedia, Google and Code Guru for education.

4.1.2 Project Management

Version Numbers

Many new users find the FOSS projects often use strange version numbering systems. For instance it is very common to see software in wide distribution that has a version number less than 1.0. For example, the web browser Firefox was widely used by version 0.6, more than a year before version 1.0 was finished. In the world of FOSS software it is generally considered important to work out all the known bugs before releasing version 1.0. While this is not a totally attainable goal, many users find early versions of software much more stable than early versions of their commercial counterparts.

Generally FOSS projects break their version numbers into 3 pieces : major version, minor update, point release. Major version is the first number in the version number; it is rare to see a free software project have a major version greater than 2 (although GNU Emacs is currently on version 21, so it is not unheard of). The minor update is the second number (the x in 2.x). A change in the number often signifies a significant update of the program. The third number (the y in 2.x.y) generally indicates a small update to fix a bug, or security problem. Thèse numbers get very high, often over 30 or 40 overtime. When a software project is well established most of their updates will come in the form of point releases.

Version numbers may also carry extra meanings. For instance ever since the Linux kernel went to version 2, it has been the practice of the design team to use odd numbers for development kernels, and even numbers for stable kernels. Therefore while it is common to see 2.2, 2.4, and 2.6 all in use today, 2.1, 2.3, 2.5 are almost no where to be seen. There are still teams that work on supporting bug/security fixes to the 2.0, 2.2, 2.4 and 2.6 kernels. As of March 2005, this policy was under review by the primary authors of the Linux kernel, however there are many projects that use similar numbering schemes, and so it holds as a useful example.

When a software project changes the major version number, this generally indicates a complete re-write of the software, or at least an extensive over haul. The Apache web server started a version 2.0 in 2003, after many years of 1.3.x versions. Apache2 is a near total re-write of Apache, which provides many new features, and significantly improved the underlying code base. The apache foundation still maintains the 1.3.x code base, although most efforts for new code are done on the 2.0.x code base.

Writers of software may completely re-write a program, improve software or unnecessarily inflate perfectly good software. If software works then there is little need to upgrade.

Also upgrading may solve some problems and add new ones. To give you an example 'Abi Word' is a fine word processor but it crashed on me. The complete package in Open Office has never done this nor has notepad or WordPad. New improved 'notepads' have occasionally crashed. So I stopped being seduced by what has many features. Any software that has the hidden feature of crashing is a liability. I have used Miranda IM without problem; others find it does not work.

4.2 OPEN SOURCE HARDWARE

Open source hardware refers to computer and electronic hardware that is designed in the same fashion as free and open source software. Open source hardware is part of the open source culture that takes the open source ideas to fields other than software. An example of this is the Computer project.

Some of the impetus for the development of open source hardware was initiated in 2002 through the Challenge to Silicon Valley issued by Kofi Annan. Because the nature of hardware is different than software, and because the concept of open source hardware is relatively new, no exact definition of open source hardware has emerged.

Because hardware has direct variable costs associated with it, no open source software definition can directly be applied without modification. Instead, the term open source hardware has primarily been used to reflect the use of free/open source software with the hardware and the free release of information regarding the hardware, often including the release of schematics, design, sizes and other information about the hardware. In anyway, it includes the hardware design and element distribution on the motherboard (*i.e.*, a notebook where one can replace elements).

With the rise of reconfigurable logic devices, the sharing of logic designs is also a form of open source hardware. Instead of sharing the schematics, HDL code is shared. This is different from free/open source software. HDL descriptions are commonly used to set up SoC systems either in FPGAs or directly in ASIC designs. HDL modules, when distributed, are called semiconductor intellectual property cores, or IP cores.

How can Hardware be 'Open' ?

Open-ness in hardware terms can have a whole range of meanings. In all the cases listed below, some hardware is open and some is not—but the trend is for open-ness to become more and more limited, restricting the freedom of designers to create or implement their own designs and even of programmers to write the programs they wish. Truly open hardware would have to satisfy all the requirements below :

1. Information on using the hardware must be available

It sounds crazy that people could sell hardware and not tell you how to use it, but it is actually a growing trend. If a company sells any device which interfaces to a computer without publishing the interface specs, they then have a monopoly on interface software (or can sell the monopoly to a software company). Win Modems and Win Printers - which also cannot be supported by Linux—are a related problem. This aspect of open-ness in hardware is so closely linked with work on free software that the FSF, Debian, and FreeBSD are all among the sponsors for the Open Hardware Certification program which is a self-certification program for hardware manufacturers. By certifying a hardware device as *Open*, the manufacturer makes a set of promises about the availability of documentation for programming the device-driver interface of a specific hardware device.... sufficient documentation for the device must be available for a competent systems programmer to write a device-driver.

2. The design of the hardware must be available

Designs can be free in exactly the same senses as software can be free.

If the design is published others can learn from it, improve on it, or even second-source the same device. Much digital hardware has never been open in this sense, creating a whole industry of reverse-engineering and patent claims and counter claims. But there have been exceptions; most notably, the SPARC architecture. Here the lessons from open source software as a tool for companies with a minority market share have been successfully imported to hardware.

Although many designs have always been patented, there is also a long traditional of engineers borrowing and improving on designs that just 'float around'. Many of these can be found in various places on the Internet, but few of them have been gpl-ed or otherwise protected as `free' designs. The attempt to create IP design libraries which are available only for sale will tend to destroy this tradition (one such IP company is already `giving' away the Strasburg library as a free offer ...).

3. Design software for hardware must be available

For many devices this has never been a problem — until recently. For the old 74 series logic devices, enough information was always made available for people to be able to create free design tools. Processor manufacturers have always published their processor Instruction Set Architectures, so it has always been possible to write free compilers. Now it seems that even this may change - the ISA for the Philips Tri media Processor is not available (it is a compressed VLIW and they consider the compression algorithm a trade secret).

But for other types of hardware, information about the underlying technologies is a commercial secret so that only the companies which own these secrets can create libraries or even efficient design tools which use them. This applies both to some types of VLSI design and to programmable logic : in the days of the first PALs, internal structure and programming details were widely published in order to expand the market. Now no manufacturer publishes the bit-stream format for programming FPGAs (the one exception, the Xilinx XC6200, now seems to have been dropped). As a result, the only design software available for these devices has been commercial software, and it has not been possible to create free software to make up for some of the deficiencies in these tools.

4.3 OPEN SOURCE DESIGN

Open design is the application of open source methods to the creation of physical products, machines and systems.

4.3.1 Definitions

Many of the arguments over free hardware design consist of people from software and hardware backgrounds talking at cross-purposes. One cause of this is the simple fact that the word 'software' refers both to source code and executables, while the words 'hardware' and 'hardware design' clearly refer to two different things. Using the word 'hardware' as short-hand for both design and physical object is a recipe for confusion. The following terms have all been used in discussions of this topic.

- *Free hardware design* refers to a design which can be freely copied, distributed, modified, and manufactured. It does not imply that the design cannot also be sold, or that any hardware implementation of the design will be free of cost. All the same arguments about the meaning of 'freedom' between supporters of the Free Software Foundation, and the supporters of BSD style licensing for software unfortunately carry over to hardware designs.

What is a 'free hardware design' ?

Perhaps the easiest way to define it is by looking at what it is not—by looking at current commercial design practice.

1. Commercial design practice

- Designs are owned by the company which creates them. Ownership is protected by 3 sets of laws : copyright, trade secret, and patent. It is often not even possible to see a design without signing a non-disclosure agreement.

- Designers cannot legally build on older designs unless their company owns the right to use these designs. Larger companies hold 'patent pools', which they use as bargaining counters with one another, and which block new entrants from the market. This is particularly important for developing countries.
- Where the design is for a basic building block (*e.g.*, an FPGA, or a cell library), design software can only be written by those entitled to know the secret information. EDA software is either written in-house (*e.g.*, for FPGAs) or by software companies that have agreements with the man- factures. Even where EDA software is generic, end users often have to purchase the right to use specific libraries. The result is that EDA software is ridiculously expensive; all except the largest companies (or universities) are barred from using them by cost.
- Designs are driven by marketing departments. The two main goals are minimizing time to market (estimated to reduce by 30% per year for VLSI designs) and minimizing manufacturing costs.
- Users of the final product have no rights to know hcw they work.

The combined effect is to create a closed caste of designers producing unintelligible products for a passive population of consumers so what would free designs look like by comparison ?

2. Free Design Practice

- Designs are owned by the people who create them. Ownership is protected by copyright law only. The intention is to make designs as widely available as possible.
- There is every incentive to build on older designs, to collaborate with as wide a spread of people as possible, and to make the designs widely known. NGOs in developing countries are not locked out, but encouraged to reuse designs.
- Design software is free software, so that anyone who wishes to can participate.
- Designs are driven by the wishes of their creators. The end goal can be whatever they wish.
- Users of the end product cannot only know how it works, but are encouraged to create improvements or modify it for their own purposes.

If this list were fully realized, knowledge of hardware design would become more diffused through society, destroying absolute barriers between 'creator' and 'consumer'. Designs that people wanted could be produced, rather than designs planned for people to buy.

In practice, some of the features of this list are already realities, and some are becoming so. It's often assumed that 'free hardware design' is beginning only now, as a side effect of the free software movement; in fact, many of these ideas are anything but new, and free hardware design was born with free software.

- *Libre hardware design* refers to the same class of design as *free hardware design*, but tries to make it clear that the word *free* refers to freedom, not price. The term sounds very clumsy to many English ears, but is of course natural for French speakers (and translations of it are natural to speakers of most languages, which do not use one word in both *free beer* and *free speech*).

- *Open source hardware* refers to hardware for which all the design information is made available to the general public. Open source hardware may be based on a **free** *hardware design*, or the design on which it is based may be restricted in someway.
- *Open Hardware* is a trademark of the Open Hardware Specification Program. It is a limited form of *open source hardware*, for which the requirement is that :
  - I. Sufficient documentation on the device must be available for a competent systems programmer to write a device-driver. The documentation must cover all of the features of the device-driver interface that any user would be expected to employ. This includes input/output and control functions and auxiliary functions such as performance measurement or self-test diagnostics. Details of on-board firmware and the hardware implementation need not be disclosed except when necessary to make it possible to program a driver for the device.
  - II. That is, only a limited amount of information about the design need be available; possibly not enough, for example, to attempt a repair.
- *Free hardware* is a term occasionally used as a synonym for *open source hardware*. It is a tempting term, since 'hardware' appears to be directly parallel to 'software', but suffers from blurring the distinction between design and implementation. The term *free hardware* is particularly confusing since it implies that the physical hardware, rather than its' design, is somehow free. This is not normally true in the cost sense, and is meaningless (except metaphorically) in a social sense. It seems simpler to avoid this term completely, except in its cost meaning, as with the free computers given away by various social organizations.

4.3.2 Sources of the Open Design Movement

The principles of open design are derived from the Free Software and Open Source movements. In 1997, Eric S. Raymond, Tim O'Reilly and Larry Augustin established "Open Source" as an alternative expression to "Free Software," and in 1997, Bruce Perens published the Open Source Definition. In late 1998, Dr. Sepehr Kiani (a Ph.D. in mechanical engineering from MIT) realized that designers could benefit from Open Source policies, and in early 1999, he convinced Dr. Ryan Vallance and Dr. Samir Nayfeh of the potential benefits of open design in machine design applications. Together they established the Open Design Foundation (ODF) as a non-profit corporation, and set out to develop an Open Design Definition.

The idea of open design was taken up, either simultaneously or subsequently, by several other groups and individuals. The principles of open design are closely similar to those of Open source hardware design, which emerged in March 1998, when Reinoud Lamberts of the University of Delft proposed on his "Open Design Circuits" website the creation of a hardware design community in the spirit of free software.

4.3.3 An Introduction to Open Source Hardware Development

This topic introduces a new trend in hardware design and development—open source hardware. It defines open source hardware design terms, features and requirements. It presents FPGA-based platforms as the most suitable for open source design implementation. It also discusses open source hardware business models.

Open source hardware is proposed as a bridge for the technological, educational and cultural gaps between developing and developed countries. Open source hardware organizations are introduced with statistics of activities. The role of the Internet with respect to hardware open-ness is introduced.

Open source hardware's challenges, problems and suggested solutions are described. The paper aims to introduce open source hardware to the electronic engineering community as an interesting topic of practice, study and research.

1. Introduction and motivation

Open source software has become an important part of the software development process. A hardware-software analogy allows consideration of open source hardware. HDLs resemble conventional software programming languages, and programmable implementation platforms resemble general-purpose processors.

An open source phenomenon has several properties that make it interesting for study, and relevant for the discipline of engineering design. Open source eschews traditional engineering concepts such as planning and prototyping in favor of a more organic approach. For instance, the open source Linux kernel is one engineering feat that reaches high quality.

The economics of open source defies conventional economic principles, because participants are on volunteer basis. A COCOMO analysis of widely distributed open source programs concluded these programs would be valued at one billion U.S. dollars if they were created by conventional means. Open source is a product of the Internet, which enables open source products to produce tangible results.

The application of open source to hardware brings new benefits to the hardware development process. Open source hardware would reduce development time and design cost. Open source IP cores could be reused, in black box or white box modes. The white box model allows designers to customize a particular core to their own requirements.

2. Open source hardware definition

Open source hardware is based on publishing all necessary data about the hardware. The design specification, HDL files, simulation test benches, synthesis results, utilization instructions and interfaces to other systems should be documented. The open-ness of necessary design documentation and its disclosure to the public should be governed by the terms of GPL like licenses.

All information is disclosed for free, according to the terms of GPL like licenses. The EDA tools used to develop open hardware should also be open. Open-ness of resources is a must to allow the community to reuse, develop and improve open designs.

3. Open source hardware implementation

Conventional hardware implementation platforms have various choices. Designs can fit in ASICs, custom silicon, FPGAs, and CPLDs. The question is, what suits open source hardware design ?

The hardware-software analogy points to programmable implementation platforms; hence the answer is programmable logic devices such as PLDs, FPGAs, CPLDs and FPAAs. The analogy between software and hardware implementations applies to different aspects in the development process. Software programs run on general-purpose processors, but open hardware designs fit on programmable logic devices.

Software assemblers generate assembly code based on a processor's instruction set. Hardware synthesis tools generate a net list of a particular device, using a digital or analog library. Software compilers generate binary code format from an assembly of set of processor's instruction set. The programming elements of an FPGA generate a bit-stream format from a net list of device's component library.

The dynamic reconfigurability of FPGAs optimizes the performance of hardware designs using real-time dynamic loading and unloading of hardware components on the programmable logic array. This analogy between software and hardware execution and implementation phases helps prove the feasibility of adopting an open source hardware strategy.

Table 4.1 : Hardware/software implementation analogy

Software	*Hardware*
General-Purpose-Processor	PLD, FPGA, CPLD, FPAA
Assembler	Synthesis Tool
Assembler Code	Net list
Instruction Set	Target Library Components
Compiler	Device Programmer
Binary Code Format	Bit Stream format
Dynamic Instruction Set Computers (DISC)	Dynamic Reconfigurable Devices

4. Business models

Open source hardware has a set of business models that include the following :

- **Design distribution :** Companies can pack sets of designs and sell the distribution just like Linux distributions. The Open Technology CD-ROM is an example of this method.
- **Design technical support :** Experts can give support for Open designs. Asics. is a company that follows this model by releasing IP cores and charging customers for technical support.
- **Design implementation :** Companies can implement the designs, sell them and pay royalties to original designers, according to their release license.
- **Releasing :** The release of open designs under the control of GPL-compatible licenses can occur whenever a silicon implementation is considered commercially.

5. Open source hardware roadmap

The open source hardware roadmap can be divided into three main stages as follows :

Phase I (Primary)

The primary stage objective is to start the development of a set of simple and generic FPGA-based prototyping boards that can be used to test and implement simple open source IP cores. Open EDA development tools would be used, such that designers can provide feedback to open source tools developers. The communication between FPGA-based board designers, open IP core designers, and open EDA developers will improve the whole development process of open source hardware and lead to the next phase.

Phase II (Advanced)

This advanced stage assumes that open source hardware publicity has taken place. Designers will release advanced open source designs, including FPGA prototyping boards. The market demand for prototyping boards will boom, which encourages vendors to produce volumes at low prices. The low price exists because the board designs are originally open source, and there is large market demand.

The vendors could produce open source device programming tools in order to enlarge their market base. The objective of this stage is to allow an open source hardware user to download open designs from Internet, and implement designs on prototyping boards, just as computer users download open source software and run it on general-purpose processors in personal computers.

Phase III (Runtime configuration)

At this stage, the complexity and density of designs would reach the limitations of conventional programmable logic devices. The dynamic reconfigurability of certain programmable devices is characterized by their ability to reconfigure subsets of their logic and routing resources at runtime, while continuing to operate normally. This intrinsic dynamic reconfiguration results in accommodation of complex and dense designs while maintaining high performance.

The objective of this phase is open source complex systems design and implementation. This assumes a seamless architecture of system models in which boundaries between software and hardware vanish. For instance, there is an effort to run a Linux kernel as a pure hardware platform that depends mainly on dynamic reconfigurability.

6. High-tech promotions in developing countries

Open source hardware can contribute to bridging the technological, educational and cultural gaps between developing and developed countries. Open source can help build a high-tech base in these regions due to the following considerations :

1. Open source hardware is an open resource for industrial and academic fields.
2. Lack of high-tech activities and firms.
3. Lack of expertise in the high-tech field.
4. Open source allows interaction with a wide spectrum of experts in high-tech fields all over the world.
5. HDL designs that address programmable logic devices based implementation platforms can be affordable, as chip manufacturing is beyond economic capabilities.
6. Open source might help focus the spotlight on high-tech talents and qualifications in developing countries that are hidden due to market constraints.

7. Open source hardware organizations

This section introduces organizations that adopted the open source hardware model. It provides statistics of activities that run under the Handasa Arabia, Open Cores, and Open collector organizations.

The organizational work is a result of volunteer engineers' efforts to manage the operations and projects under development. An open hardware design of a RISC architecture processor, open RISC1K, is used by some commercial companies that embed the design in their platforms.

The following table could be considered as a performance indicator for open source hardware. The statistics provide a sample of Handasa Arabia, Open Cores and Open collector activities.

Table 4.2 : Open source organization statistics

Activity	*Statistics*
Designers	860
Projects	210
Mailing List	18
News Posters	85
Sponsor Firms	9

8. New computational engines and the Internet

Open source hardware could produce a new generation of computers and the Internet. Computational engines might change from traditional architectures that are based on software instructions that execute on hardware resources, into algorithms that process hardware functions that load and unload dynamically on to a programmable logic platform.

Future personal computers might be built from FPGA-based boards that contain connectors to the external world. Hardware designers will be able to code modules or cores for specific FPGA computing machines or future computers. The Internet, the fundamental framework for open source designers, might be affected by the concept of dynamic reconfiguration and open source hardware design. FPGA prototyping boards can be connected to the Internet to act as free computing and debugging machines.

The future might give rise to a new Internet service called "Hardware Computing Resource Protocol" or HCRP. This may enable developers to design their algorithms, which are based on hardware cores, and upload them to these machines to run and implement them. The open source designs, open source computational resources, and global networking introduce a new era of innovative technologies and applications.

9. Challenges and suggested solutions

There are problems that face designers and prevent them from developing open source hardware.

- **Cost of EDA tools**

  Designers can't afford the cost of EDA tools. The suggested solution is to pursue development of open source EDA tools and improve them with feedback from the design community. Alliance [19]and gEDA [20] are good models for open EDA tools.

- **Manufacturing cost**

  Hardware manufacturing is relatively expensive. The suggested solution is implementation on FPGA-based prototyping boards or simulation of designs using formal verification techniques.

- **Design protection**

  The suggested solution is the protection of the open designs using GPL-like licenses that reserve rights for original designers, according to particular terms and rules.

- **Market**

  Market competition is mainly based on patents and intellectual property that maintain all rights for the originator firm. Companies may oppose aspects of open source that generate alternatives for commercially protected products.

  The suggested solution is that companies might take advantage of open source as a way of bridging the gap for time and cost absorbed in R&D. The researchers might find they don't have to reinvent already existing wheels. Companies may find adoption of an open source design with large base of customers as a win-win deal. Companies can refine the open source design with affordable prices and make use of bug fixing provided from the community. The end result is cutting-edge reliable products with affordable prices.

- **Credibility**

  Open source has to build confidence. The suggested solution is that designers produce high quality and completely documented designs. It will be only a matter of time to convince the user community of the credibility of open designs. For instance, the Linux operating system has become reliable and competitive due to efforts exerted to enhance quality and performance from the developing community.

4.4 OPEN SOURCE TEACHING (OST)

Open Source Teaching (OST) is a platform that utilizes emerging technologies to facilitate shared learning and the development of communities. OST redefines the relationship between learners by eliminating the barriers of time and distance. OST provides learners with simultaneously real-time and time-independent access to the ideas of people with varying degrees of experience, expertise, points of view, knowledge, and skills.

Open source teaching provides new strategies and opportunities for individuals to engage in the shared investigation of common challenges. These methods are applied using emerging communication platforms and generally include components of the following :

- Shared communication using an open source web space, available to all users, including the direct archiving and tracking of individual comments by all users.

- An open source induction and user agreement, outlining the fundamental truths for communication within each shared web space.
- Archived record of communication and dialogue, providing a common basis for learning and discussion among all users, including the direct tracking of files, which are accessed.
- The investigation of relevant research, current events, challenges, and case studies related to the academic, professional, or social challenge.

A final shared work product that requires shared collaboration among teams of participants and the collective community for the assigned web space.

4.4.1 What is it About ?

The open source idea has proved outstandingly successful in the development of Linux, the free ware version of the Unix programming language. In this case, a group of interested people voluntarily co-operated together for reasons other than a short-term cash reward.

In our project, interested teachers from a number of Universities will co-operate to produce teaching materials that are freely available to all. The chosen topic for this project is Visual Basic but, if successful, it should work for almost any subject.

4.4.2 How does it Work ?

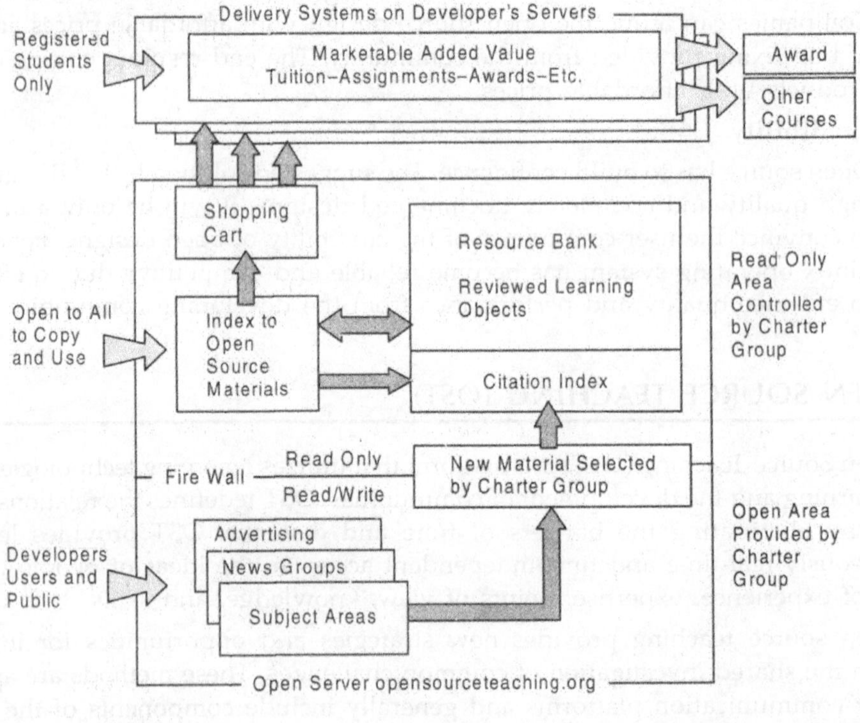

Fig. 4.1. Outline structure of open source teaching method.

The open source learning material is held in a *Resource Bank* on the 'www.opensourceteaching.org' server and is protected behind a firewall. Anyone can read, copy or use it, subject to certain restrictions, sometimes known as *Copyleft*. Only the *Charter Group* can edit material in this area.

4.4.3 Delivery of Courses

An institution, company or individual can set up a *Delivery System* to use any of the material on the website as they see fit, completely free of charge, subject only to *Copyleft* conditions. How material is delivered; how much is used or what value is added depends on the purpose the end user has in mind. They can only charge for the value added and the costs of delivery. Any changes to the original material must be acknowledged.

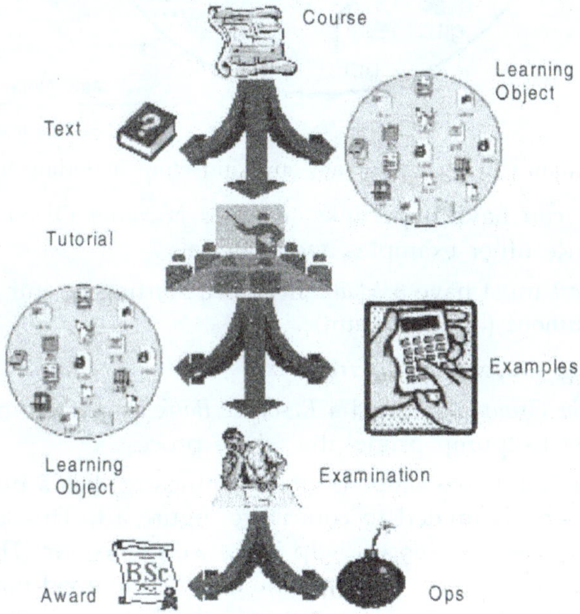

Fig. 4.2. One of many possible course delivery structures.

Individuals may use the material to learn about Visual Basic on their own but without receiving any support or qualification.

4.4.4 What are Learning Objects ?

A *Learning Object* is the basic unit that teaches a single idea or skill. It is a collection of just about any type of files and each file is called an *Atom*. Each Atom shows something and they are linked together to produce an overall multimedia effect.

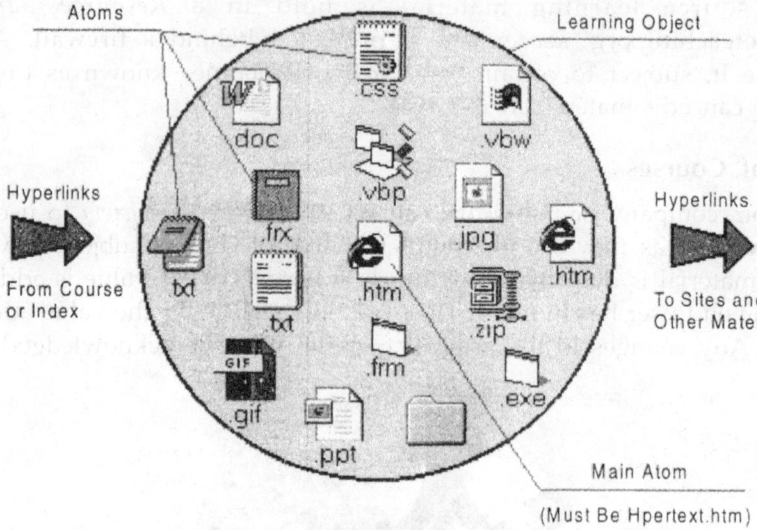

Fig. 4.3. The learning can object contain any kind atom including learning objects.

A *Learning Object* can have hyperlinks to other *Learning Objects*, data, help files or external sites to reference other examples and materials.

Each *Learning Object* must have a *Main Atom* as a starting or entry point and currently this is an Internet document (.html or .htm).

Where do the Learning Objects come from ?

Initially, the *Charter Group* will build a *Resource Bank* of suitable materials to make the site of sufficient interest to 'pump prime' the whole process.

The *Open Learning Server* (www.opensourceteaching.org) has a public area outside the firewall to which everyone is invited to contribute, figure 4.1. This area contains bulletin boards, news groups, theme conferences, help lines, web links, etc. The *Charter Group* will sift through these areas (cherry pick) and are able to promote good material to the *Resource Bank*. These open areas are also a resource, but only the *Resource Bank* is stable and subject to strict quality control. The promotion of material is a mark of excellence.

The *Charter Group* has a significant task to :

- Edit the material;
- Apply quality control;
- Ensure that material fits into the index system;
- Keep control of revisions and version changes.

4.4.5 Who Would Use It ?

The Open University would sell these materials as a training pack or build it into one or more courses. In this case the value added could include :

- Tutorials (face to face or virtual);
- Readers, guides and other teaching material;
- Conferences;

- Assignments;
- Assessment;
- Award of qualification.

The University of Ulster would use it in a teaching lab environment. Staff with less specific knowledge could facilitate the course, even if they could not have written it. In this case the value added could be :

- Tutorials;
- Assignments;
- Assessment;
- Provision of rooms and computer equipment;
- Award of qualification.

Industry or commerce could tailor it to specific training needs. In this case the value added could be :

- Training;
- Services to other departments or companies.

The participating groups may seem to have differing needs. For example, the Open University's courses in the *'Going Digital'* series would be much more general than UUJ's 'hard engineering' courses. It is up to the *Charter Group* to provide a *Resource Bank* for a wide range of end uses including VBA and Office automation.

4.4.6 How is it Used ?

The key features of the structure in figure 4.1 are the 'index to materials' and the 'shopping cart'. The index will be structured in such a way as to allow the learning objects and atoms to be examined and 'tagged' if selected for use.

Not all materials will be able to be viewed directly, *e.g.*, a Visual Basic project file (.vbp) can only be meaningfully viewed in the VB editor. However, the learning object files should be able to run with many of their embedded dependent files. The index will also list any dependent files that are required by the main file being viewed, *e.g.*, images, sounds etc.

Tagged items would be automatically added to the shopping cart, together with the complete set of dependent files. At the end of the session all tagged items would be zipped for the user to download. If desired, the Metadata files that describe the file and its dependent files can also be added to the basket.

It may be necessary to download some or all of the database tools, so that the user can keep track of a large number of files by reading the Metadata. This would simplify building the delivery system. Indeed, a tool for building the course is an obvious next step.

4.4.7 What are the Driving Forces ?

What cultural and social forces are at work that will make the system effective ? That it worked in the case of Linux is undeniable. People contribute to open source because :

- Of approbation by peers;
- Being part of a center of excellence can make an individual more productive than working alone;

- It provides access to a source of good practice and material;
- It leads to a work load reduction;
- It provides a kite mark for courses for Teaching Quality Assessment;
- They wish to contribute to a self-organizing community that may change 'the system'.

Citation Index

If the project is successful, this teaching method could grow to be a major movement in teaching. Making a contribution to this type of reviewed teaching resource could become an important recognition of professional competence. At the moment, there is no equivalent to the refereed research publication for teaching staff. The citation index could become such an equivalent.

It is essential to build a prominent 'citation index' into the materials index so that recognition of contributions is obvious to all. This provides recognition, benefit and further motivation to contributors.

4.4.8 How is the Resource Bank Structured ?

The user can select a set of required *Learning Objects* from the *Resource Bank* index by viewing the object directly or by scanning through the *Meta Files.*

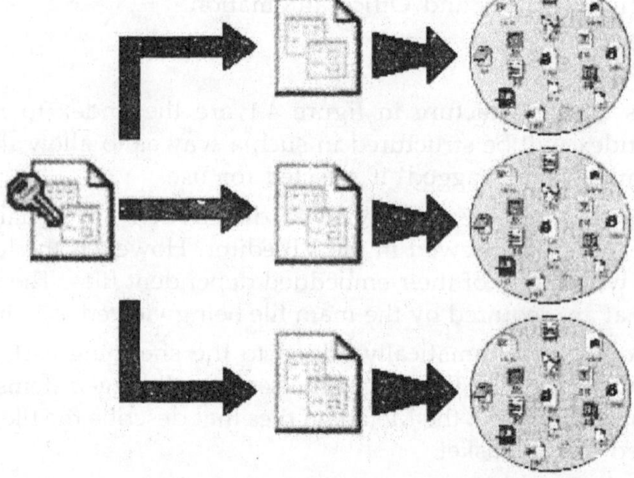

Fig. 4.4. Simplified database structure.

The Meta files contain the following data for each object :

- Name
- Caption describing the ideas or skills to be learned
- Previous knowledge required
- Level
- Learning outcomes
- Next suitable objects to study (if known)

- Location
- Files list
- Source
- Author(s) name

These Meta file data are a sub set of IEEE P1484 Learning Object Metadata specifications.

4.5 PAJAMAS MEDIA/BRIEFLY KNOWN AS OPEN SOURCE MEDIA

Pajamas Media, briefly known as *Open Source Media*, is a startup company founded in 2004 by mystery writer, screenwriter and blogger Roger L. Simon, and Charles Johnson of Little Green Footballs "with the intention of... aggregating blogs to increase corporate advertising and creating our own professional news service."

4.5.1 History

Pajamas Media completed its first round of venture capital funding on November 14, 2005; its launch and official rebranding as "Open Source Media" took place November 16. Launch festivities included a keynote address by former *New York Times* journalist Judith Miller.

Pajamas Media Board members include many prominent bloggers and journalists, including "Instapundit" Glenn Reynolds, CNBC's Larry Kudlow, Michael Barone of *U.S. News & World Report*, David Corn of *The Nation* and Claudia Rosett (who helped break the United Nations' "Oil for Food" controversy).

Now over two years old, Pajamas Media has correspondents in 48 countries and is beginning to syndicate original content in the manner of a news service, one of the first new media companies to do this. It has also added a list of Pajamas press bloggers including historian Victor Davis Hanson, journalist Ron Rosenbaum and the actor Ron Silver.

4.5.2 7 Rules for Open Source Media

1. **Freely accessible** : Available to stream, or download without a fee. Should be available via direct download and P2P media, so it is not behind a gateway.
2. **Freely available** : Permanently available without DRM, or release windows. The end user able to share the work without restriction.
3. **Freely viewable** : Available in multiple formats, and to be converted freely (in the case of video works, for example, as dvd, xvid/divx, mp4, and HD formats).

   The above qualities are essential for open content. Open source content adds to the cultural commons by making creation of new content from the work.
4. **Giving source files** : Source media, such as rushes and raw graphics files should be archived and available for other creators to work with.
5. **Allowing remixing** : Materials should be licensed explicitly to allow derivative work (*e.g.*, other works based on the script, or video mashups, and remix edits) for at least non-commercial/artistic purposes. Creative Commons and other licenses are available for flexible copyrighting.

Open Plus adds more opportunities for participation and involvement in the work whether as a creator, or as part of what used to be called 'the audience'.

6. **Reveal the process :** Allowing access to not only the final source media, but work-in-progress material and software files, adding another layer of transparency and documentation.
7. **Open contribution :** Adding ways to influence and participate in the creation of the original work through various types of community/audience involvement (opportunities such as open crewing, direct feedback or contribution mechanisms).

SUMMARY

Open source hardware refers to computer and electronic hardware that is designed in the same fashion as free and open source software. Open source hardware is part of the open source culture that takes the open source ideas to fields other than software. An example of this is the Computer project.

Many of the arguments over free hardware design consist of people from software and hardware backgrounds talking at cross-purposes. One cause of this is the simple fact that the word 'software' refers both to source code and executables, while the words 'hardware' and 'hardware design' clearly refer to two different things. Using the word 'hardware' as shorthand for both design and physical object is a recipe for confusion. The following terms have all been used in discussions of this topic.

Open Source Teaching (OST) is a platform that utilizes emerging technologies to facilitate shared learning and the development of communities. OST redefines the relationship between learners by eliminating the barriers of time and distance. OST provides learners with simultaneously real-time and time-independent access to the ideas of people with varying degrees of experience, expertise, points of view, knowledge, and skills.

Pajamas Media, briefly known as *Open Source Media*, is a startup company founded in 2004 by mystery writer, screenwriter and blogger Roger L. Simon, and Charles Johnson of Little Green Footballs "with the intention of... aggregating blogs to increase corporate advertising and creating our own professional news service."

REVIEW QUESTIONS

1. What is open source project and how we manage the project ?
2. What is open source hardware ?
3. What is open source design ? What is need of this ?
4. What is open source teaching and explain it ?
5. What is open source media ?
6. What are the rules for open source media ?
7. Explain the open source hardware development.
8. What are the steps for starting open source project ?

❑❑❑

Chapter 5 OPEN SOURCE ETHICS

5.1 OPEN SOURCE VERSUS CLOSED SOURCE

Richard Stallman's organization is called the Free Software Foundation, not the Open Source Software Foundation. There's a reference to "FSF's mission to preserve, protect and promote the freedom to use, study, copy, modify, and redistribute computer software." This is missionary zeal. However, it's not the reason for the success of open source software. It is critically important that we think clearly bookmaking money through traditional methods, such as sale of the use of individual copies and patent royalty payment, is more difficult and sometimes impractical with open source software. Some closed-source advocates see open source software as damaging to the market of commercial software. This complaint is countered by a large number of alternative funding streams such as :

1. Giving away the software and charging for installation and support (used by many Linux distributions).
2. Make the software available as open source so that people will be more likely to purchase a related product or service you do sell (*e.g.*, OpenOffice.org vs. Star Office).
3. Cost avoidance/cost sharing : many developers need a product, so it makes sense to share development costs (this is the genesis of the X Window System and the Apache web server).

Studies about security in open source software versus closed-source software show that closed-source software have fewer advisories but open source software usually has less time between flaw discovery and a patch or fix. Advocates of closed source argue that since no one is responsible for open source software, there is no incentive or guarantee it will be fixed, and there is nobody to take responsibility for negligence. Open source advocates argue that since the source code of closed-source software is not available, there is no way to know what security vulnerabilities or bugs may exist. However, having the source code for a program could also make it easier for a malicious person to discover security vulnerabilities that they can take advantage of (instead of reporting or fixing them).

Proprietary/ Close Source S/W	*Open Source S/W*
Licensor distributes object code only; source code is kept a trade secret.	Licensor distributed source code.
Modifications are prohibited.	Modification are permitted.
All upgrades, support and development are done by licensor.	Licensee may do its own development and support or hire any third party to do it.
Fees are for the software license, Maintenance, and upgrades.	Fees, if any, are for integration, packing, support, and consulting.
Sublicensing is prohibited, or is a very limited right.	Sublicensing id permitted; licensee may have to distribute the source code to program and modification.
Microsoft Windows is an example of Close Source S/W.	Wikipedia is an example of Open Source S/W.

Open source (or free software) and **closed source** (or proprietary software) are two approaches to the control, exploitation and commercializing of computer software. Open source approaches differ from the proprietary model of software licensing by allowing other individuals and organizations to view, modify and redistribute the source code. This is in the tradition of the early times of computing (before 1980) when software wasn't licensed at all.

5.1.1 Background

Computer software is an unusual commodity. Once written, it can be copied and reproduced for very little cost, and can have great commercial value. However, the original source code created by the authors, if publicized, would allow anyone to duplicate and extend their work easily. The commercialization of software through the 1970s and 1980s lead to program code hidden from anyone outside the company that developed the software and the code is treated as a trade secret.

Under the *closed source* model, source code must be hidden from the public and competitors, who might otherwise reproduce, study or modify the code, either to resell the product, learn from the product or for other reasons. Software companies that follow the closed source model see it as a way to protect their products from software piracy or misuse, from reverse engineering and duplication, and to maintain competitive advantage and vendor lock-in. Closed source software usually is developed and maintained by a relatively small team who produce their "product" in a compiled executable state, which is what the market is allowed access to. Microsoft, the owner and developer of Windows and Microsoft Office, along with other major software companies, have long been proponents of this business model, although their business models have shifted with time.

The *open source* model allows for any user to view and modify a product's source code. Organizations and individuals that adhere to this model believe that the benefit that they gain from improvements to their software provided by the community of software developers is more important than protecting their competitive advantage. Common advantages cited by proponents for having such a structure are expressed in terms of trust, acceptance, teamwork and quality.

Most of the open source software is licensed under what is often termed a "copy left" license, a term which emphasizes the license's reversal of the principles of copyright. A traditional license is used to limit freedoms, which the free software movement considers essential, the "four software freedoms", taking them away from the users either completely ("you may not distribute the software") or partially ("you can use the software for an evaluation period of 30 days; after that you must either pay a license registration fee or discontinue the software"). By contrast a copy Left license protects the "four software freedoms" by explicitly granting them and then explicitly prohibiting anyone to strip them away when redistributing the package or reusing the code in it to make derivative works. However there are few open source software packages licensed under a license that grants the four software freedoms but allows redistributors to remove them if they wish. Such licenses are sometimes called *permissive software licenses* (for example in). An example of such a license is the BSD license which allows derivative software to be sold as closed source products, as long as they give credit to the original designers.

Open source can and is commercialized, both by purely open source companies such as Red Hat and more traditional software companies such as IBM and Novell. The archetypal open source software is the Linux operating system.

5.1.2 Collaboration and Project Management

Closed source projects ("CS") tend to collaborate either only to a limited or peripheral degree with third parties (other than project co-members), or under non-disclosure agreements. Corporate development is usually run by teams or structured groups, with workload, agendas, intended results, and deadlines, centrally agreed, and use paid developers to achieve these goals as required.

Open source projects ("OS") by contrast can be voluntary for many of those involved, and who are doing it for fun (however, an increasingly large amount of open source code is written by paid programmers). New code is developed and reviewed in a less formal process by many people in some cases hundreds of thousands, or millions and since many of these are intimately familiar with the system concerned, the quality of review and final writing tends to be extremely high on such projects and the speed of development can be very fast. Collaborative work is also resource efficient, since duplication of effort is avoided.

CS and OS projects tend to view their *priorities* as different. CS projects tend to work to deadlines, the date at which (for corporate, market or investor purposes) a new product or update must be released, or a new feature made available. OS projects, lacking investor pressure, tend to be more actively interested in how to do a job well, as well as produce it quickly, and in producing work to a high standard. However, feature creep is often prevalent in various smaller OS projects where the project fails to lock down milestones for releases which lead to frequent unpolished releases that are user unfriendly. This is not unique to OS projects, but as CS projects are driven by the market their releases do tend to be cleaner for the user (even if they end up slower and messier under the hood).

Example :

- *Microsoft Windows is closed source,* it is the most common operating system on personal computers and a de facto standard on these. Proponents would tend to agree that most versions of Windows have contained major changes to previous versions. Because it is developed by one company, it can be centrally managed and co-ordinated, and there are fewer "odd gaps" in its development as such. However against this, a huge effort has gone into protecting and preventing others from benefiting from this work in unintended ways, there has been much conflict over "hidden code" allegations, and security and quality have consistently been criticized by independent third parties over the years.
- *Wikipedia itself is open source,* both its software and the actual content, is collaborative. In five years it grew from under 1000 articles, to millions of articles, and its software is continually updated by a developer community that spans the world. The software is as a result very robust, since millions of people have access to it and any untoward happening has been analyzed by many developers at a moment's notice. The information contained is broader, more comprehensive and more in-depth than any corporate team could produce, and grows extremely fast in quality and scope, and there is a huge user base of millions of contributors, however as there is no central control, there are many articles not yet up to the intended long term standard and no article can be 100% relied upon without additional checking by the user.

5.1.3 Commercialization

The primary mechanisms for making money from closed-source software all seem to involve imposition of artificial scarcity constraints on something that, by its nature, can be very easily and cheaply copied and distributed. It has famously been said that "information wants to be free"; closed-source vendors would counter this by saying that "information providers want to be paid". Thus, they impose various limitations on what can be done with their software, first of all by usually not giving customers access to the source code, and then backing this up by restrictions on copying, enforced using both legal (copyright law) and technological measures (copy protection and digital rights management). Finally, there are a series of arguments against the commercialization of open source at all. One such argument is made in a position paper by Packet Trap Networks.

Thus, in closed-source software, there is an element of the design which means that the product is designed to *prevent* the customer from doing some actions that the company feels would result in compromise of their source code, even if this is something that isn't source compromising, or something the consumer wishes to do.

Open source, on the other hand, abandons all such attempts at forcing the customer to do things in a certain way. Instead, the revenue model is based solely on what customers can be persuaded to pay for of their own free will.

Another important factor in the closed-source revenue model involves fending off competitors (both actual and potential) by continually *raising the barriers to entry*. Thus, new versions of the software are continually being introduced, with lots of new features being added. Competitors then have to come up with their own answers to these new features (otherwise they will not be seen to "remain competitive"), which they have to reinvent essentially from scratch, which adds to their own costs. Typically these features are added with little thought for their impact on the conceptual integrity of the overall product, leading to the well-known phenomenon of software bloat.

Another problem with the addition of these features is that they often add to the software vendor's own costs; when they try to adapt the product to new markets and new applications, then the more feature-ridden the product is, the less flexible and adaptable it becomes. For example, operating systems built on the Linux kernel are available for a wider range of processor architectures than Microsoft Windows, including PowerPC and SPARC. None of these can match the sheer popularity of the x86 architecture, nevertheless they do have significant numbers of users; Windows remains unavailable for these alternative architectures, although there have been such ports of it in the past.

The most obvious complaint against open source software revolves around the fact that making money through some traditional methods, such as the sale of the use of individual copies and patent royalty payments, is much more difficult and sometimes impractical with open source software. Moreover, many see the introduction of open source software as damaging to the market for commercial software. Most software development companies sell licenses to use individual copies of software as their primary source of income, using a combination of copyright, patent, trademark and trade secret laws (collectively called intellectual property rights laws). Fees from sale and licensing of commercial software are the primary source of income for companies that sell software.

Additionally, some companies with large research and development teams develop extensive patent portfolios, with the purpose of making money from patent royalties. These companies can charge licensing fees for the use of their patents in software, however open source distribution creates the potential for an unlimited number of derived works using the patented technology without payment to the patent holder.

This complaint is countered by a large number of alternative funding streams, which are actually better-connected to the real costs of creating and maintaining software. After all, the cost of making a copy of a software program is essentially zero, so per-use fees are perhaps unreasonable. At one time, open source software development was almost entirely volunteer-driven, and although this is true for many small projects, many alternative funding streams have been identified and employed for open source software :

- Give away the program and charge for installation and support (used by many Linux distributions).
- "Commoditize complements" : make a product cheaper or free so that people are more likely to purchase a related product or service you do sell (this is a primary reason for OpenOffice.org; Sun gives away the office suite to encourage users to buy their computer hardware). This is similar to The Gillette Company giving away razor handles so they could make money on razor blades, or Radio Shack giving away : Cue Cat scanners.
- Cost avoidance/cost sharing : many developers need a product, so it makes sense to share development costs (this is the genesis of the X Window System and the Apache web server).

Increasingly, open source software is developed by commercial organizations. In 2004, Andrew Morton noted that 37,000 of the 38,000 recent patches in the Linux kernel were not created by developers directly paid to develop the Linux kernel. Many projects, such as the X Window System and Apache, have had commercial development as a primary source of improvements since their inception. This trend has accelerated overtime.

Additionally, it is worth noting that open source programmers may have non-financial reasons for developing software. An analogy is that of Wikipedia, where people contribute without expecting compensation.

5.1.4 End User Support

Computer software is complex enough that users frequently need help with it even after they have got it set up and working to begin with. Software also invariably has *bugs* in it, which may adversely impact the users' ability to get work done and so need to be fixed. A user may also see areas in which the functionality of the software may be improved, to help not just that user but others as well.

Closed-source software vendors typically provide a "one-stop shop" for all support matters : since the vendor developed the software (and appropriately licensed any included components that were developed by others), the vendor also provides all necessary support functions. Nobody else can provide the level of support that the original vendor does, simply because nobody else has the requisite access to the source code (not just to understand how it works, but to make modifications and fix bugs).

This kind of model works well up to a certain point. However, as the number of customers increases, its effectiveness decreases. The better-known PC software packages of today have customer bases numbered in the millions. With that many users, support needs to be delegated to a group of people separate from the software developers (otherwise the developers would have no time to work on the software). This group increases development costs, and invariably, not all bugs may be fixed fast enough to remain profitable. Another problem when a closed source project is this big is hackers trying to compromise other users' systems, often outnumbering the bug-fixers. (However, some say that it is easier to find bugs in open source software, as bugs can be more easily found with source code.

Open source offers an alternative model, where easy access to the source code allows the proliferation of a multitude of alternative support organizations, each remaining small enough to remain responsive to the needs of its own set of customers. With ready access to the source code, any programmer can find a bug or shortcoming in the software, and submit a patch for it all the way back to the original software developers, who in turn can very quickly decide whether the patch is worth accepting or not. It is often said that the more eyes looking for bugs reduce them, and with more people looking for bugs, than looking to exploit them, it is no wonder bug fixes may be faster for open source projects.

5.1.5 Innovation

Open source software has often been accused of being more derivative than innovative. This is true to some extent, mostly in the desktop arena. For example, GIMP is in many ways a reinvention of the functionality of Photoshop, while OpenOffice.org is primarily designed as a plug-compatible replacement for Microsoft Office.

Many of the largest well-known open source projects are either legacy code (*e.g.*, FreeBSD or Apache) developed a long time ago independently of the free software movement, or by companies like Netscape (which open sourced its code with the hope that they can compete better), or by companies like MySQL which use open source to lure customers for its more expensive licensed product. However, it is notable that most of these projects have seen major or even complete re-writes (in the case of the Mozilla and Apache 2 code, for example,) and do not contain much of the original code.

However, one should not overlook the many innovations that have come, and continue to come, from the open source world :

- GCC is a set of compilers for C and other languages that support more different processor architectures, for both native and cross-compilation, than any other compiler.
- The Linux kernel is available for nearly two dozen different major processor architectures. The runner-up for most widely ported kernel, the NetBSD kernel, is also open source.
- Mozilla Firefox is a Web browser which has managed to take increasing market share from Microsoft's Internet Explorer, to the extent that version 7 of Internet Explorer offers many features similar to those already in Firefox. Firefox, however, copies many features from closed-source browsers such as Opera.
- Beowulf MPI is an open source framework used for building parallel-processing applications that run on Linux and other UNIX-like operating systems. It has proved itself so powerful that Microsoft has adopted it as a crucial part of its own efforts to establish a presence in the supercomputing market.
- The Gmail Filesystem is a good example of the collaborative nature of much open source development. Building on FUSE (which allows filesystems to be implemented in userspace, instead of as code that needs to be loaded into the kernel) combined with libgmail, which is a Python library for programmatic access to a user's Gmail message store, the result is the ability to use the multiple gigabytes of Gmail message space as a fileserver accessible from anywhere on the Internet.
- Perl, the pioneering open source scripting language, made popular many features, like regular expressions and associative arrays, that were unusual at the time. The newer Python language continues this innovation, with features like functional constructs and class-dictionary unification.
- draw is an open source tool for decoding RAW-format images from a variety of digital cameras, which can produce better-quality output than the closed-source tools provided by the camera vendors themselves.
- Nicholas Negroponte's $100 laptop will use Linux as its operating system. The decision was made after months of discussions with vendors of closed-source alternatives.
- A number of laptop models are available with a particular emphasis on multimedia capabilities. While these invariably come preinstalled with a copy of Microsoft Windows, some of them also offer an alternative "fast-boot" mode based on Linux. This gets around the long time it can take to boot up Windows.

- JACK is an audio-routing architecture that has been found sufficiently useful to be ported to Apple's Mac OS X.

5.1.6 Compatibility and Interoperability

One issue that needs to be watched with software as it evolves is the need to maintain compatibility with other software, whether via common data formats, communication protocols or APIs. Closed-source software has a particular problem with APIs, since old, obsolete ones may need to be supported essentially forever, because they are still being used by other software that has never been updated.

For instance, consider the migration from 16-bit to 32-bit x86 processor architectures. Microsoft brought out its first 32-bit version of Windows, Windows NT 3.1 in 1993, yet it wasn't until 2001, with the release of Windows XP, that it was able to put out a mass-market 32-bit OS that did away with most of the backward compatibility with 16-bit code. Now there is the next transition, to 64-bit processor architectures. Windows XP Professional x64 Edition was released in 2005, but full 64-bit support in the way of applications and hardware drivers still remains thin on the ground, and the migration looks likely to be at least as protracted as the 16-to-32-bit one.

Contrast the situation with Linux. That has been available on a range of processor architectures, including 64-bit ones, since early in its history. Now that 64-bit processors are commonplace in the mass market, all the major Linux distributions offer full 64-bit-native versions, running full 64-bit binaries and using full 64-bit drivers.

5.1.7 User Freedoms to Make Use of Software

The politics of Open Source is an area that is so controversial; often even Open Source advocates themselves cannot agree what it should be.

The free software movement demands the following four freedoms :

- Freedom 0 : The freedom to run the program for any purpose.
- Freedom 1 : The freedom to study and modify the program.
- Freedom 2 : The freedom to copy the program so you can help your neighbour.
- Freedom 3 : The freedom to improve the program, and release your improvements to the public, so that the whole community benefits.

Freedom 3 includes the freedom for language communities to localize software into their own languages, and to adapt it to local cultural and legal requirements.

However, one thing all are agreed on is that Open Source software is never designed to *prevent* users from doing things they might legitimately want to do.

5.1.8 Integration and Overall "Feel"

When people compare the user experience with using Microsoft Windows versus typical Linux distributions as a desktop system, they generally agree that Windows works in a more seamless fashion. Every bit of the system was produced by one company, so naturally the parts work together well. A typical Linux distort, on the other hand, is a combination of pieces from a large number of independent groups : the Linux kernel itself, basic operating system infrastructure from the GNU Project, basic GUI functions from X.Org on top of which one may run window managers or alternatively more elaborate GUI environments such as GNOME or KDE, and so on.

But on the other hand, all the different open source groups have a strong interest in having their projects work well together. They achieve this by having a fondness for open interoperability standards, such as those promoted by Freedesktop.org and the Linux Standard Base.

This cooperation between different groups naturally has to be conducted on a more structured basis than that between different departments of the same company. This turns out to have benefits in some respects.

An example of why integration needs to be done on a carefully-structured basis, compare the systems for applying updates to operating system installations in Windows versus typical open source operating systems. In versions of Windows up to XP/2003, updates (patches) are applied to the OS as a monolithic whole :

One of the new features under consideration for the next version of the Windows Installer is the ability to uninstall a patch. Currently you must uninstall the whole product or use a hack anti-patch style mechanism. Currently patches are applied by MSI in the order they are received at the client, not the order they were created by the author. This can get really nasty in some scenarios, because applying patches in the wrong order can actually result in files being down.

Most Linux distributions, as well as the BSD operating systems, on the other hand, include package management systems as standard. The various components of the installation are carefully separated into individual *packages*, with clearly-defined *dependencies* between them. An attempt to upgrade a package on which another package depends will trigger a message to that effect, perhaps with an offer to automatically upgrade the latter package as well. Two packages that do not depend on each other can be independently upgraded, and if a problem is revealed with the new version of one of them, it can be independently reverted, regardless of the order in which the two were upgraded.

Since the package management systems are open source and public, it is straightforward for third parties to set up additional package repositories (such as Packman for SUSE Linux) that integrate cleanly with the original vendor/developer provided ones.

A complication arises from the abundance of alternate free-software programs to meet a given need. For example, multimedia frameworks like GStreamer, Xine and Mplayer compared to the one centralized API, DirectShow, on Windows. In Windows, any media software can play any file format as long as the appropriate DirectShow codes have been installed. In Linux, the appropriate codec must support not only the correct file format, but also the right framework : codecs for one framework are not compatible with another. This can lead to an inconsistent user experience, where some player software can play certain files, but other software cannot. The issue of DRM further complicates things. Only closed-source Operating Systems, most notably Windows Vista, and closed-source media players can play DRM protected content. This is something which is unlikely to ever get support in open source software as the purpose of DRM is to limit the rights of the user, which is antithetical to the open source movement.

5.1.9 Security

Open source advocates usually believe that open source programs are more secure, mostly because flaws in the code can be seen and fixed by anyone. Different studies reach different conclusions about security through obscurity versus open source. Also note that proprietary software companies may not always release advisories for all bugs in their software. Closed source advocates, including Microsoft corporation, argue that since no one is responsible for open source, there is no way to know whether it has been fixed. Open Source advocates argue back that no one knows what bugs exist in a closed source product, since there is no one independent and credible checking in depth claims made by neither its vendor nor any open process addressing problems whose quality can be examined by 3rd parties.

Some people believe that closed source software is more secure than open source software. With any given piece of software, it's much easier for a black hat to find and exploit security holes in any given piece of software when he has the source code than without it. For example, many open source web programs using PHP have serious security problems and although these problems are being fixed, they are only fixed when affected end users prompt the developers about the problem.

Other people believe that open source software is more secure than closed source software. The availability of open source code leads to faster discovery of security issues, and faster resolution of these issues. They point to the exploitation of proprietary software such as Internet Explorer. But others claim that such software is exploited because it has a large market share—making it an attractive target for attackers—and claim that open source software would also be exploited if it attracted the attention of those attackers. Open source advocates often counter by pointing to Apache, which is more popular than its main competitor, Microsoft IIS, but is also exploited less often. This argument is analogous to one in cryptography : it is believed that a secure encryption scheme has to be able to withstand attacks from people who have access to the code, and that security through obscurity is not a good thing. Though security and software development are different things, they can have the same goal (security).

Flaws certainly occur in both closed-source and open source software. However it has frequently been the case that a patch to fix one security problem in closed-source software has created another problem or failed to fix the actual problem, and other times a vendor may leave a known flaw unlatched for months or even years at a time. These sorts of issues seem to be less common in open source software.

5.2 OPEN SOURCE GOVERNMENT

Open source governance advocates the application of the philosophies of the free software movement to democratic principles, in order to enable any interested citizen to add to the creation of new policy as with a wiki document. Legislation is democratically opened to the general citizenry in this way, allowing policy development to benefit from the collected wisdom of the people as a whole.

Some envision this form of governance as a post-national "virtual state" governing structure, where policy-setting is decoupled from territorial management. Some models are significantly more sophisticated than a wiki, incorporating levels of control or scoring to mediate disputes. In any event, the idea demonstrates the still untapped potential of how open source philosophies can merge with government.

The core principle is the concept of a "central codebase" in the form of a set of policies that are maintained in a public registry and that are *infinitely reproducible*. "Distributions" of this policy-base are released (periodically or dynamically) for use in localities, which can apply "patches" to customize them for their own use. Localities are also able to cease subscribing to the central policy-base and "fork" it or adopt someone else's policy-base.

In effect, the government stems from emergent co-operation and self-correction among members of a community. As the policies are put into practice in a number of localities, problems and issues are identified and solved, and where appropriate communicated back to the core. Because so much information must be gathered for the overall decision-making process to succeed, however, technology may provide important forces leading to the type of empowerment needed for participation in this kind of government, especially those technological tools that enable community narratives and correspond to the accretion of knowledge.

1. **Open Source Government** : Primarily refers to use of open source software technologies in traditional government organization and government operations such as voting.
2. **Open Politics** : It is also known as Open Source Politics. It's a term used to describe a political process that uses Internet technologies such as blogs, e-mail and polling to provide for a rapid feedback mechanism between political organization of the Open Source Politics which relates to the development of public under a set of rules and processes similar to the Open Source Software Movement.

5.3 THE ETHICS OF OPEN SOURCE

There are a few people who believe that open source software is somehow morally superior to closed source software. Richard Stallman is one. To him, the issue is one of freedom versus slave "Ruth" this. The real reason for the success of open source is not the missionary zeal of Stallman and others, but a more humdrum factor called commoditization. In industry, something is a commodity if it is widely available from many suppliers and relatively homogenous. Bread is a commodity, and so is a teabag and a kettle. The kettle is an interesting case, because it comes in different shapes, colors and sizes, but you're going to be reluctant to spend too much on a kettle because you know that ultimately they all do the same thing, which is to boil water. And this last point is critical. You can make money selling commodities, but not very much, because if you try to charge a premium someone else will quickly undercut you.

There is a process of commoditization happening in software as well. We know what constitutes the bread-and-butter of the computing world. Operating systems, web servers, e-mail clients, database managers, spreadsheets, word processors, and so on. They may not be as easy to make as kettles, but the problems they pose are now well-known and they are available from multiple suppliers. What then should be their cost ? Well, probably not very much. Consider a common tool like a word processor. How many people need a word processor ? Almost everyone So, if everyone who needs a word processor pools their resources, you can easily make a very good word processor which then belongs to everyone. It makes enormous sense, not in terms of politics or religion, but in sheer commercial terms. Put another way, it makes little sense for everyone individually to pay hundreds of pounds each for a word processor license, when the technology required to provide this piece of software is commonplace.

Of course, the problem with this sort of reasoning is that it requires organization and communication. The key enabler is the internet. This extraordinary network provides both communication and distribution. It enables the pooling of resources, management of source code, distribution of both code and binaries, and peer-to-peer support. With hindsight, something along the lines of Linux and Open Office has been inevitable ever since the Internet took off.

What we are seeing with the open source movement is commoditization of software to match what has already taken place with hardware. Ironically, Microsoft—my first mention of the M word—built its success in part on the commoditization of the PC. It forced down hardware prices, and make Microsoft's hardware platform by far the cheapest. What Microsoft conspicuously failed to do was to reduce the operating system and application cost in line with falling hardware prices. The result is an increasing discrepancy that strengthens the incentive to look for alternatives.

It is easy to see how well this logic applies to what you might call bread-and-butter software. Web servers, e-mail clients, database managers, office productivity applications, even programming languages. However, it breaks down as software becomes more specialists. What about software for dental practitioners or estate agents, can they find or resource free software to meet their needs ? Possibly not. And when it comes to custom software to manage specific business needs, again commoditization does not apply. Following that logic through, we should expect software essentials to be free or very cheap, but will still have to pay commercial rates for the skills to develop custom solutions. There's also the matter of knowing how to configure and support software. We should expect then that specialist software will always be costly, and that computer services are a good way to make money, but that making all your money by selling standard operating system or application software is going to be difficult.

Of course those companies who do make their money in such a way will do their best to resist the trend. They can do so in various ways. First, they can add so many premium features that you don't mind paying extra. In other words, the proprietary item offers more than the free equivalent. Vendors are doing this with varying degrees of success. I'd rather store my data on Oracle, DB2 or SQL Server than on MySQL, PostgresSQL or Firebird, the open source version of Borland's Interface. However, if you just want a simple database server to run behind a small-scale website, the benefits of the premium solution are zero. Equally, Microsoft works strenuously to keep Office ahead of its open source competition. Last year I attended a press conference about the new release of Office, called Office 2003. I stuck my hand up and asked how the company intended to persuade users who simply typed letters and the minutes of meetings that the new features offered anything of value to them. The Office product manager was very offended, responding along the lines that "Office 2003 is not about writing letters and the minutes of meetings. It is about enhanced collaboration and improved productivity"—that's not an exact quote, but it is close. Unfortunately for Microsoft, a lot of people do just type simple documents. Put another way, if only those people who really use the advanced features purchased Office, Microsoft's business model would disappear.

The problem for all these vendors, whether Oracle, IBM or Microsoft, is that with these core products the open source community can quickly catch up. If enough people press for a particular feature, it will undoubtedly appear. My conclusion is that the downward pressure on prices for commodity software products will continue. Services on the other hand will remain a strong profit centre. If like IBM you make most of your money from services that's fine; it also happens to be the business model of open source companies like Red Hat.

Software vendors have other strategies. The favorite is called vendor lock-in. What this means is that the customer might like to move to a different product, perhaps with a cheaper or free license, but they cannot because it is too costly. Database administrators and programmers suffer badly from this. Typically, moving complex database applications to another DBMS is difficult, because vendor-specific features and optimizations mean that queries and stored procedures have to be re-written. In this case, you might say that the vendor lock-in is the features of the database manager that go outside standard ANSI SQL. Another aspect of vendor lock-in is in the guise of integration. Microsoft is a master of this, making sure that the Windows operating system, the Exchange messaging server and the Office productivity applications all work better together than any of its competitors can manage. It becomes hard to shift away to something different. There are also things like document compatibility. Many people use Microsoft Office because they know that everyone has to produce documents that Office can read, while the reverse may not be true. However, vendor lock-in never works over the long-term. If there are better and cheaper solutions out there, eventually either you will find them or your competitors will.

1. Morals

Ethics and morals are respectively akin to theory and practice. Ethics denotes the theory of right action and the greater good, while morals indicate their practice. "Moral" has a dual meaning. The first indicates a person's comprehension of morality and his capacity to put it into practice. In this meaning, the antonym is "amoral", indicating an inability to distinguish between right and wrong. The second denotes the active practice of those values. In this sense, the antonym is "immoral", referring to actions that violate ethical principles.

Personal ethics signifies a moral code applicable to individuals, while social ethics means moral theory applied to groups. Social ethics can be synonymous with social and political philosophy, in as much as it is the foundation of a good society or state.

Ethics is not limited to specific acts and defined moral codes, but encompasses the whole of moral ideals and behaviors, a person's philosophy of life (or *Weltanschauung*).

2. Greek philosophy

- **Socrates**

  Socrates was one of the first Greek philosophers to encourage both scholars and the common citizen to turn their attention from the outside world to the condition of man. Knowledge having a bearing on human life was placed highest, all other knowledge being secondary. Self-knowledge was considered necessary for success and inherently an essential good. A self-aware person will act completely within their capabilities to their pinnacle, while an ignorant person will flounder and encounter difficulty. To Socrates, a person must become aware of every fact (and its context) relevant to his existence, if he wishes to attain self-knowledge. He posited that people will naturally do what is good, if they know what is right. Evil or bad actions are the result of ignorance. If a criminal were truly aware of the mental and spiritual consequences of his actions, he would neither commit nor even consider committing them. Any person who knows what is truly right will automatically do it, according to Socrates. While he equated knowledge with virtue, he similarly equated virtue with happiness. The truly wise man will know what is right, do what is good and therefore be happy.

- **Aristotle**

  Aristotle posited an ethical system that may be termed "self-realizations". When a person acts in accordance with their nature and realizes their full potential, they will do well and be content. At birth, a baby is not a person, but a potential person. In order to become a "real" person, the child's inherent potential must be realized. Unhappiness and frustration are caused by the unrealized potential of a person, leading to failed goals and a poor life. Aristotle said, "Nature does nothing in vain." Therefore, it is imperative for persons to act in accordance with their nature and develop their latent talents, in order to be content and complete. Happiness was held to be the ultimate goal. All other things, such as civic life or wealth, are merely means to the end. Self-realization, the awareness of one's nature and the development of one's talents, is the surest path to happiness.

  Aristotle asserted that man had three natures : vegetable (physical), animal (emotional) and rational (mental). Physical nature can be assuaged through exercise and care, emotional nature through indulgence of instinct and urges, and mental through human reason and developed potential. Rational development was considered the most important, as essential to philosophical self-awareness and as uniquely human. Moderation was encouraged, with the extremes seen as degraded and immoral. For example, courage is the moderate virtue between the extremes of cowardice and recklessness. Man should not simply live, but live well with conduct governed by moderate virtue. This is regarded as difficult, as virtue denotes doing the right thing, to the right person, at the right time, to the proper extent, in the correct fashion, for the right reason.

- **Hedonism**

  Hedonism posits that the principal ethic is maximizing pleasure and minimizing pain. There are several schools of Hedonist thought ranging from those advocating the indulgence of even momentary desires to those teaching a pursuit of spiritual bliss. In their consideration of consequences, they range from those advocating self-gratification regardless of the pain and expense to others, to those stating that the most ethical pursuit maximizes pleasure and happiness for the most people.

- **Cyrenaic hedonism**

  Founded by Aristippus, Cyrenaics supported immediate gratification. "Eat, drink and be merry, for tomorrow we die." Even fleeting desires should be indulged, for fear the opportunity should be forever lost. There was little to no concern with the future, the present dominating in the pursuit for immediate pleasure. Cyrenaic hedonism encouraged the pursuit of enjoyment and indulgence without hesitation, believing pleasure to be the only good.

- **Epicureanism**

  Epicurus rejected the extremism of the Cyrenaics, believing some pleasures and indulgences to be detrimental to human beings. Epicureans observed that indiscriminate indulgence sometimes resulted in negative consequences. Some experiences were therefore rejected out of hand, and some unpleasant experiences endured in the present to ensure a better life in the future. The *summum bonum*, or greatest good, to Epicurus was prudence, exercised through moderation and caution. Excessive indulgence can be destructive to pleasure and can even lead to pain. For example, eating one food too often will cause a person to lose taste for it. Eating too much food at once will lead to discomfort and ill-health. Pain and fear were to be avoided. Living was essentially good, barring pain and illness. Death was not to be feared. Fear was considered the source of most unhappiness. Conquering the fear of death would naturally lead to a happier life. Epicurus reasoned if there was an afterlife and immortality, the fear of death was irrational. If there was no life after death, then the person would not be alive to suffer, fear or worry; he would be non-existent in death. It is irrational to fret over circumstances that do not exist, such as one's state in death in the absence of an afterlife.

- **Epictetus**

  The Stoic philosopher Epictetus posited that the greatest good was contentment and serenity. Peace of mind was of the highest value. Self-mastery over one's desires and emotions leads to spiritual peace. The "unconquerable will" is central to this philosophy. The individual will should be independent and inviolate. Allowing a person to disturb the mental equilibrium is in essence offering you in slavery. If a person is free to anger you at will, you have no control over your internal world, and therefore no freedom. Freedom from material attachments is also necessary. If a thing breaks, the person should not be upset, but realize it was a thing that could break. Similarly, if someone should die, those close to them should hold to their serenity because the loved one was made of flesh and blood destined to death. Stoic philosophy says to accept things that cannot be changed, resigning oneself to existence and enduring in a rational fashion. Death is not feared. People do not "lose" their life, but instead "return", for they are returning to God (who initially gave what the person is as a person). Epictetus said difficult problems in life should not be avoided, but rather embraced. They are spiritual exercises needed for the health of the spirit, just as physical exercise is required for the health of the body. He also stated that sex and sexual desire are to be avoided as the greatest threat to the integrity and equilibrium of a man's mind. Abstinence is highly desirable. Epictetus said remaining abstinent in the face of temptation was a victory for which a man could be proud.

Meta-ethics

Meta-ethics is concerned primarily with the *meaning* of ethical judgments and/or prescriptions and with the notion of which properties, if any, are responsible for the truth or validity thereof. Meta-ethics as a discipline gained attention with G.E. Moore's famous work *Principia Ethical* from 1903 in which Moore first addressed what he referred to as *the naturalistic fallacy*. Moore's rebuttal of naturalistic ethics, his Open Question Argument sparked an interest within the analytic branch of western philosophy to concern oneself with second order questions about ethics; specifically the semantics, epistemology and ontology of ethics.

The semantics of ethics divides naturally into descriptivism and non-descriptivism. The former position advocates the idea that prescriptive language (including ethical commands and duties) is a subdivision of descriptive language and has meaning in virtue of the same kind of properties as descriptive propositions, whereas the latter contends that ethical propositions are irreducible in the sense that their meaning cannot be explicated sufficiently in terms of truth-conditions.

Correspondingly, the epistemology of ethics divides into cognitivism and non-cognitivism; a distinction that is often perceived as equivalent to that between descriptivists and non-descriptivists. Non-cognitivism may be understood as the claim that ethical claims reach beyond the scope of human cognition or as the (weaker) claim that ethics is concerned with action rather than with knowledge. Cognitivism can then be seen as the claim that ethics is essentially concerned with judgments of the same kind as knowledge judgments; namely about matters of fact.

The ontology of ethics is concerned with the idea of value-bearing properties, *i.e.*, the kind of things or stuffs that would correspond to or be referred to by ethical propositions. Non-descriptivists and non-cognitivists will generally tend to argue that ethics do not require a specific ontology, since ethical propositions do not refer to objects in the same way that descriptive propositions do. Such a position may sometimes be called anti-realist. Realists on the other hand are left with having to explain what kind of entities, properties or states are relevant for ethics, and why they have the normative status characteristic of ethics.

Descriptive ethics

Descriptive ethics is a value-free approach to ethics which examines ethics not from a top-down *a priori* perspective but rather observations of actual choices made by moral agents in practice. Some philosophers rely on descriptive ethics and choices made and unchallenged by a society or culture to derive categories, which typically vary by context. This can lead to situational ethics and situated ethics. These philosophers often view aesthetics, etiquette, and arbitration as more fundamental, percolating "bottom up" to imply the existence of, rather than explicitly prescribe, theories of value or of conduct. The study of descriptive ethics may include examinations of the following :

- Ethical codes applied by various groups. Some consider aesthetics itself the basis of ethics – and a personal moral core developed through art and storytelling as very influential in one's later ethical choices.
- Informal theories of etiquette which tend to be less rigorous and more situational. Some consider etiquette a simple negative ethics, *i.e.*, where can one evade an uncomfortable truth without doing wrong ? One notable advocate of this view is

Judith Martin ("Miss Manners"). According to this view, ethics is more a summary of common sense social decisions.

- Practices in arbitration and law, *e.g.*, the claim that ethics itself is a matter of balancing "right versus right," *i.e.*, putting priorities on two things that are both right, but which must be traded off carefully in each situation.
- Observed choices made by ordinary people, without expert aid or advice, who vote, buy, and decide what is worth valuing. This is a major concern of sociology, political science, and economics.

Applied ethics

Applied ethics is a discipline of philosophy that attempts to apply ethical theory to real-life situations. The lines of distinction between meta-ethics, normative ethics, and applied ethics are often blurry. For example, the issue of abortion can be seen as an applied ethical topic since it involves a specific type of controversial behaviour. But it can also depend on more general normative principles, such as possible rights of self-rule and right to life, principles which are often litmus tests for determining the morality of that procedure. The issue also rests on meta-ethical issues such as, "where do rights come from ?" and "what kind of beings have rights ?"

Another concept which blurs ethics is moral luck. A drunk driver may safely reach home without injuring anyone, or he might accidentally kill a child who runs out into the street while he is driving home. The action of driving while drunk is usually seen as equally wrong in each case, but its dependence on chance affects the degree to which the driver is held responsible.

5.4 SOCIAL AND FINANCIAL IMPACTS OF OPEN SOURCE TECHNOLOGY

There is no doubt that technological change brings about social change. The Industrial revolution saw many people displaced from their land, to find work in crowded city factories. Serfdom was abolished and the population shifted from villages to the cities. Strong family ties, self sufficiency and the right to occupy land were replaced with uncertain tenancy of land, dependency on trade and a weakening of the family unit.

Economically, goods and money abounded, and trade flourished. The merchant class profited from the wealth that was generated on the backs of the displaced population of urban workers. Children were sent to work in factories, in order for families to make enough money to live. The peasant class worked long hard hours in poor conditions with no security. The Industrial revolution led to the alienation of the working class and although many union battles have since led to the adoption of better working conditions, the effects of the Industrial revolution remain. The family unit is even more vulnerable today with soaring divorce rates, high rates of teenage suicide, most of society are either heavily mortgaged to banks or paying high rents, and no one can be self-sufficient in a world governed by free trade.

Advances in technology, is generally not equitably shared within society. People with money have more opportunity to acquire technology, which enables them to acquire even more wealth.

Technology leads to greater social economic division. Laborers are viewed as commodities and expendable. Technology leads to alienation because it can create jobs that require no specialist knowledge.

To date, since the industrial revolution we have seen technology used to the detriment of society. The right to occupy land has become a privilege that must be worked for and earned and now the battle is on to control all the world's food and textiles through genetically modified seeds and animals. The insidious part of GM is that there is no recall once it is released into the environment. Salmon that will grow ten times faster than normal salmon will destroy river systems, as their unfair genetically modified advantage will see all smaller life forms extinguished and genetically modified crops that are dependent on pesticides will contaminate organic, heritage seeds that have sustained people for thousands of years. Seeds will no longer be able to be harvested and replanted but the farmer will have to buy new seed every year from GM seed makers. This fight is more important that the fight over **open source** because it involves the right of people everywhere to have clean, safe food that has not been genetically altered. Essentially GM is a tax on everyone because a patent will be on every seed and seeds are made to be sterile the following year. This is something to become angry about. The greedy corporations and individuals that want control over our food, water and land, do not care about the irreversible damage to the environment. People and animals that they cause.

We have the right to eat tomatoes that are free of fish DNA, meat and milk that is free of human DNA, pigs that haven't been grown to harvest anthrax antibodies. They will never be able to prove the safety of GM food and no long-term studies have been done. Nor will GM solve the problem of soil erosion, and pollution of rivers from artificial fertilizers and pesticides. Only a return to responsible organic and biodynamic farming practices will solve these problems. The 50 harmful effects of GM food Courts are not keen to pursue pesticide makers for poisoning farmers, or GM seed makers for monopolizing the world's seeds through patents, (through genetic engineering that not only renders the seed worthless for replanting the next year but also contaminates non-GM crops by cross pollination.

The internet in its current form was developed as a free exchange of information, unregulated by any one government or owned by any one person or company. In its raw form it was the playground of hackers and computer geeks, who challenged the status quo. It brings about a new era, the technological revolution. The free flow of information has brought about technological advances at an unprecedented rate and has made many rich and brought companies who failed to adapt to a standstill.

How will this technological revolution impact on our society ? If the industrial revolution is any thing to go by, there will be winners and losers to technological revolution.

E-commerce will affect the middle man and allow direct trade with consumers. Efficiency brings about lower prices for the consumer, but it is more accurate to argue that efficiency brings about greater wealth for shareholders, directors and owners. The intrinsic weave of social interactions of trade, can be disentangled and made into a horizontal supply chain. E-commerce will create efficiencies that effectively remove the need for a long supply chain but at the expense of social relationships.

The effect of e-commerce and the internet will impact on every society on the earth. Already, the barriers of trade between individuals in different countries are non-existent. Company contact details are searchable through powerful search engines, and trade can commerce between two individuals who would otherwise never have met. The internet dissolves national boundaries, and the consequences for cities that have developed as centers of administration and trade will be disastrous, if they do not embrace the technological advances in communication and trade that the internet brings. While at the same time, free trade means fierce competition without the protection of award wages. People are reduced to consumers and suppliers.

Resisting the tide of technological change is impossible. Of course it is possible to do business without a website or e-mail or mobile phone or a fax machine. People have been doing business well before any of these gadgets were invented. But business today is about competition, and technology is about leverage. Technology can lead to alienation if it is not widely dispersed in society. The Industrial age saw the concentration of technology in the hands of the rich and powerful, allowing them to dominate and subdue the population into harsh working conditions and the social impact of the internet and computers is only just beginning, will it challenge the status quo or will it lead to greater population control ?

The latter is probably more likely, and many will look on this time as the golden age of the internet. Already technology like digital TV is being pushed in the guise of better quality but the benefits to those who own the systems is that they will be able to track what you watch, when you watch it, whether or not you switch off an ad, and perhaps even whether that pizza ad makes you pick up the phone and call for a pizza. Knowledge is power, and with access to tapping phone lines, reading e-mails, reading your credit card statements, knowing by GPS where you are by tracking your mobile phone, it can be a scary world, if all that knowledge and power were to be used to oppress and control.

On the upside, technology has made the developed world a richer place to the detriment of the environment. Machines have allowed people to move away from physical work, so that now in Australia there are 100,000 accountants and 85,000 farmers. Perhaps, technology has gone too far, and there are more people counting beans than growing them!

5.4.1 Impact of Technology on Government

The legal system is dependent on local jurisdictions under common law. Historically, one has to remember that before the age of the internet, airplanes and telephones, the vast majority of business was done locally. Technology has rapidly changed the way people do business but there has not adapted to the changes. There is no one body that governs international trade.

What are the Implications ?

If you buy a product from a local supplier in your State, and it turns out that the item is faulty, you can go back to your supplier to work out repair or replacement and if they don't help you, you can take the matter to local Trades office or file legal action in your state. If however, you buy a product outside your jurisdiction, you must file a claim in the State, where the supplier is located. You can only use a lawyer in the State where you file your action; your local lawyer can only act as a consultant and has no authority to represent you in court or to serve papers.

Therefore, we have a world which is governed by local laws and yet the businesses and individuals are now actively trading outside of their local area.

Governments are trying to make laws about content on the internet but have no jurisdiction to enforce those laws. This has created havens in small developing countries, that are happy to accept companies that want to run online gambling websites that may be outlawed in their jurisdiction or companies that wish to reduce their tax liabilities by opening up bank accounts in developing countries.

We see arising now a homogenizing of local laws on issues like SPAM, and even sending a international letter from anywhere in the world involves the completion of almost identical forms, Governments are making agreements, in an attempt to be relevant in a world where people are able to trade more freely and where digital communication has enabled businesses to work, almost without physical boundaries.

5.4.2 Business Names and the Internet

In the beginning, it was easy to start a new business. You would go to your local business registration office in your State and apply for a business name. If it was taken, you would choose another name. Most people do not realize that a business name is only valid for the State that it is registered in and the only way to protect your business name is to incorporate a company. In Australia, you would lodge forms with ASIC to incorporate a company and you then have rights to use your business name exclusively in Australia and its territories.

However, with the birth of the internet, your Australian company name may be the same as the name of a company overseas.

This has resulted in legal action being taken, as companies tussle of business names and the rights to use those names and a court system that is unable to deal effectively with international disputes over business names and has resulted in greater costs to people who want to start a business as they must register multiple domain names, take about international trademarks and find a name that has not already been taken. Even if they contact lawyers to register all the domain names and trademarks to avoid disputes (both local and international), legal action can still be taken against them. And when it comes to justice, money wins almost every time, unless companies want to relocate to safe havens in developing countries where they cannot be pursued in court.

5.4.3 Impact of Technology on Corporate IT Department

The Open Source movement is gradually impacting corporate IT departments at major corporations worldwide. Various forces internal and external to the software industry are supporting this trend. In this Colum, I will try to explore some of the reasons why open source is becoming more acceptable to corporate IT department as following :

1. Trends
2. Current Economic Environment
3. New Hires

5.5 SHARED SOFTWARE

Shared Software is a different term used to describe free software open source software and possibly also software that is not formally covered by the definition of either, but that is in some other way shared rather than owned.

The way to develop and use software more effectively is to share it with others. Sharing is symmetric. If we share our software, we are sharing my software and that seems to be twice as powerful as one way reusing.

If we start calling it sharing instead of reusing, it changes the tone of the exposition. For starters sharing is a much more high-minded, noble and ethical thing than reusing which sounds more hackneyed and shopworn and it sounds better precisely because it signifies that there is a reciprocal understanding in order to share, you have an obligation to contribute as well as consume and your contribution becomes available for others to build upon increasing value for all. Think too of the difference in morel. Do you want you're to be reused ? Or do you want your expertise ?

Investment banks and ventures capitalists raise capital form lots of individual or institution and let them ownership of companies. Insurance companies let people share risk. Everybody contributes a premium and most people expect that they want get a pay out.

Examples of shared software are :

- CICS : Transaction Control Manager
- EOS : Report archive and distribution
- PL/1 : Compiler and run time libraries
- Cobol : Compiler and run time libraries
- DB2 : Adabas and other Database software

5.6 SHARED SOURCE

Shared source is Microsoft's framework for *sharing* computer program source code with individuals and organizations. Microsoft's Shared Source Initiative includes a spectrum of technologies and licenses. Most of its offerings are available for download by anyone. For these programs there are eligibility criteria to be met.

The licenses associated with the offerings range from allowing only viewing of the code for reference, to allowing it to be modified and redistributed for commercial or non-commercial purposes.

5.6.1 Benefits of Shared Source

The common benefit of all the Shared Source programs is the availability of source code for reference when developing complementary systems. For example, having the source code to significant portions of an operating system aids application developers in maintaining stability and consistency in their own programs. The availability of source code also permits review and auditing from a security perspective, something which some large corporations and governments are now mandating.

Some of the Shared Source licenses share many of the benefits (and drawbacks) of open source licenses. The Microsoft Public License and Microsoft Reciprocal License have been approved by the Open Source Initiative as open source licenses.

Other Shared Source licenses allow the copyright holder to retain much tighter control over the use of their product than open source licenses, which generally include the voluntary abdication of many of the author's rights. From the perspective of companies which are used to developing proprietary software, this is a smaller transition to make, and may be seen as an interim step to full open source disclosure.

Microsoft's Shared Source Initiative has been imitated by other companies such as RISC OS Open Limited.

5.6.2 Notable Shared Source Programs

1. **Microsoft Enterprise Source Licensing Program**

   Microsoft gives enterprise customers viewing access to some parts of some versions of the Microsoft Windows operating systems. The ESLP license agreement is among the most restrictive of the licenses associated with Shared Source programs, allowing no modifications of the code.

2. **Microsoft Windows Academic Program**

   The Windows Academic Program provides universities worldwide with concepts, Windows kernel source code, and projects useful for integrating core Windows kernel technologies into teaching and research.

3. **Microsoft Shared Source Common Language Infrastructure**

   The first widely-distributed shared source program is Shared Source CLI, the shared source implementation of the Common Language Infrastructure. The licensing permits non-commercial modification and distribution of the source code, as long as all distributions include the original license, or one encompassing the original terms.

   Microsoft Shared Source Common Language Infrastructure is neither free software according to the Free Software Foundation, nor OSI-approved open source.

4. **Windows Installer XML (WiX)**

   WiX is a toolset for advanced Windows developers that build Windows installation packages from XML source code. The first Microsoft Shared Source offering to be released on Source Forge, the WiX toolset is licensed under the Common Public License (CPL).

5. **ASP.Net AJAX Control Toolkit**

   The ASP.Net AJAX Control Toolkit is a set of controls and extenders that use AJAX technologies to enable developers to easily improve the client experience on their websites. The ASP.Net AJAX Control Toolkit, licensed under the Microsoft Public license (MS-PL), is accessible on Code Plex, Microsoft's online community development portal for collaborative software development projects.

5.6.3 Notable Shared Source Licenses

1. Open Source Licenses

- **Microsoft Public License (Ms-PL)**

  This is the least restrictive of the Microsoft licenses and allows for distribution of *compiled* derived code for either commercial or non-commercial purposes under any license that complies with the Ms-PL. Redistribution of the source code itself is permitted only under the Ms-PL. Initially titled *Microsoft Permissive License*, it was renamed to *Microsoft Public License* while being reviewed for approval by the OSI. The license was approved on October 12, 2007.

- **Microsoft Reciprocal License (Ms-RL)**

  This Microsoft license allows for distribution of derived code so long as the modified source files are included and retain the Ms-RL. The Ms-RL allows those files in the distribution that do not contain code originally licensed under Ms-RL to be licensed according to the intellectual property creator's choosing. This equivalent to the CDDL or LGPL (GPL with a typical "linking exception"). Initially known as the *Microsoft Community License*, it was renamed during the OSI approval process.

  On December 9, 2005, the Ms-RL license was submitted to the Open Source Initiative for approval by John Cowan. OSI then contacted Microsoft and asked if they wanted OSI to proceed. Microsoft replied that they did not wish to be reactive and that they needed time to review such a decision. Then at OSCON in July 2007 Bill Hilf announced that Microsoft had now formally submitted Ms-PL and Ms-RL to OSI for approval. It was eventually approved October 12, 2007 along with the Ms-PL.

2. Proprietary Licenses

- **Microsoft Reference Source License (Ms-RSL)**

  This is the most restrictive of the Microsoft Source Licenses. The source code is made available to view for reference purposes only. Developers may not distribute or modify the code for commercial or non-commercial purposes. The license has previously been abbreviated *Ms-RL*, but *Ms-RL* now refers to the *Microsoft Reciprocal License*.

- **Microsoft Limited Public License (Ms-LPL)**

  This is a version of the Microsoft Permissive License in which rights are only granted to developers of Microsoft Windows-based software. This license is not open source, as defined by the OSI, because it violates the stipulation that open source licenses must be technology-neutral.

- **Microsoft Limited Reciprocal License (Ms-LRL)**

  This is a version of the Microsoft Reciprocal License in which rights are only granted when developing software for a Microsoft Windows platform. Like the Ms-LPL, this license is not open source because it is not technology-neutral.

SUMMARY

Open Source : Richard Stallman's organization is called the Free Software Foundation, not the Open Source Software Foundation. There's a reference to "FSF's mission to preserve, protect and promote the freedom to use, study, copy, modify, and redistribute computer software." This is missionary zeal.

Open Source Government : Primarily refers to use of open source software technologies in traditional government organization and government operations such as voting.

Open Politics : It is also known as Open Source Politics. It's a term used to describe a political process that uses Internet technologies such as blogs, e-mail and polling to provide for a rapid feedback mechanism between political organization of the Open Source Politics which relates to the development of public under a set of rules and processes similar to the Open Source Software Movement.

The ethics of Open Source : There are a few people who believe that open source software is somehow morally superior to closed source software. Richard Stallman is one. To him, the issue is one of freedom versus slave rut this. The real reason for the success of open source is not the missionary zeal of Stallman and others, but a more humdrum factor called commoditization.

Shared Software : is a different term used to describe free software open source software and possibly also software that is not formally covered by the definition of either, but that is in some other way shared rather than owned.

Shared Source : is Microsoft's framework for *sharing* computer program source code with individuals and organizations. Microsoft's Shared Source Initiative includes a spectrum of technologies and licenses. Most of its offerings are available for download by anyone. For these programs there are eligibility criteria to be met.

REVIEW QUESTIONS

1. Give Difference between Open Source and close source software.
2. What is open source government ?
3. Explain the shared software.
4. Explain the social and financial impacts of technology.
5. Explain the social and financial impacts of technology on government.
6. Explain the shared software and give its examples.
7. Explain the shared source in detail.
8. Explain the ethics of open source technology.
9. Write short note on the following :
   1. Benefits of Shared Source
   2. Open source Impact on IT department.

□□□

INDEX

□□□